# WILD

# CIVILITY

---

*The English Comic Spirit on*

*the Restoration Stage*

# WILD CIVILITY

## The English Comic Spirit
## on the Restoration Stage

### VIRGINIA OGDEN BIRDSALL

*Indiana University Press*

BLOOMINGTON / LONDON

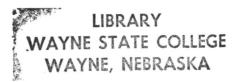

*for*  Carol, Hugh, and Meredith—*players all.*

A winning wave, deserving note,
In the tempestuous petticoat:
A careless shoe-string, in whose tie
I see a wild civility:
Do more bewitch me than when art
Is too precise in every part.

—Robert Herrick

# CONTENTS

# CONTENTS

# WILD

# CIVILITY

*The English Comic Spirit on*

*the Restoration Stage*

# [ I ]

# *Prologue*

---

TEMPORAL things will have their weight in the World,
and though Zeal may prevail for a time, and get the better in
a Skirmish, yet the War endeth generally on the side of
Flesh and Blood, and will do so until Mankind is another thing
than it is at present.

—SIR GEORGE SAVILE, *Marquis of Halifax*

THE RESTORATION OF CHARLES II TO THE ENGLISH THRONE IN 1660 seems to have produced little corresponding restoration of old optimisms regarding man's angelic and heroic potential. The return of the monarchy and the aristocracy had come only after a period of social and religious upheaval which marked the death of a great many illusions; and the expansive possibilities which had seemed so infinite in the age of Elizabeth had dwindled until the courts of kings had come to resemble drawing rooms. Seemingly the aristocratic world of Charles II's courtiers had closed in upon itself and, assuming a monopoly of the London theaters, had insured that English drama would become as narrow and superficial as were the lives that the courtiers themselves had chosen to lead. The "heroes" of their comedies seemed scarcely heroes at all. They were rakes, libertines, wits, gallants, painted with realistic strokes from living models; and court society, so one critical argument goes, merely thronged to the theater to see and admire themselves upon a stage.

Are the comedies of Etherege, Wycherley, and Congreve simply to be accepted then as faithful representations of the life of the times—social studies in "manners," as a highly influential group of earlier twentieth-century critics would have it, or intellectual studies in cynicism and disillusion, as a more recent emphasis would conclude? In the light of the imaginative critical approaches of the past fifteen or twenty years, it is at any rate no longer easy to dismiss this whole important body of English comedy with L. C. Knights' summary adjectives, "trivial, gross, and dull,"[1] nor with John Wain's damning judgment of it as "trifling" and wholly lacking in "artistic morality."[2] The greatest of the Restoration playwrights were, as has been increasingly recognized, decidedly not triflers. What has not been sufficiently acknowledged is that they were conscious artists—and indeed artists who hold precisely the "consistent attitude toward problems of conduct" which Wain denies to them. If that consistency has eluded a good many latter-day audiences, it is probably because it is of a rather unorthodox kind—a consistency based on the traditional comic view of the relationship between "morality" and the individualistic spirit.

One may hazard it as a reason for past critical injustices that Restoration comedy has been frequently categorized wrongly as to ancestry. On the one hand, the plays of Etherege, Wycherley, and Congreve simply do not fit comfortably into the comedy-romance tradition of Lyly, Shakespeare, and Shirley into which they have often been forced, and it cannot be anything but misleading to suggest that they are essentially corrective comedies—that their heroes, like many of those in earlier and later romantic comedy, are in the course of the action in some way educated or "tamed."

Yet it is equally misleading to regard these plays as mavericks so far as any English tradition is concerned. Too often, critics in search of literary antecedents specifically comic have looked abroad to Molière, just as those seeking the source of what they have called the "manners" emphasis have turned to an examination of the Frenchified court of Charles I's queen, with its dedication to the *précieux* conventions. The more closely the purported Molière influence has been examined, however, the less genuine it has come to seem. And the more the "artfulness" of the heroes and heroines has been discussed in terms of the *précieux* mode and of form, decorum, and artificiality, the less such a tradition seems to have to do with their most essential characteristics.

The fact is that beneath their mannered, polite-society surfaces, the comedies of Etherege, Wycherley, and Congreve are, when viewed properly as comedy, quite recognizably English in theme and spirit, and this special English quality lies at the root of their meaning and their morality. How comedy is defined has a certain amount to do with the national boundaries within which it appears; and in the case of English and French comedy there is a particularly notable difference. French comedy has tended to stand with society against the deviating individual, while in England, for whatever complex reasons, the audience has always expected of their comedies an almost categorically opposite stance—a stance (with a good deal of classical precedent) in which social or moral authority is gleefully and triumphantly challenged by the defiant individual.[3] And just such an individual is the rake-hero of Restoration comedy.

At the formidable risk, therefore, of disagreeing with George Meredith's poetic tribute to "silvery laughter" as the ultimate expression of the comic genius (Molière was, it must be remembered, his ideal comic playwright), it might well be maintained that the most typical *English* laughter is, while less "silvery" and less "humane," at once more individualistic, more earthy, more *human*. Robust and tough-mindedly realistic, the English comic spirit is often none too kindly and is dedicated first of all to challenge and to release from rigid and stultifying creeds and institutions, whether these have to do with Puritanism, with social affectation, with codes of honor, or whatever. Against them it sets its own laughing, boisterous irreverence—its wish, in Eric Bentley's words, "to desecrate the household gods"[4]—and is bent on asserting the élan vital of the individual in opposition to all superficially formalizing dictates. Indeed Baudelaire, in defining the special character of English comedy (in this instance pantomime), talks of "comic savagery" and goes on to conclude that "the distinctive mark of this type of the comic was *violence*," that everything "was expressed in the same way, with passionate gusto; it was the dizzy height of hyperbole."[5]

In early English drama the principal comic character, more often than not, had been a rogue who, by means of asides or soliloquies, established a rapport with the roguish propensities latent in the members of his audience and invited them to laugh with him at the spectacle before them. He was, so to speak, one of them. He sprang from the everyday, prosaic world that they knew and was of the earth earthy. And much the same sort of figure, albeit with a sophisticated difference, was the rake-hero of Restoration comedy. He belonged undeniably to his own historical period, as comic figures have always belonged to the particular social scene which produces them, but he shared also in a comic tradition as old as English drama—a tradition of comic "heroes" who were shrewd, double-dealing rascals dedicated to the cause of their own freedom and prosperity. The first comic playwright to achieve any prominence in England had been the Wakefield master, and from the moment when his "mery lad" Pikeharness rebelled mischievously against Cain in *The Killing of Abel* and the irrepressible and none-too-admirable Mak arrived among the gullible shepherds of *The Second Shepherds Play* and began to work his trickery on them to serve his own nefarious purposes, English comedy had found its "hero."

Indeed Louis Cazamian finds the same spirit abroad in England even earlier, for he sees the "realism of the Riddles" as a "new spirit, racy, spontaneous, audacious, coarse," arising in spite of "the authority of aristocratic and religious influences."[6] After Pikeharness and Mak as possessors of the "new spirit, racy, spontaneous, audacious, coarse," came the so-called Vices of the morality plays,[7] and after them, Mathew Merygreeke of *Ralph Roister Doister* and Diccon the Bedlam of *Gammer Gurton's Needle* (both still recognizably English even with the parasite and tricky-slave elements from Roman comedy now added to the characterization).[8] Then, of course, came Shakespeare's Falstaff of *Henry IV,* parts one and two—to be followed a half century later by the witty rakes of Restoration comedy, not so changed as we might expect, for all their gentility of surface.

In conventional terms it may be true that low comedy has given way to high in the process (physical violence, horseplay, and open vulgarity having largely disappeared). But the question at once arises as to whether the line between the two ought really to be drawn so sharply with reference to the development of English comedy. For one thing, the best of the early Vices, and those predominantly comic in potential, had themselves been in some degree *eirons* as well as buffoons, thus revealing witty as well as farcical aspects. For another, even though the rebellion is clearly more intellectualized in the case of the rake-heroes, similar social and moral repressions still give rise to that rebellion. And finally, may it not be legitimately argued that the wit of these rake-heroes (and in fact all true wit) is in some sense verbal farce—with physical aggressiveness transferred into the intellectual sphere and with coarseness disguised, in the best Freudian tradition, in order to gain admission to the drawing room?

In order to understand the role of the rakes, then—and especially to come to some means of assessing the charges of immorality and grossness which have been repeatedly flung at them—we must first acknowledge the essentially devilish, bad-boy nature of the English comic spirit in general. The parentage of the Vices themselves has been variously traced to the Devil, to the Bad Angel, and to assorted agents of evil in the early mysteries and moralities; and whichever be chosen, it is clear that theirs was no innocent merriment. The rake-heroes have an obvious precedent for their "immorality," and when Macaulay arraigned Restoration comedy as "earthly, sensual, devilish,"[9] and Dr. Johnson said of Congreve's plays that the "ultimate effect is to present pleasure in alliance with vice, and to relax those obligations by which life ought to be regulated,"[10] both were putting the Restoration comic dramatists at the very center of the English comic tradition.

What Cazamian says of *Hyckescorner* is, in fact, true to a greater or less degree of all the plays in which a typical English comic protagonist figures: "We catch in it a rebellion of instinct and natural mirth against the repression of a faith too strictly bound up with the fear of hell. The naughty characters speak with a strangely genuine and free voice. . . . A Rabelaisian note of frank, almost pagan, naturalism more than once rings out between the accents of perfunctory orthodoxy; and that slyly double inspiration is the source of what we may well call 'humor of release.' "[11] As we laugh in delighted responsiveness with the mischievous, high-spirited troublemakers, who are expressing for us our own fundamental humanness, we are perhaps, in line with the catharsis theory, giving a safe and socially harmless release to repressed instincts within ourselves. But at the same time we have accorded tacit approval to the dynamic, self-centered life force which has challenged the repressive status quo.

At his most highly developed comic heights, the early English comic protagonist is the laugher, and we laugh along with him at what he makes of other people and not at what they make of him. In his own comic world defeat is never more than temporary, and he invariably turns it the next minute into victory. He is the principal actor and the principal artist on his own comic stage, as the rake-heroes of Restoration comedy were later to be on theirs. There are two vital factors, however, which set the rake-hero apart from most of his devilish predecessors. The first has to do with that more intellectual quality of his rebellion already touched on. The second lies in the key word "hero." Heretofore the comic rogue had occupied the central position in the comic action, but not the central position in the drama as a whole. He could hardly, in the overall context of a morality or history play, be allowed to emerge as the victor, even if his *dramatic* victory was patent. But figures like Dorimant and Horner and Mirabell (and Harriet and Millamant as well) belong to a world purely comic and hence they do win. They create their own morality, which has little to do with conventional morals and which may be termed a morality of honesty or of integrity in the most basic meaning of the word. They are triumphant in their reassertion of the spirit of Silenus—"the satyr-god of comedy leading the ecstatic 'chorus of natural beings who as it were live ineradicably behind every civilization.' "[12] Confronted with a world which lacks any sense of cosmic orderliness and abstract moral certainty and which has committed itself to civilized forms largely derivative and hollow, they make *their* spirit prevail. And it is their ultimate achievement that they succeed in creating their own harmonies out of the dissonances of experience and in establishing between themselves and their society a vital and dynamic relationship.[13]

# [II]

# *Dramatis Personæ*

WHERE the spirit of comedy has departed, company becomes
constraint, reserve eats up the spirit, and people fall into a
penurious melancholy in their scruple to be always exact, sane,
and reasonable, never to mourn, never to glow, never to betray
a passion or a weakness, nor venture to utter a thought they
might not wish to harbour for ever.

—GEORGE SANTAYANA, *"The Comic Mask"*

## *The Rake-hero as Player*

AT LEAST ONE CRITIC OF RESTORATION COMEDY HAS COMMENTED ON
the fact that each of Etherege's three comedies begins in the morning, and no one can have failed to notice the importance which all
the greatest of the Restoration comic dramatists attach to youth.
Whatever the degree of social polish, their heroes and heroines invariably possess a defiantly youthful vigor and a determination to
create around themselves a fresh and challenging morning world
which will afford the fullest scope for their varied personalities.
Theirs is no jaded sophistication. On the contrary, the most crucial
thing about them is that they are all highly imaginative creators
and that their creativeness takes the form of playing in both inter-
related senses of the word. Seeing themselves and their world with
unillusioned clarity, they become at once dramatic artists, acting
out roles in a drama of their own devising, and artists of their

[9]

supremely subtle game of life, insistently dictating the rules according to which that game must be played.

Their starting point is, in accordance with their youthfulness, a kind of innocent apprehension of themselves in regard to their own basic instincts and desires. Paradoxically perhaps, it is also a devilish apprehension (*The Country Wife,* for example, defines Horner as both "innocent" and "devil"), since once we have entered adulthood, any return to the innocent indulgences of childhood must always be thought of in some such terms as sin or vice or surrender to temptation. Like earlier rogues of English comedy the rake-hero is thus, for all his subtlety and sophisticated veneer, in some sense a childlike figure who is playing a game. He is a mischief-maker, a prideful rebel, a showman, a shameless egotist, an actor complete with disguises, a clever manipulator of the world he lives in, and above all an artist.

But it is his identity as a player of games that we must examine first, since that aspect of his nature not only dictates most of his actions and characteristics but lies at the root of his creativeness, his artistry. Nearly everyone who has written on the subject of comedy has recognized its "play" quality, and most critics of Restoration comedy in particular have at some point commented on the manners game being played. They have, however, usually become so preoccupied thereafter with a search for values in the plays that they have neglected the central thematic concern with the value of "play" in its own right. The fact is that at bottom we find implicit in the works of all three playwrights much the same conclusions regarding the play function which are to be found explicitly analyzed in Johan Huizinga's *Homo Ludens.* Huizinga begins his book by asserting that play is in itself "a *significant* function—that is to say, there is some sense to it. In play there is something 'at play' which transcends the immediate needs of life and imparts meaning to the action."[1] And he goes on to show the basic resemblance between play and virtually all forms of creativity. Play activity involves what he calls "a certain 'imagination' of reality," and becomes a "cultural factor in life."[2] That is, it entails some sort of innovation—some *re-creation* or *re-forming* process.[3] And further, in identifying the creative function of poetry with "a function even more primordial than culture itself, namely play,"

Huizinga points out that both functions assume the same kind of mood and that either can be defined as "an activity which proceeds within certain limits of time and space, in a visible order, according to rules freely accepted, and outside the sphere of necessity or material utility. The play-mood is one of rapture and enthusiasm, and is sacred or festive in accordance with the occasion. A feeling of exaltation and tension accompanies the action, mirth and relaxation follow."[4]

All of these characteristics without exception—the playground, the rules, the nonutility, the tension—have also been at one time or another insisted on as requisite characteristics of comedy and indeed of all drama. But are they not also factors which we have come to associate with a notable number of the individual comic protagonists *within* English drama? In short, may it not be argued that we are often confronted with English comedy which is, at least in part, actually *about* the efforts of a protagonist to make of his own life and the life about him a dynamic, coherent, harmonious drama? As devised by such figures as the Vices, the "play" was, of course, more or less rudimentary. In the hands of the rake-heroes, however, it achieves a high degree of sophistication and refinement.

We may object that Charles Lamb, in that part of his celebrated defense of Restoration comedy in which he talks of "artificiality" and a "Utopia of gallantry" and removes the plays into a sphere which "has no reference whatever to the world that is," tends too much to deny to them any meaningful cultural function. But the fact remains that he must be credited with having set criticism on a track which later critics would have done well not to abandon so scornfully. He did know a playground when he saw one, and he knew that as often as not the comic spirit has nothing to do with correction but is rather issuing an invitation to the audience to join a protagonist in a spirit of wholehearted play. Like many later writers on comedy, Lamb recognized the importance of emphasizing the nonutilitarian nature of the comic art. The psychologist James Sully was to define play a century later as "free activity entered upon for its own sake" and as being "free from external restraint, and from the sense of compulsion—of a 'must' at the ear, whether embodied in the voice of a master or in that of a higher self—which accompanies the attitude of the worker."[5] And Lamb had seen the world created on the Restoration comic stage in similar terms, describing it as "that happy breathing-place from the burthen of a perpetual moral questioning," and going on to warn: "in our anxiety that our morality should not take cold, we wrap it up in a great blanket surtout of precaution against the breeze and sunshine."

If we balk at a complete agreement with Lamb at this point, it is because he emphasizes too exclusively the escapist view and interprets morality too narrowly—and because the playground on which the Restoration comic protagonists play achieves a much higher and more subtle form than he acknowledges. "I am glad for a season," he writes, "to take an airing beyond the diocese of the strict conscience,—not to live always in the precincts of the law courts—but now and then, for a dream-while or so, to imagine a world with no meddling restrictions." Huizinga too sees play as a function "never imposed by physical necessity or moral duty" and remarks that here "we have the first main characteristic of play: that it is free, is in fact, freedom."[6] But just what this freedom signifies has been, in Lamb's discussion, simply ignored. As Bentley protests, Lamb seems to think he has said all there is to say when he has called Restoration comedy farce instead of satire and has associated it with the gay and the fantastic, while in reality he has opened up a whole new area for speculation, since farces by their very nature involve aggressiveness and are filled with Freudian overtones.[7]

And further, what Lamb does not acknowledge is the thematic emphasis in Restoration comedy not only on freedom but on discipline. For Huizinga freedom is only "the *first* main characteristic" of play, and the fact is that if the comedies with which we are here concerned were nothing more than what Lamb defines as a "scenic representation of disorder," we would all finally have to agree as to their triviality. Like Huizinga, however, all of the great Restoration comedies repeatedly insist by implication on order as of the very essence of play: "it creates order, *is* order."[8] At the same time that the play world within each of the comedies challenges a present state of things which has become sterile or confining, the players are simultaneously establishing a new world of their own.

Creation involves bringing into being a new kind of order, dynamic and not static, expressive and not repressive.[9]

However sophisticated the play-activity may become, however finished its form, it is still genuine play so long as it remains harmoniously expressive of basic human energies. The gap between such freewheeling, roguish vice-figures as Udall's Mathew Merygreeke and Stevenson's Diccon on the one hand and those polished sophisticates Dorimant, Horner, and Mirabell on the other is perhaps a wide one; and yet the Restoration rakes have their free-ranging, devilish substratum, just as the most highly developed comic Vices have in their make-up a substantial ingredient of smooth, controlled savoir-faire. Both elements are crucial, for as the Restoration comedies themselves often tell us, if form not expressive of an underlying energy is sterile and meaningless, energy without form remains chaotic.

What the freedom of the comic hero involves is a release of his energies; but once achieved, that freedom itself presents a new challenge. As Havelock Ellis insists: "The freedom of art by no means involves the easiness of art. It may rather, indeed, be said the difficulty increases with freedom, for to make things in accordance with patterns is ever the easiest task."[10] In short, it is much simpler to accept existence within a status quo than to *live*. "To dare, to take risks, to bear uncertainty, to endure tension—" says Huizinga, "these are the essence of the play spirit."[11]

But if released energies, lacking controlling form, can be simply dissipated, it is obvious that they can also be manipulated to achieving wholly negative ends; they can be encouraged to explode not to the controlled end of forward-moving creativity, but to the wholly opposite end of general destruction, with the vice-figures becoming ancestors not of a Falstaff but of an Iago.

It is a distinction which must be taken up later in greater detail, but at this point we may simply note that if we examine a character such as Diccon in *Gammer Gurton's Needle,* we see the comic, creative potential wholly dominant. Diccon conducts his revels in a language full of gross excremental images. (The play is astonishingly well supplied with references to "turds," "backsides," and "black holes.") Yet he exercises such joyous imaginative control over that elemental existence that he succeeds in making a true game of it and, in terms of the play's prevailing metaphor, turns darkness into light. He is a comic accepter, always on the side of life.

To discover a similarity of creative role in the Restoration rake-heroes may, perhaps, not seem so procrustean an undertaking if we approach Dorimant and Mirabell by way of their wilder cousins Sir Frederick Frollick and Horner. In Etherege's comedies, for example, the methods of aggressive game-playing alter noticeably as Sir Frederick gives way to Courtall and Courtall to Dorimant—with the overstatement of farce changing to the understatement of wit and with the final comic triumph in *The Man of Mode* at once more difficult of achievement and more subtly and expertly brought about. Like Diccon, Sir Frederick and Horner live in a rather grossly physical world—a world seemingly reduced at times to a preoccupation with sexual disease and one which challenges such forms as honor as persistently as Falstaff's. Each controls his surroundings with undeniable vitality and artistry, but the differences are obvious between a Diccon or a Horner on the one hand and a Dorimant or a Mirabell on the other, and the reason for those differences is surely much the same as that suggested by Lane Cooper to explain "the difference between the broad humor of the Elizabethans and the innuendo of a Congreve. The innuendo of the Restoration *is* more like the language a gentleman would permit himself to use in private than are the obscenity and personal abuse of a Falstaff."[12] Yet whatever the disparities of technique, the game being played always entails in both cases the fundamental unity of energy and form.

Clearly the playground is not a place to which anyone ought to repair simply in pursuit of relaxation. On the contrary, it is of the essence of the play spirit that there be no letting up of control. Playing well requires both intensity and adaptability, both being positive and creative elements. The typical English comic protagonist is constantly called upon for the maximum intensity of participation within the narrow space of himself and within the narrow time of the present moment. And he possesses a resiliency that is essentially childlike, for the form which the comic hero as artist seeks is not rigid but flexible and contains within itself crucial characteristics of seeking and expansion.

Release from formalization and the creation of new form become a part of one *process*—a dynamic process in which tension is central. The form of play in which this process can most readily be apprehended is probably dancing, which Huizinga defines as "pure play."[13] The dancer gives release, freedom, expression to the instinctive forces welling up within him and at the same time controls those forces through form. Energies become disciplined rhythms. It is what Havelock Ellis calls the dance of *life*—"imparting strength and adding organised harmony."[14]

Because dance represents a creation of vital form, it is not surprising to find it associated with fertility rites in Greek drama or to find Ellis emphasizing its love and courtship associations: "In innumerable parts of the world the season of love is a time which the nubile of each sex devote to dancing in each other's presence, sometimes one sex, sometimes the other, sometimes both, in the frantic effort to display all the force and energy, the skill and endurance, the beauty and grace, which at this moment are yearning within them to be poured into the stream of the race's life."[15] It is just in this spirit that Isabella exclaims at the conclusion of Dryden's *The Wild Gallant:* "Come Nuncle, 'tis in vain to hold out now 'tis past remedy: 'Tis like the last Act of a Play, when People must marry and if Fathers will not consent then, they should throw oranges at 'em from the Galleries; why should you stand off to help us from a Dance?"

The appearance of "merry song and dance" in connection with so many of the Vices of the morality plays suggests the play spirit which frequently inspires them. In the *Interlude of the Four Elements* we find Sensual Appetite summoning a band of entertainers to sing and dance; in *Like Will to Like,* Nicol Newfangle is, according to the stage direction, to have "a gittern or some other instrument (if it may be); but if he have not, they must dance about the place all three, and sing this song that followeth, which must be done also, although they have an instrument." In *Wyt and Science* a stage direction such as "the minstrels play and Honest Recreacion and Wyt dance" is typical, and in *Wisdom* there are several songs. As might be anticipated, the elements of singing and dancing become more prominent and more integral as the morality preoccupation fades. Hence Mathew Merygreeke is frequently accompanied by his group of musicians who, significantly, sing two marriage songs, and Diccon is appropriately given a scene in an alehouse, where the taverners lend their voices to the roisterous drinking song, "Back and syde, go bare, go bare."

Lest it be objected, at this point, that song and dance are nothing more than primitive expressions of high spirits which might be expected to appear quite naturally in these comparatively primitive plays, it should be pointed out that both Havelock Ellis and Huizinga often cite the musical preoccupations of primitive cultures to illustrate the artistic basis on which they rise. Perhaps indeed any human being who insists on confronting face to face the raw materials of existence is potentially an artist. What comic protagonists like Diccon and Dorimant do is to make of their own social existence a dance of life, to reassert their own primitive energies artistically in the face of some social or moral rigidity which threatens to deny their creative humanity. In short, they are "players," and they insist upon making the "plays" in which they have the leading roles ones of their own devising.

## The Rake-hero as Vice

IN UNDERTAKING A MORE DETAILED EXAMINATION of the behavior and the general characteristics which may establish the vice-figure as possessing a recognizable kinship with the Restoration rake-hero, we may do best to mention first the extent to which both are supremely conscious of themselves as practicing artists. When Gayley asserted of the Vice that "he found a house of correction and he left a stage,"[16] he was thinking presumably in dramatic terms and meant to point up the importance of introducing onto the stage a dynamic figure. But in a broader reference, the statement suggests much more, for is not this one way of defining precisely what the play spirit, and the archetypal comic hero who embodies it, has done in every age? Refusing to be bound by dead forms, he has irrepressibly operated to turn the environment he encounters into a playground filled with challenges to his skills.

Thus it is that in their comic aspect the vice-figures are, more often than not, fully conscious entertainers, bent upon making of their world a pageant—dedicated to putting on a good show.[17]

Bernard Spivack pertinently points out that "in one of the Martin-Marprelate tracts the Vice is referred to as though he were, not simply a metaphorical fiction of the stage, but another struggling playwright or actor of the times: . . . 'vices make plaies of Church matters.'" And earlier in this same passage he has remarked on the "proprietary attitude" which the Vice maintains toward his own play.[18] When we turn from these comparatively early plays to figures like Heywood's Mery Reporte and Udall's Mathew Mery-greeke and then to Falstaff and to Ben Jonson's Brainworm and Face, the similarity of function is striking. And cannot much the same preoccupation be readily recognized also in Sir Frederick Frollick, in Dorimant, in Horner, in Mirabell—and in Etherege's Harriet, Wycherley's Hippolita, and Congreve's Millamant as well? Each of them, although with a good deal more subtlety and less bombast, is a "showman." Each, as Ola Winslow says of the Vice, "stands to the main action in the relation of manipulator."[19]

And further, what Spivack says of the "histrionic intimacy of the Vice with his audience,"[20] can be frequently said also of the Restoration rakes. The apron of their stage still allowed them to stand among their audience,[21] and the members of that audience are constantly being invited to keep in mind that the stage has become, in thematic terms, a playground. They are, in effect, invited to take sides with the hero or the heroine and hence to become involved in the game even while they retain their awareness that it *is* a game.

In describing the manipulative role of the Vice, Spivack brings out clearly his relationship with the audience—his means of making them privy to his stratagems:

> In the later moralities and hybrid plays, the whole design of which consists of a succession of his stratagems illustrating his ability to deceive and dominate, and extending from him upon the other characters like spokes from a hub, he occupies the stage almost constantly, prefacing and concluding each part of his activity with his explanatory and triumphant monologues. He not only tells the audience what he is about to do, but also predicts the consequences of his various stratagems, describes off-stage developments, heralds the entrances of his separate victims, and when they leave he usually remains behind to supply the commentary, dramatic and moral, which is always a fundamental part of his office.[22]

Much the same description might be applied to the mode of operation of a Dorimant, a Horner, or a Mirabell, so long as we understand first the special kind of "moral" they draw and then recognize that the "explanatory" and "triumphant" passages are more often delivered not in monologues but, more dramatically, in dialogues with a confidant and that the occasional use of asides is the chief method of establishing a *direct* player-audience rapport.

The stratagems of the Vice are variously carried forward by disguise, pretense, and trickery. It has been suggested, indeed, that he can trace his name to his having at one time worn a mask (*vis, visage*);[23] and whatever the origin of his name, it is undoubtedly true, as Spivack says, that a "part of the Vice's talent in deceit is his virtuosity in the art of false faces. 'Two faces in a hode couertly I bere,' says Cloaked Collusion in *Magnificence,* and his comment on himself applies to the Vice generally. He has one countenance for his dupe and another for his audience, and the rapid transformation of his features, depending on which way his business lies, is a standard and sensational part of his repertory."[24] The equal aptness of the description to Dorimant or Harriet, to Horner or Hippolita, to Mirabell or Millamant, need hardly be heavily underlined.

The Vices find dissimulation useful for much the same reason as do the rake-heroes, and for all of Spivack's negative emphasis, a great many of them use it to similar positive, life-asserting ends. The typical comic protagonist is too clever to attempt breaking down the defenses of morality, sobriety, propriety by attacking them directly. Rather, he makes use of disguise and pretense to get behind those defenses. Such is his means of gaining acceptance so that he may play his game as he will and enjoy the world on his own terms—so that, in short, he may keep himself *alive*. It is always his contention that outward forms should give scope for and ultimately express inner realities, and his disguises and deceptions by no means contradict this fundamental position. His dissimulating is simply his mode of attacking constraint, his means to assuring his own free expression (and sometimes also his means of holding falsities up to laughter by an imitation of their absurdities).

In the particular case of the rake-hero, the aim of self-expression clearly ties in with the Hobbesian conviction that art, far from covering up nature, should express it—that the artist should turn to nature, to experience, to the reality he knows for his materials. It is just such a conviction that lies behind not only the actions of the rake-hero but his mode of dress and his language as well. He knows that clothes, for all their superficial concealing function, may be made to *express* the real substance beneath (and indeed this is precisely what Dorimant and Harriet insist upon in their numerous references to their own grooming). And in his use of language he shares with Hobbes's ideal artist the concern for what Dryden termed a "propriety of thoughts and words."[25]

As comic artist, then, while he is always acting one part or another for purposes of either parody or maneuver, it is his real aim to define and even create a self which will leave no aspect of his essential nature out of account; and in recognizing this aim, we are also brought to recognize another of his important characteristics: that he always maintains a certain degree of objectivity and self-consciousness regarding his own actions. As Oscar Wilde says, "the work that seems to us to be the most natural and simple product of its time is always the result of the most self-conscious effort. . . . there is no fine art without self-consciousness."[26]

Inevitably, moreover, the creation of a self also involves the creation and control of a world which will give that self scope. Thus it is that the rake-hero shares with the vice-figure a seemingly inexhaustible talent for improvisation. He is continually creating the conflict situations, physical, intellectual, and emotional, which constitute the action of the comedy in which he acts. He always seeks to remain the author of his own "play"—the controller of his own world which he struggles to make dominant. And this is as true of a farcical rogue like Mathew Merygreeke as of a refined gentleman like Dorimant. "We shall have sport anon," says Merygreeke, and his genuine creativeness is clearly evinced in the scene where he symbolically brings life out of death by turning his mock corpse, complete with funeral procession, into a mock bridegroom, complete with marriage march—and a glib Lazarus reference slipped in.

Each of these protagonists is, paradoxically, a bad boy because he insists on leading the good life which to him is life itself. And here the reasons for the rake-hero's immorality (another of the key factors contributing to an identification of him with the comic Vice) become obvious. Comedy is, after all, always concerned in some way with the fertility theme. "The same impulse that drove people, even in prehistoric times, to enact fertility rites and celebrate all phases of their biological existence," says Susanne Langer, "sustains their eternal interest in comedy." And she continues: "It is in the nature of comedy to be erotic, risqué, and sensuous if not sensual, impious, and even wicked."[27] In short, the comic protagonist is, in conventional terms, immoral because of his life or creativity emphasis. Coarseness, vulgarity, obscenity are not indulged in for their own sakes;[28] and carping critics who see the new game being played on the Restoration stage as one wholly lacking in rules—a kind of sexual free-for-all[29]—overlook completely the underlying implications. The fact is that the Restoration comic hero does not turn the world of inherited rules upside down merely for the smutty or destructive fun of it. If he is self-consciously wicked, it is because the prevailing system has proved repressive of his élan vital and hence prompts him to demand more flexible and expressive forms. For him the only true morality is living well and fully. He is the artist in living who, in Havelock Ellis's words, sees "the slavery to rigid formulas" as "the death of all high moral responsibility. Life must always be a great adventure, with risks on every hand; a clear-sighted eye, a many-sided sympathy, a fine daring, an endless patience, are for ever necessary to all good living. With such qualities alone may the artist in life reach success; without them even the most devoted slave to formulas can only meet disaster."[30]

Immorality, then, is a crucial and positive ingredient of Restoration comedy. Yet critics who have attacked it on this ground have at least this to be said for them: that they are thereby implicitly acknowledging the genuine sexual content of the plays. Criticism in the twentieth century, however, has taken a far more arbitrary turn; and curiously enough, it has now become necessary to argue the case for the presence of sex in the Restoration comic world. Where George Meredith had seen "cynical licentiousness," L. C. Knights, for example, now sees no true licentiousness at all. Restoration comedy, he states, "far from being outspoken, hovers on the outskirts of sexual relations, and sees nothing but the titillation of appetite. . . . Sex is a hook baited with tempting morsels; it is a thirst quencher; it is a cordial; it is a dish to feed on; it is a bunch of grapes; it is anything but sex."[31] What, then, would he have us make of all the sexually charged wit in the plays, not to mention a stage direction such as that in *The Man of Mode* having to do with "Handy tying up Linnen" or the healthy desires of Margery Pinchwife, to cite only two of the more obvious and open sexual references?

And what would John Palmer make of such passages? Palmer actually defends Restoration comedy on much the same basis that Knights condemns it; he counters the charge of immorality by denying that any immorality exists within the plays. Thus he sees "sex used merely as a comic convention upon which an ingenious plot was able to turn," and goes on to maintain that we find a "stage-direction, such as *Offers to throw her down,* meaning no more, so far as sex excitement went, than *Walks left centre,*" and "a comic hero tumbling the wife of his friend with as little sex significance to the deed as though he were tumbling upstairs or losing his watch and chain." It is all merely "comic machinery . . . colorless, dispassionate."[32] If such were really the case, Restoration comedy would indeed be the dull affair that Knights pronounces it to be and Congreve's characters only the "Dutch dolls" that Palmer seems to find so harmlessly appealing.

It is difficult to counter such arguments except by suggesting that apparently one man's sex may be another man's titillation and then to insist, in the face of all assertions to the contrary, that Restoration comedy *is* "about" sex, that it is about the sexual relationship with everything that relationship implies of hostility, aggression, and power as well as physical attraction and love. By "love," however, the Restoration playwrights mean an emotion which includes the sexual instincts as an essential ingredient, as opposed to what we may call emotionalism, romance, or sentimentality, which leaves that instinct largely out of account. In the comedies of this period, and especially those of Etherege and Wycherley which followed hard on the Restoration, there is a recognition that in their sophisticated society sex, as often as not, was being falsified. In the name of romance and Platonic love, it had become so idealized that the reality of instinct (of lust if you will)

had been denied. And what the rake-hero of the comedies does—
with the tough-minded realism which seems always to be at the
core of the English comic spirit—is to put the animal vitality back
into the male-female relationship, not to the exclusion of emotion
but of emotionalism or sentimentality. John Palmer objects to Vanbrugh because his "indecencies are Aphrodisiac."[33] But so, it must
be insisted, are Etherege's and Wycherley's. The true objection to
both Vanbrugh and Farquhar is that both are basically dishonest
in that they want to be at one and the same time unrealistically
romantic and unromantically realistic. And the audience is caught
in the middle, having to respond now in one way and now in
another.

What may seem a similar dilemma also confronts a Wycherley
audience, and it is a problem which will have to be contended with
in a later chapter. To make an exception of Wycherley, however, is
not to say that his plays are therefore less effective comically than
those of Etherege and Congreve. They are simply rather different
for the reason that, having drawn a dividing line between his
comic and his "romantic" worlds, he does not really concern himself, within the comic one, with the ultimate emotional conflict
which develops when one strong-willed, proudly individualistic
adventurer in life comes face to face with another one of the opposite sex. In Wycherley we find no "pair of witty lovers,"[34] although Hippolita and Gerrard, Ranger and Lydia have their fleeting
moments.

In one sense it is on this account easier to conceive of his comic
heroes as possessing similarities to the Vice than in the case of
Etherege and Congreve. Perhaps because the love-power conflict
has largely been left out, they are less far removed from the world
of masculine tavern vulgarity. Theirs is, more often than not, a
world of male conversation into which women do not enter on
equal terms, and consequently there is little emotional involvement beyond the exclusively sexual. There are no genuine sex-
battles in such a world, and the challenge that confronts a Dorimant
or a Mirabell on one side and a Harriet and a Millamant on the
other is seldom even given. Horner belongs, at least on one side
of his rather complex nature, among the boys in the back room,
and he can make his world dance to the tune he calls in much the

same free-spirited, devil-may-care way of his comic predecessors, with no one to offer any serious challenge to his supremacy.

That there is rarely any explicit vulgarity or coarseness in the dialogues between Etherege's and Congreve's lovers is readily understandable once we recognize the inevitable repressions dictated by the drawing-room environment. The different kinds of vulgarity possible or desirable in a tavern on the one hand and in a drawing room on the other ought to be as obvious as are the corresponding differences in the amount of repression to be overcome. There may have been women present in the tavern playground but there were no ladies, and Falstaffian comedy could indulge in what Meredith calls "frank filth" because it is almost purely masculine. In the drawing-room playground, however, there are both ladies and gentlemen (the latter category presumably having little meaning apart from the former), with a resulting alteration in the degree of directness possible. And here we cannot do better than to turn to Freud for a clarification:

> Not until we come to the refined and cultured does the formal determination of wit arise. The obscenity becomes witty and is tolerated only if it is witty. The technical means of which it mostly makes use is allusion, i.e., substitution through a trifle, something remotely related, which the listener reconstructs in his imagination as a full-fledged and direct obscenity. The greater the disproportion between what is directly offered in the obscenity and what is necessarily aroused by it in the mind of the listener, the finer is the witticism and the higher it may venture in good society. . . . It now becomes comprehensible what wit accomplishes through this service of its tendency. It makes possible the gratification of a craving (lewd or hostile) despite a hindrance which stands in the way; it eludes the hindrance and so derives a pleasure from a source that has become inaccessible on account of the hindrance. The hindrance in the way is really nothing more than the higher degree of culture and education which correspondingly increases the inability of the woman to tolerate the stark sex.[35]

Thus when we move into the more refined, drawing-room world of Etherege and Congreve, we may at first seem to have moved out of the comic sphere peopled by outspoken rogues and back into the sphere occupied by Lyly's witty lovers and Shakespeare's gay heroes and heroines. But for Etherege's and Congreve's heroes and heroines, the central preoccupation is not *love* so much as *freedom* and *life*. Love for them is not the end of the struggle but the beginning of the most intense struggle of all. It is the ultimate challenge to their pride, their individualism, their view of themselves as the artistic shapers of their own lives. Hence, the area in which Shakespeare's three comedies of love anticipate those of the Restoration has to do not with their romantic aspects but with their comic ones —and specifically with a wittily antagonistic couple like Beatrice and Benedick, and even more clearly with a heroine like Rosalind. Rosalind, with Touchstone by her side, is, for all her romantic surroundings, as much in touch with the earth and with the realities of things as are Harriet and Millamant, and she challenges the unreality of sighing romantic love in a way that anticipates Harriet's later challenge, although somewhat less militantly. With her characteristics of hard-headed common sense and earthy self-awareness, she belongs to that English comic tradition of contentious individualism which eternally calls into question every abstraction not tested on the pulses.

In Etherege's and Congreve's comic world, however, she would have encountered a counter-challenge which she does not really find in her own, for in that later milieu both heroes and heroines are characterized by complete self-knowledge. In the tradition of their kind, they both know exactly what they are and exactly what their world is. Each is, in his or her own special way, a type of Susanne Langer's comic hero: "his fight is with obstacles and enemies, which his strength, wisdom, virtue, or other assets let him overcome. It is a fight with the uncongenial world, which he shapes to his own fortunes."[36] The difference between the gay Restoration couples and earlier dramatic couples with whom they have been compared—including Shakespeare's Beatrice and Benedick as well as Shirley's Carol and Fairfield—lies largely in this area of self-awareness and control. Almost invariably in the past the love conflict has had to do with an "education" in self-awareness administered by one lover to the other (Rosaline to Biron, Fairfield to Carol, Rosalind to Orlando) or with the manipulation by other people in their world of both of them (Beatrice and Benedick). But Harriet and Dorimant, Millamant and Mirabell always retain their world's strings in their own competent hands, and all are open-eyed from the start. Harriet, for example, does not "educate" Dorimant. What she does is to come to terms with him as he does with her in an uneasy truce, after a pitched battle of the sexes.

In this connection it is especially important to realize that the witty exchanges between the Restoration lovers are not, as so many critics have maintained, dryly intellectual and consciously formalized in the Lylyian manner. Their wit at its best possesses a heavy emotional charge. It expresses sexual aggressiveness or hostility or desire for approval kept under tight control. But however brittle and clever the intellectual surface, the emotional content never lies far below, and its explosive potential always fills the atmosphere. Thus the wit is functioning at once to give release or expression to vital energies and to impose a form and rhythm on those energies. Each lover has found in the other a worthy adversary—one who knows how to play the game of life and love as it should be played. And it is in the witty dialogue that the game or contest is very largely carried out.

Indeed wit as it is employed by the comic heroes and heroines of the Restoration achieves much the same kind of creative vitality on the level of language that the comedy itself achieves on the level of action. Congreve's heroes and heroines no more "talk for talk's sake"[37] than do Etherege's. The *way* in which they talk precisely expresses the way in which they respond to and control their worlds. And here again their kinship with the vice-figure becomes apparent. The Vice too, although in a considerably less finished manner, is a player with words, a punster, an ironist. If, until Falstaff, his success in this area is not especially marked, the seeds for a later development are undeniably present. For him, as for the rake-hero, word play constitutes what James Sully defines as a "playful impulse to get as far away as possible from rule and restriction, to turn things topsy-turvy, to seize on the extravagant and wildly capricious," and it has "a close kinship with make-believe."[38]

And not only does the talk of the comic protagonists reveal their fundamental aggressiveness, but it is, as are they in their individual ways, inventive, mischievous, spontaneous, deceitful, ironic, dynamic. Far from being a purely detached "intellectual exercise,"[39] such wit is firmly anchored in instinct. Bernard Harris, in one of the best studies to have appeared on the subject of the language of Restoration comedy, puts it this way:

> To all that Bonamy Dobrée so well said about Congreve's rhythm, its flexibility and point, one might only want to add that it is the articulation not only of an "incomparable beauty" and "seductive gentleness" but of an inexhaustible human energy. The "refinement" is fuelled upon gross matter and when it neglects the origin of the supply the comic creation collapses as violently as does the verbal poise of Lady Wishfort when she discovers Foible's deceit. . . . The balance lost here, and strenuously being restored at the close of the play, may serve to represent that major theme of Restoration social comedy which engages in so many ways with the refined and the raw. . . . The tension between reason and appetite . . . is achieved in the prose of Congreve.[40]

It is imperative that this emphasis on "inexhaustible human energy" and upon a " 'refinement' fuelled upon gross matter" be kept prominently in mind in considering the function of wit in Restoration comedy. And it is equally imperative to remember its fundamentally combative and aggressive quality. Words, as they are used by the Restoration comic protagonists, have become a part of the life of their wielders. The mind has been brought into play in the service of energetic expression. Minds have become tennis rackets with words for balls—except that the ball is likely without warning to change into a shuttlecock or a feather or a spring. Critics have at various times commented significantly on the unstable meanings of words in both Etherege and Wycherley; the real import of abstractions is forever being challenged; generalities undercut; paradox piled on paradox.[41] The player has to be everywhere on the court at once. His opponent is forever trying to defeat him by upsetting his equilibrium, throwing him off balance, taking him by surprise, deceiving his expectations, and he must not only get his racket on the ball but send it back with a spin or a smash or an over-the-head lob of his own. And to keep up the pace he must have agility, control, a bag of tricks at his command, and a talent for anticipation. His wit, in short, is essentially a Hobbesian "Celerity of Imagining."[42] And the resulting tension should be obvious. Yet the hero must not give himself away by appearing fatigued. His art must seem artless. Always aware of himself as a player before an audience, he makes his wit a part of his perform-ance, his comic self-consciousness and self-definition.

The synthesis he achieves, however, is never final. It is, in fact, never more than momentary. A successful witticism always seems, as it is uttered, to have constituted a "passing shot." It seems to have delivered the final sword-thrust, to have contributed the last word on a subject. But in the world of comedy, every witty thrust is at the same time a victory and a challenge to new conflict. Comic wit thus expresses verbally that dynamic quality which characterizes the comic protagonists themselves. The tension on the verbal play-ground never lets down; the battle is never finally won.

It has been said of Diccon that he "is a 'dynamic' character who lives...by his wits."[43] So too do the Restoration comic heroes, but it is equally true that they *live* by their *wit*. They not only act but think and talk dramatically. Not only do they "seize the day." They seize every moment and fill it with dramatic tension. "Instead of treating his ideas as mere symbols," says Bergson, "the wit sees them, he hears them and, above all, makes them converse with one another like persons."[44] In short, he gives them life, and they in turn affirm his own.

The typical English comic protagonist thus goes beyond the role of *eiron* reserved in comedy for the fool and the clown, for at the same time that he stands outside the scene as entertainer and man of wit, he is also an *insider*. At the same time that he is "in front of the curtain," he is also an actor on a stage. His wit is simultaneously a wry or rebellious commentary and an expression of his own ele-mental drives toward self-assertion and self-definition, and his witty observations draw their life and force from the instinctual and emo-tional needs which prompt them. Mathew Merygreeke, for exam-ple, does not merely direct the "dance of life"; he dances it as well. Having devised and staged the war games with the help of Mistress Custance, he becomes a delighted player in them and turns up in the thick of the fight. And Dorimant is quite obviously a player of the love game as well as an expert commentator on it.

Such a comic protagonist will always, moreover, be his own best audience. He views the world *he* has made and his own role in it with pardonable pride—indeed with the colossal self-assurance which must characterize the spirit daring enough to challenge all the world in the name of a fragile self and to make it over on his own terms. And when he laughs it is with a devilish, rather Baudelairean laughter. ("Laughter comes from the idea of one's *own* superiority. A Satanic idea if there ever was one!")[45] Not surprisingly, one of the central Vices in Medwall's *Nature* is actually named Pride, and his opening lines shamelessly ask that we admire him. And Falstaff's egotism is as overblown as his frame. It is a key aspect of their relationship with the audience that such comic heroes invite us to admire their prowess as they, with a kind of artistic detachment, admire it themselves. Theirs is the player's pride in performance and the egotism of the victor. "Joy, arising from imagination of a man's own power and ability," said Hobbes, "is that exultation of the mind which is called GLORYING: which if grounded upon the experience of his own former actions, is the same with Confidence: but if grounded on the flattery of others, or onely supposed by himself, for delight in the consequences of it, is called Vaine-Glory."[46] In such terms the typical English comic hero is a bona fide "glorier."

The Hobbesian emphasis on "power" here is also of importance to an understanding of the way in which a Merygreeke, a Falstaff, a Dorimant molds his world to himself. Havelock Ellis cautions us to "remember that the distinction between the 'creative' and the 'possessive' impulses, although convenient, is superficial." And he goes on: "In creation we have not really put aside the possessive instinct, we may even have intensified it. For it has been reasonably argued that it is precisely the deep urgency of the impulse to possess which stirs the creative artist. He creates because that is the best way, or the only way, of gratifying his passionate desire to possess."[47] The comic hero who would create a world, then, must in effect possess it. He must, like his parasite counterparts, have an "ambition to rule," and he must have it "in his power" to do with life what he will.[48] In Restoration comedy the power instinct and the sex instinct are, in fact, really working in the same direction and indeed cannot be legitimately separated.

And perhaps at this point—while we are considering the mode of operation of the comic vice-figure and the later English comic hero as involving some desire to possess and dominate, to assert superiority, to achieve power—we may do well to return for a moment to a consideration of that vexing question already touched upon: the question of what there is to distinguish him from an Ambidexter (*Cambises*) or an Iago, each of whom also belongs to the Vice family and is also a detached artist, "making sport" and delightedly creating conflict. Is not the comic hero here under consideration also in some sense a "villain"? Is he not "wicked"? Does he not work (or play his game) with a kind of cold-blooded calculation or policy? Is he not fundamentally Machiavellian and very often cruel? If Iago is persistently associated with the devil, so, almost as insistently, are Falstaff and Dorimant and Horner. Clearly the vice-figure possesses a double potential, and Eric Bentley has hinted at the nature of this doubleness in concluding that the "knave in farce is the equivalent of the villain in melodrama. 'Passions spin the plot.' If the passion that spins the melodramatic plot is sheer wickedness, the passion that spins the farcical plot is that younger brother of wickedness, the spirit of mischief."[49]

But after all, one role is not really "equivalent" to the other, and the distinction to be made between knave and villain rests upon two basic considerations: first, the kind of passions which each in spinning his plot seeks to release, and second, the ends to which he practices his art. Vice-figures like Ambidexter and villains like Iago clearly belong to a tragic or melodramatic scene. Symbolically they represent the destructive passions in human nature—and most notably hatred and jealousy—and these are the passions they seek to unleash in others. Their role is that of artists of destruction devising and staging a scene of general chaos. And because of their essentially negative dedication, the principal targets of their attack are, as might be expected, those sources of life represented by family unity and love. Thus, in defining the actions of the four Shakespearean villains whom he regards as inheritors of this "vicious" tradition, Spivack writes:

> It is not simply coincidence that Aaron by contriving the rape of Lavinia, destroys virginity and defeats the consummation of chaste love in marriage; that Richard seduces Lady Anne out of the bonds of matrimonial piety that tied her to the memory of her dead husband; that the slander manipulated by Don John is an aggression against the values of chastity and matrimony; that Iago destroys

the bond of love and marriage which, in the persons of Desdemona and Othello, unites transcendent virtues—love and purity with valor and magnanimity. Neither is it chance that all four gleefully demonstrate their skill in divorcing lover from lover, husband from wife, child from father, brother from brother, ruler from subject, friend from friend.[50]

Interestingly enough, similar characters are to be found in the comedies of Etherege, Wycherley, and Congreve. But they are not the comic heroes and heroines. Rather they are the characters who, out of their own passions of hatred and jealousy, seek to release the same passions in the world they occupy in order to destroy it; and especially in the plays of Congreve they are patently the characters of melodrama: Maskwell and Lady Touchwood in *The Double-Dealer*, Fainall and Mrs. Marwood in *The Way of the World*. But Spivack's particular preoccupation with Iago's ancestry has led him to overemphasize the destructive aspects of the early Vices and to ignore the fact that, in Northrop Frye's words, "as a rule the vice's activity is, in spite of his name, benevolent."[51] Even Frye's "in spite of" qualification must be called into question, however, since certain human vices, certain kinds of "devilishness" may, as already suggested, have a positive as well as a negative potential. Mrs. Langer sees the identification of devil and clown as "a historical accident, due to the peculiar Christian conception that identifies the devil with the flesh, and sin with lust." And she goes on: "For there is no denying that the Fool is a red-blooded fellow; he is, in fact, close to the animal world; . . . He is all motion, whim, and impulse—the 'libido' itself."[52] The English comic hero (who bears, of course, a close kinship with the fool) is "devilish" in a positive, life-asserting sense, and he reveals through his character and actions the constructive possibilities of at least some of the human vices. His sphere of action is, significantly, the same as that of his negative counterpart, for more often than not he too attacks "family unity and love" (Bentley's "household gods"). But he does so only when they have abandoned their creative potential, when they have proved to be repressive of vitality or have become mere words and forms, empty of any genuinely constructive promise, and hence no longer sources of life but deadening restrictions. And his motives for attack are wholly opposite from those of an Iago, for he seeks to put in the place of the existing family or society new marriages and unities of his own devising.

Oscar Wilde is clearly writing *in* the English comic spirit as well as about it when he asserts:

> What is termed Sin is an essential element of progress. Without it the world would stagnate, or grow old, or become colorless. By its curiosity, Sin increases the experience of the race. Through its intensified assertion of individualism, it saves us from monotony of type. In its rejection of the current notions about morality, it is one with the higher ethics. And as for the virtues! What are the virtues? Nature, M. Renan tells us, cares little about chastity, and it may be that it is to the shame of the Magdalen, and not to their own purity, that the Lucretias of modern life owe their freedom from stain. Charity, as even those of whose religion it makes a formal part have been compelled to acknowledge, creates a multitude of evils. The mere existence of conscience, that faculty of which people prate so much nowadays, and are so ignorantly proud, is a sign of our imperfect development. It must be merged in instinct before we become fine. Self-denial is simply a method by which man arrests his progress.[53]

The heroes of Restoration comedy use the word "sin" much as Wilde is using it here. It is partly true, of course, that they are, as Sypher puts it, "making game of 'serious' life"—that "comic rites are necessarily impious, for comedy is sacrilege as well as release."[54] But in using words like "sin," "wickedness," and "devil"—and in reveling in the thought of themselves as sinful, wicked, and devilish —they are not only defiantly challenging Christian morality but they are expressing precisely what they are. In the early morality plays the comic spirits were called not only Vice but more specific names like Pride, Sensuality, and Riot—those instincts with whose total repression "the world would stagnate, or grow old, or become colorless."

And since youth is the period in which the instinctual life most insistently asserts itself, the play spirit here in question tends always to be a youthful spirit. Thus we ought at this point to be looking for one final similarity between the Vices and the rake-heroes which we do indeed find: that all of them are, if not chronologically at least in spirit, youthful. The example of Falstaff is too obvious to require more than passing mention. With the early Vices the case is less clear, merely for the reason that they have only a metaphorical or allegorical existence. Yet in the great majority of cases, the human figure of whom they represent one side is a young man, whether he be named Wit, Mankind, or Lusty Juventus. As for the situation in Restoration comedy, one critic has found the youth emphasis pervasive enough to support a full-scale study, and has finally concluded that nowhere do we find a body of comedy in which there is such a wholesale rejection and even villification of age in favor of youth. Even the aging Etherege still maintained this attitude, as evidenced by his writing from his post at Ratisbon: "Let us take care our years do not sour us with any of the common vices of age; let us still preserve our good humour and our good nature, to make us welcome near those young people who possess that plentiful estate we have pretty well run out of, that we may help them rail at the morose and cry out with Falstaff: 'down with them that hate us (youth)!'"[55]

## The Rake-hero as Libertine

To TURN FROM THE SELF-CONTAINED WORLD of the Restoration comedies to the historically definable world from which they sprang is to be at once struck with the remarkable extent to which the emotional and intellectual atmosphere of the court of Charles II evinced a comic potential. The fact that a robust, earthy comedy hitherto confined to low-life characters and tavern surroundings was now finding a place in a social milieu once almost wholly given over to pastoral and romantic comedies may well, indeed, be explained finally in terms of a rather extraordinary historical accident. The intellectual climate of the Restoration period, at least in one of its multiple aspects and that which largely prevailed in court society, was one in which a spirit of skepticism, libertinism, Machiavellianism flourished, in which man was seen by Hobbes and his followers in all his naturalistic crudeness, and in which a classical respect for tradition was giving way to a preference for trying philosophies at the bar of experience. In short, a great many of the ingredients which, when combined in past English comedy, had made up the vigorous self-assertiveness and rebelliousness of the comic protagonist, were actually present among the members of the Restoration court.

But if the specific comic role of the rake-hero of the stage is to be fully comprehended, some familiarity is also necessary with the causes of his particular rebellion, as they had their root in the repressive, life-denying conventions to be found in actual court circles. These conventions, as might be expected in an aristocratic milieu, tended to be primarily social rather than moral or religious. Neither Puritanism in particular nor middle-class morality in general was, after all, much of a force to be reckoned with at court. What *was* apparently still a formidable force, despite the lapse of years since the domination of Charles I's French queen, was that highly artificial *précieux* love convention based largely on Platonic and chivalric ideals. By the laws of that convention lovers were expected to whine and sigh at the feet of the beloved. "Basically," as one literary historian describes it, "it was a form of ceremonious social intercourse which derived its attitudes, postures, and special vocabulary from the belief that beautiful and virtuous ladies have a semi-divine status, to which their male satellites . . . can be drawn by due worship of these ladies and the cultivation of refinement, honor, virtue, superficial learning, and a certain stereotyped wit."[56] The words "belief" and "worship" are significant. The male-female relationship was, according to this tradition, a sacred, a religious matter, and even the most recalcitrant male might hope to experience a "conversion" when the "flaming darts" from a lady's eyes penetrated to his very soul.

That the religious ideas of love, honor, virtue, constancy lingered on into the Restoration period is amply attested to by their continuing dominance in the world of heroic tragedy. But, as John Wilson says, "in matters of love the Wits were atheists." And he goes on to suggest that the influence of such writers as Horace, Lucretius, and their own Hobbes, as well as the tendency to think of human behavior in rational, scientific terms, left the Wits contemptuous of so irrational a belief as that required by the chivalric love tradition.[57] The question must be explored at greater length in the discussion of individual comedies, and especially those of Etherege. For the present, however, suffice it to say that in love as in philosophy, "scientific" explanations were replacing religious ones. Hence when a comic hero self-consciously uses religious terminology to describe a male-female encounter, he is ironically underlining both his atheism in religion and his atheism in love. And in the cases where he begins to use the *précieux* vocabulary in seeming earnest, the heroine invariably refuses to take her place on the pedestal and recalls him to the realities of flesh and blood.

Nor was the *précieux* stance in love the only impetus to rebellion. As empiricists, the "new" man and woman quite predictably looked upon the marriage institution itself with similar suspicion. Marriage was most often seen as a restriction imposed by society to prevent free expression of the instincts—and all the more reprehensible an institution at a time when divorces were as hard to obtain legally as marriages were easy.[58] It was, moreover, an institution which, established in the name of morality, had become in skeptical eyes grossly immoral by becoming simply on the one hand a means for economic gain (matches being arranged by parents with an eye to greater accumulations of land and wealth)[59] or on the other a means of allowing men and women to use one another like pieces of property.

In the comedies of the period marriage was often for these reasons equated with confinement in the country, the country representing to the skeptical and rebellious mind a traditional, an unchanging pattern of life and thought and being associated, moreover, in literary tradition with the romantic, pastoral world and with that Golden Age of simplicity and innocence for which men had dreamingly yearned in a more idealistic age but which could only seem now a prettified falsification. For a generation that disbelieved in human innocence in the traditional sense, Arcadia would inevitably have seemed as much a fraud and a delusion as did the whole conception of romantic and Platonic love. Said Congreve, "Believe it, Men have ever been the same,/And all the Golden Age is but a Dream."[60]

Like so many other traditional assumptions, the Arcadian was being insistently measured against the realities of experience. Thus it was that mock-pastoral often replaced pastoral, and that the time-honored rural-urban antithesis could be audaciously turned upside down. "Shakespeare's type of romantic comedy," writes

Northrop Frye, "follows a tradition established by Peele and developed by Greene and Lyly, which has affinities with the medieval tradition of the seasonal ritual-play. We may call it the drama of the green world, its plot being assimilated to the ritual theme of the triumph of life and love over the waste land."[61] In these terms what we find in Restoration comedy amounts to a wholesale inversion. The rural atmosphere has become a "waste land," no longer fresh and green but sterile. And the "green world" is now the town, the urban setting, which possesses genuine "fertility." It is only in the country that a Pinchwife can safely expect to practice his brand of marital tyranny and can effectively repress the youthful exuberance of a Margery. The very title of the play makes an association of ideas which appears again and again in Restoration comedy. Margery is a "country wife," and her innocence is an ignorance of the possibilities for living which has been fostered in her country home and in her marital confinement. In pastoral (and traditionally moralistic) terminology she is presumably corrupted. But in terms of what might be called the higher morality of comedy, she is released and given life.

In opposition to the advocates for a pastoral or romantic approach to love, moreover, the Restoration courtiers disbelieved altogether in timelessness, and they hard-headedly set against such sentimentalism their own much-discussed *carpe diem* philosophy. They did not have "world enough and time" that they might waste it on whining and sighing and declarations of constancy. They saw, as men possessed by the comic spirit have always seen, that, in Susanne Langer's words, "no matter how people contrive to become reconciled to their mortality, it puts its stamp on their conception of life: since the instinctive struggle to go on living is bound to meet defeat in the end, they look for *as much life as possible* between birth and death—for adventure, variety and intensity of experience, and the sense of growth."[62] It is just in this sense that the English comic spirit is eternally young. In seeking never to lose the "sense of growth," the comic protagonist rejects the oppressive past—symbolized in Restoration comedies by traditional institutions, by the country, and by age—and maintains a state of precarious balance in the present, always knowing that that balance may be at any moment upset and a new center of equilibrium required. He seeks to possess life without being controlled and possessed by it. No doubt a sober second thought would show him that life can be stable and serene, and age and tradition worthy of veneration and respect. But he has nothing to do with sober second thoughts. He does not yearn toward a past or an unattainable ideal, but accepts the raw stuff of humanity for what it is and makes the most of it. And *carpe diem* is his watchword:

> Then since we lovers mortal are,
> Ask not how long our love will last;
> But while it does let us take care
> Each minute be with pleasure pass'd;
> Were it not madness to deny
> To live, because we're sure to die?

Etherege

And if such was the view of the Restoration courtiers and their comic heroes, it was equally the view of their ladies, although they might make application of the philosophy with a difference. Whether treated as a piece of property on the one hand or as an angel of light on the other, a witty and intelligent woman like a Harriet or a Millamant, in possession of a new-found equality of status, insisted that her basic humanity not be ignored. Characterized by a new independence, she was also characterized by a determination to exert individualistic power equal to that of the male and above all to remain her own woman. No wonder that she faced the prospect of marriage with "dubiety"[63] when it loomed as a loss of both freedom and power. She may not have been a libertine in the usual sense of the word (even the broad-minded seventeenth-century aristocratic world could not quite bring itself to that), but she was certainly so in the sense that she stubbornly demanded from the world all it had to give of psychic pleasure and satisfaction.

Within the world of the comedies, then, it is not surprising that what both the rake-heroes and their emancipated ladies are seeking in the play sphere is genuine self-expression on their own terms. Lionel Trilling, in the course of an assessment of Freud, points out that "the ego is the aspect of the mind that deals with the object-

world, and one of its important functions is the pleasurable entertainment of the idea of adventure. But if part of the object-world is
closed off by interdiction, and if the impulse to adventure is checked
by a restrictive culture, the free functioning of the ego is im-
paired."[64] The rake-heroes and their heroines are, in these terms,
looking not only toward the release from old restrictions but also
toward the creation of a new culture in order to "make a coherent
life."

The nature of the playground on which they meet is one which
the Hobbesian spirit of the time must have done much to shape,
and the word "pleasure" unquestionably sounds the keynote. In
deliberately flinging their own pleasure-seeking individuality in
the teeth of social repression, the rakes could have found their
justification in the Hobbesian view, for Hobbes of course placed
the pleasure-giving passions at the very source of life. "This motion,
which is called appetite . . ." he wrote, "seemeth to be a corrobora-
tion of vital motion, and a help thereunto." Of both Gassendi and
Hobbes, Thorpe says:

> They regard pleasure as something positive, something which is the
> object of desire, and good because it is desired. The psychology
> which led up to this ethical valuation is therefore the reverse of the
> traditional. It recognizes desire as both natural and good. It refuses
> to distinguish between the lower and the higher types of desire, but
> regards all desire as fundamentally the striving of the organism after
> its satisfaction. . . . This then is the new point of view, a fresh
> conception of the natural man, a dynamic standpoint that sees in
> every person an eternal striving which creates the ends it strives to
> attain.[65]

Clearly enough, the pursuit of pleasure to Hobbes is creative,
life-giving, vital; and it is, as Thorpe later points out, closely allied
in his thinking to the life of the imagination:

> For since pleasure and desire are engendered by an imagination of
> a good to come, imaginative response is a way both to the passion
> of pleasure and to the passion of appetite for new and continued
> activity. But imaginative response is itself both motion and the result
> of motion engendered by the same sort of pleasure and appetite it

promotes. Now Hobbes clearly regards man's happiness as dependent upon a continuation of this sort of circular, reciprocal process, motion and pleasure and appetite ever producing more motion and pleasure and appetite.[66]

But it is important to stress in this connection that (whatever may have been the case with Charles II's courtiers) the life of pleasure for the comic heroes and heroines with whom we are dealing has little to do with mere self-abandonment or self-indulgence any more than has play. On the contrary, it constitutes, to use Gourmont's words, "a human creation, a delicate art, to which, as for music or painting, only a few are apt."[67] The true "art" of a Dorimant or a Harriet, a Mirabell or a Millamant has to do with the creation of an elegant life-style in which the passions are not denied but accommodated as vital sources for extending and enriching experience. "The principal wits of all the plays," says one commentator, "are supposed to possess or be close to acquiring *le je ne sais quoi*—an inexplicable interior harmony resulting in an indescribably elegant deportment."[68] And his libertinism or pursuit of pleasure has to do with a good deal more than carnal appetite. Indeed, what William Temple had to say about the "Libertine" nature of the poetic genius is peculiarly applicable to him:

> The truth is, there is something in the Genius of Poetry too Libertine to be confined to so many Rules; and whoever goes about to subject it to such Constraints loses both its Spirit and Grace, which are ever Native, and never learnt, even of the best Masters. 'Tis as if, to make excellent Honey, you should cut off the Wings of your Bees. ... They must range through Fields as well as Gardens, choose such Flowers as they please, and by Proprieties and Scents they only know and distinguish. They must work up their Cells with Admirable Art, extract their Honey with infinite Labour, and sever it from the Wax with such Distinction and Choyce as belongs to none but themselves to perform or to judge.[69]

Like play, the comic art encloses human impulses, in Huizinga's words, "within certain bounds freely accepted."[70] But within those play boundaries there must be an "eternal striving" toward happiness and full self-realization. Just as Hobbes largely denies to repose any contribution to pleasure, so the Restoration comic heroes and heroines define a Hobbesian "motion" or "agitation" as one of the first rules of their game. Happiness to Hobbes "lies not in the repose of achievement but in the excitement of pursuit."[71] Agility, then, is an essential requirement if the comic protagonists are to be and to remain participants in the comic dance which "is the rule of number and of rhythm and of measure and of order, of the controlling influence of form."[72]

Thus the rake-heroes, both as libertines and as persistent challengers who thrive on controversy, are exemplary of the Hobbesian thinking which prevailed in court circles after the Restoration. At a time when skepticism was widespread and philosophies were experimental and exploratory, the comic potential was in the very air. For the comic as for the skeptical spirit, there can be no repose. Both exist of necessity in a state of suspense. Both defy "the tyranny of results and conclusions."[73] And both are rooted in an egotism which ruthlessly tests every assumption against its own arbitrary demands. The typical English comic protagonist, whether he is called merely Vice or more specifically Diccon or Falstaff, Dorimant or Horner, confronts his world with a persistent irony; and he finally achieves, at his most successful, that ideal which has been ascribed to the humanistic Greeks: "the happy union of natural exuberance with a sense of style which does not impede but gives it a direction and a distinction."[74]

# [ III ]

# *The Beginnings in Etherege*

---

APOLOGIZE, v.i. To lay the foundation for a future offence.
DEFENCELESS, adj. Unable to attack.

—AMBROSE BIERCE, *The Devil's Dictionary*

LIKE HIS OWN SIR FREDERICK FROLLICK, YOUNG GEORGE ETHEREGE was, in 1662, only recently returned from France and was already launched upon a career of gaiety. Years later he was to cast his thoughts across the Channel from Ratisbon and was to recall those past good times. "There is not a day," he was to write wistfully to a friend, "but my thoughts dog you from the coffee-house to the play, from thence to Marylebone, always concerned for your good luck, and in pain I cannot make one with you in the sports you follow. Some of the ancients have imagined that the greatest torment of the dead was an impatient longing after what they delighted most in while they were living, and I can swear by my damnation in Germany, this hell is no jesting matter."[1] For Etherege, as for his comic heroes, life was for living, and the greatest compliment he could pay to a man was the one he had paid a year or so earlier to the Count de Lemburg: "he is a gentleman; besides his other merits he knows how to live, which is a thing most of our Doctors are to learn."[2]

It has been generally agreed that Etherege largely drew his comic heroes in his own image; and in so doing he was following the time-honored practice of those comic poets who, in Lane Cooper's

[40]

words, "naturally pass into intensified modes of their own habitual reactions."[3] He did indeed, as John Palmer asserts, find "a form for the spirit of his age," of which spirit he was himself, in many respects, exemplary.[4] But he was nonetheless a thoroughly conscious artist, and if not quite the thoughtful intellectual that certain recent critical judgments would make of him,[5] he was a developing writer with a consistent comic philosophy. Each of his three ebullient heroes possesses undeniable dramatic life; each epitomizes in his own highly individual way a triumphant life force; and each handily dominates his particular playground, with the audience taking his side in the game he devises and sharing in his meeting of successive challenges and in his ultimate victory. Other worlds are, it is true, measured against the one in which he moves, but in the end it is to him that we look for a conclusive definition of the way life should be lived. His particular mode of life, in all its devilish vitality, asserts itself at the outset and maintains itself throughout the action against all oppositions, until it finally makes its essential spirit overwhelmingly felt. As Alfred Harbage has put it: "To reform him were to ruin him; he is the new pattern of perfection."[6]

## *The Comical Revenge, or Love in a Tub*

THE AMOUNT OF CRITICAL ATTENTION given to Etherege's first play (1664) is generally felt to have more to do with its importance to the history of English comedy than with its intrinsic dramatic worth. Standing as it does at the beginning of the so-called comedy of manners tradition, it has been accorded a certain acclaim; but as a work of art, critics have tended to regard it as a dramatic hodge-podge, in which backward-looking elements (shades of Elizabethan and Jacobean roguery) combine with elements borrowed from heroic tragedy—the elements being imperfectly bonded together by a hero who anticipates, albeit a bit farcically, the rake-heroes of later Restoration comedy. Yet Sir Frederick Frollick has almost always emerged with critical accolades. If nothing else, he has been heralded as something new to the English theater, and John Wilson has paid to him and his creator an accurate tribute.

"Perhaps Etherege's first claim to fame," he writes, "is that he brought merriment back on the stage."[7]

Within recent years, however, critics like Norman Holland, Dale Underwood, and Jocelyn Powell have made out convincing cases for a "unity of concern" informing the various plot lines, and there is now less inclination to regard Sir Frederick as an isolated phenomenon in the play, having only a tenuous connection with the surrounding actions. But what, finally, is to be made of his role? Does he represent a "golden mean," "a middle way" between a high plot and a low, as both Holland and Underwood argue in their different ways? And is it true, as in Powell's interpretation, that with his "vigorous and graceful series of masquerades" he is the center of a "spectacle" through which "the experience of the play is grasped"?[8] It will be one of the central contentions of this chapter that the first of these conclusions is actually false and that the second is justified but incomplete.

As Powell's statement suggests, Sir Frederick must certainly be recognized as assuming the role of master of the revels. But crucial though this insight may be, it is yet more crucial to see that there is a great deal more to him than that. The important things about him are first that he is the original Restoration embodiment of the English comic rogue, the English comic spirit incarnate, and second (the really vital point) that Etherege's play is actually thematically concerned with depicting this spirit in the very act of gaining acceptance and dominance in a new sphere. The action of the play, which records his successful wooing of the Widow Rich, constitutes a *dramatization* of the process whereby Falstaffian tavern humor, with its boisterousness and its robust vitality, challenges and gains entry into a sophisticated and effete court world.

As the play opens, we are confronted with two separate modes of life: one is the down-to-earth, harddrinking, prosaic mode of the low plot; the other, the idealized, codified, poetic mode of Beaufort and Graciana. By birth Sir Frederick belongs to the upper world, but (and here is the important point to be acknowledged) Etherege takes great care to let us know that by experience and sympathies he belongs far more essentially to the lower one. He has already been—to use Wylie Sypher's words about Prince Hal[9]—"initiated into the company of Fools and Rogues," into "the depths of bohemia, amid whores, parasites, and cowards, a realm where Falstaff is king and priest."[10] The opening dialogue carefully underscores the fact that he has returned from France equipped only with the raw materials of existence out of which to make a world and with only the primitive man Dufoy "to counsel and to advisé him."[11]

As the play opens, a new day lies before him—and so too, with the delivery of Beaufort's invitation, does the challenge of a new world. But it is clear from the outset that Bohemia is his spiritual home. If Wheadle and Palmer are rogues and villains, so, we are plainly asked to see, is Sir Frederick. If they are drinkers, gamblers, roisterers, tricksters, so is he. Early in the play he describes Wheadle as being "of a ready Wit, pleasant Conversation, throughly skill'd in men; in a word, he knows so much of Virtue as makes him well accomplish'd for all manner of Vice." The description would serve just as well for Sir Frederick himself, and indeed he goes on to say, "I made a little debauch th'other day in their Company" (7). Like Palmer, Sir Frederick is a "Dexterous Rogue"; like Wheadle, he always has some sort of "design" afoot. And in fact there is a direct verbal parallel made between Sir Frederick's designs on the Widow Rich and those of Wheadle and Palmer upon Sir Nicholas Cully, both designs being spoken of in terms of "Anglers," "Bait," and "Fish" (8, 11).

In short, Sir Frederick knows Wheadle and Palmer because he is very much at home in their world; and he is not (as the ensuing dialogue of the scene clearly indicates) at home in Beaufort's. To Beaufort's invitation to "be my Guest at my Lord *Bevill*'s Table," he replies affirmatively, but with an important reservation: ". . . upon condition you'l excuse my errors; you know my Conversation has not been amongst ceremonious Ladies." Thus he himself plainly underlines his alien position; and in diction as well as in general preoccupations, the position becomes more and more marked, with a world of couplets continually juxtaposed to his world of earthy prose. As early as scene ii, for example, we witness a telling dialogue between Sir Frederick and Beaufort:

SIR FRED. . . . But pray, my Lord, how thrive you in your more honourable adventures? Is harvest near? When is the Sickle to be put i'th' Corn?
BEAUF. I have been hitherto so prosperous

My happiness has still out-flown my faith:
Nothing remains but Ceremonial Charms,
*Graciana's* fix'd i'th' circle of my Arms.
    SIR FRED. Then y'are a happy man for a season.
    BEAUF. For ever.
    SIR FRED. I mistrust your Mistresses Divinity; you'l find her At-
tributes but Mortal: Women, like Juglers Tricks, appear Miracles to
the ignorant; but in themselves th'are meer cheats.

The contrast between the two worlds is pointed up not only by the
prose-verse opposition but also, obviously, by the kind of diction employed in the respective references made by the two men with regard to sexual consummation. Just as Sir Frederick opposes his
"season" to Beaufort's "eternity," he uses concrete images ("harvest," "Sickle") and harsh monosyllables ("Tricks," "cheats") to
undercut Beaufort's soft abstractions.

For all its artificiality, however, we are clearly asked to believe in
the actual existence of this *précieux* realm of courtly love, of whining, sighing, honor-bound young men and of noble, equally honor-
bound ladies, much as we are asked in *Henry IV* to believe in
Hotspur's world as one possible interpretation of reality by which
men still choose to live. James Sully, in his book on laughter, describes much the kind of situation with which we are here confronted when he writes: "Nowhere, perhaps, is the elation of mirth
more distinctly audible than in [the] ridicule by an advancing age
of the discarded ways of its predecessors. Art gives us many examples of this merriment over what is decaying and growing
effete."[12]

Thus, in *The Comical Revenge* we are patently presented with
two modes of living, two ways of interpreting reality, indeed two
opposing views of human nature and potential: one, in Sully's
phrase, a "disappearing phantom," the other a present development.
One is based on abstract ideals—on a belief in human nobility; the
other is based on concrete realities—on a view of man as by nature
animalistic and a view of human relationships as a combat between
aggressors. One sees life controlled by "Heaven" or "Fate"; the
other sees fate itself as dependent on "small accidents" and as simply
another challenge to human ingenuity.[13] And the higher world
constantly suffers an undercutting in comparison to the lower, not

only at the hands of Sir Frederick but at those of Wheadle, Palmer, and Dufoy as well.

But just how does Etherege go about achieving this undercutting and establishing the thematic unity of the play? The answer is not far to seek, for a careful examination of the dialogue at once reveals certain emerging patterns of imagery in terms of which one world is made to comment upon and evaluate the other. These patterns have to do with sickness or disease, with warfare and death, and with pastoralism, and each emphasizes the same essential contrast between a vital and an effete way of life.

The disease imagery is perhaps the least pervasive and, associated as it often is with "wounds," could be regarded as an aspect of the more general warfare imagery (an association made implicitly in the play's title), but in any case its suggestiveness is surely unmistakable. Thus, for example, we hear Graciana, at the end of Act I, repining: " 'Tis cruelty to gaze on Wounds I'm sure,/ When we want Balsome to effect their Cure" (12). The "wounds" in this context are those her beauty has inflicted upon Bruce. But the "wound" being discussed at the opening of Act II is of quite another kind:

> CLARK. Methinks the wound your Master gave you last night, makes you look very thin and wan, Monsieur.
>
> DUFOY. Begar you are mistaké, it be de voundé dat my Metresse did give me long agoe.
>
> CLARK. What? some pretty little English Lady's crept into your heart?
>
> DUFOY. No, but damn'd littel English Whore is creepé into my bone begar, me could vish dat de Diable vould také her vid allé my harté.

And the scene ends with Dufoy declaring: "Begar, I do not care two Soulz if de Shamber-maid ver hangé; be it not great deal better pretendé d'affection to her, dan to tellé de hole Varldé I do take de Medicine vor de clapé; begar it be de very great deale better" (16). To which the close of the next scene counterpoints Aurelia's despairing cry: "there's nothing here does give me ease,/ But in the end will nourish my disease" (22). The rather sordid realism of the low plot thus suggests a deliberately unromantic commentary on the romantic love of the high plot—all the talk about loves of the "heart" (and unfulfilled loves, at that) being heard above a persistent undercurrent of references to raw sexuality ("love in a tub").

Meanwhile Sir Frederick's "love encounter" with the Widow in one garden is being played off against Beaufort's and Graciana's meeting in another. Both couples converse about their relationships in metaphors of wars and flames, but the differences of implication are patent:

> Wid. You cannot blame me for standing on my guard so near an Enemy.
> Sir Fred. If you are so good at that, Widow, let's see, what guard wou'd you chuse to be at shou'd the Trumpet sound a Charge to this dreadful foe?
> Wid. It is an idle Question amongst experienc'd Souldiers; but if we ever have a War, we'l never trouble the Trumpet; the Bells shall proclaim our Quarrel.
> Sir Fred. It will be most proper; they shall be rung backwards.
> Wid. Why so, Sir?
> Sir Fred. I'le have all the helps that may be to allay a dangerous fire; Widows must needs have furious flames; the bellows have been at work, and blown 'em up. (16)

On such a note Act II, scene i draws toward its unromantic conclusion, and as scene ii opens, one garden has given way to another:

> Beauf. *Graciana,* why do you condemn your Love?
> Your Beauty without that, alas! would prove
> But my destruction, an unlucky Star,
> Prognosticating ruine and despair.
> Grac. Sir, you mistake; 'tis not my Love I blame,
> But my Discretion; *Here the active flame
>                         [**Pointing to her breast.*
> Shou'd yet a longer time have been conceal'd;
> Too soon, too soon I fear it was reveal'd.
> Our weaker Sex glories in a Surprize,
> We boast the sudden Conquests of our Eyes;
> But men esteem a Foe that dares contend,
> One that with noble Courage does defend
> A wounded Heart; the Victories they gain
> They prize by their own hazard and their pain.
> Beauf. *Graciana,* can you think we take delight

To have our happiness against us fight:
Or that such goodness shou'd us men displease
As do's afford us Heav'n with greater ease?    (17)

Clearly, the references to "a Charge" and to "experienc'd Souldiers" and "War" and to "fire" and "flames" in the earlier passage have sexual implications which the Widow can hardly miss, and in fact Sir Frederick's part of the dialogue is really too unsubtle to qualify as wit and might more properly be classified as something close to ordinary smut. Hence it contrasts all the more sharply with the romanticized jargon concerning love in which Graciana indulges through her use of similar imagery ("active flame," "Conquests," "Victories").

And the warfare metaphors are carried out in the action of the play as well. Not only is it clear that Bruce and Beaufort are caught up in the chaotic aftermath of a real war, but all the actions of the high plot have to do with a kind of "civil war" within their own society. Like Hotspur, Etherege's Lovis has a passionate commitment to an abstract ideal of honor, and that commitment leads to a potentially destructive confrontation between Bruce and Beaufort. And like the life style of Falstaff, that of Etherege's rogues, based on skepticism and good-natured expediency, constitutes an indirect but heavily ironic commentary on that kind of passion. The wars, revenges, duels, deaths, and imprisonments of the high plot are turned into comic games in Sir Frederick's world. When Sir Frederick "plays dead" or marches bravely at the head of his fiddlers and link-boys, when Dufoy bursts upon the stage *"with a Helmet on his head, and a great Sword in his hand"* or suffers imprisonment in a tub, the actions not only undercut the heroism of the high plot but also express basic aggressions safely contained within the play sphere. As one critic has put it in words which have a special aptness here:

Play is a nurtural form which the behaviour of almost any human instinct may take. It is not to be distinguished in any hard and fast way from earnest, but it is relatively distinguished from this by requiring the modification, more or less, of the *natural* end-result of a behaviour-cycle. The natural end-result of the behaviour of fighting is killing your adversary; the playful end-result of this behaviour is winning on points. The satisfaction of play is the satisfaction of

[47]

primitive impulses which the gradual advance of civilization has circumscribed. It is a less intense satisfaction than that provided by earnest, but it makes up for this loss in intensity by a gain in security; in play, whether one wins or loses, one lives to fight another day.[14]

But the wars waged by Sir Frederick are still more positive than this. Thriving on troublemaking to his own life-affirming ends, he is always, as Beaufort once phrases it, "at wars with the Women" (5), in what is plainly a sexual sense, and his armed assault on the Widow's lodging is anticipated by an earlier assault upon the house of Wheadle's mistress—with the sex implications of all the "assault" and "house" imagery made quite obvious. "A civil Gentleman," sneers Jenny, "will come to a Ladies Lodging at two a clock in the morning, and knock as if it were upon life and death; a Midwife was never knock'd up with more fury"(4). Her remark, offhand as it may seem, could hardly define the comic challenge more clearly. It is, indeed, a matter of life and death, and the "Midwife" reference has a particular appropriateness.

Jenny has not at this point, however, yet finished her abusive tirade. "These were not all your Heroick actions;" she continues, "pray tell the Consequence, how you march'd bravely at the rere of an Army of Link-boys; upon the sudden, how you gave defiance, and then wag'd a bloody war with the Constable; and having vanquish'd that dreadful enemy, how you committed a general massacre on the glass windows: are not these most honourable atchievements . . . ?" The comic vitality of Sir Frederick's war games, his defiance of traditional conceptions of law and order, and the picture drawn of him as an insistently anti-heroic mocker of Beaufort's love-and-honor world could hardly be more heavily underscored. And further, does not this irate description of one battle simultaneously constitute a part of Jenny's own attack in the "battle" she is currently waging with Sir Frederick—a battle which, as usual, Sir Frederick wins hands down?

    SIR FRED. Good sweet *Jenny,* let's come to a Treaty; do but hear what Articles I'le propose.
    MAID. A Womans heart's too tender to be an enemy to Peace.    (6)

The scene in which Sir Frederick stages his funeral procession supplies, moreover, yet another parallel to and commentary on the high plot, parodying as it does Bruce's near death and suggesting the way in which the comic hero challenges even death. Like Falstaff, Sir Frederick is only playing dead, and like Mathew Merygreeke, he finally transforms his funeral into a wedding march. Out of the lawlessness of his world Sir Frederick contrives his own vital laws for living, and out of the hostilities and antagonisms he contrives his own harmonies. The special symbolic significance of his retinue has to do, of course, with their persistent double nature: soldiers, pallbearers, or bailiffs (all agents of death or imprisonment) on the surface but always at bottom the same fiddlers—with their real badges of identity *"tuck'd under their Cloaks."* With a snap of the fingers Sir Frederick can turn death into life, dissonance into harmony.

The number of references in the high plot to "destruction," "ruine," "despair," "pain," "sorrow," "tears," "bleeding hearts," "fatal wounds" suggests, by contrast, how prevailingly negative are its preoccupations. In such a world the passions ultimately lead to "wounds" in dead earnest, and significantly it is Sir Frederick who finally puts a stop to the destruction by restraining Lovis as he is about to fall on his sword. "Forbear, Sir;" he says wryly, "the Frollick's not to go round, as I take it" (55).

Nor is the pastoral emphasis in the high plot any less negative, as witness the song sung by Aurelia and Letitia early in the play:

> *When* Phillis *watch'd her harmless Sheep*
>    *Not one poor Lamb was made a prey;*
> *Yet she had cause enough to weep,*
>    *Her silly heart did go astray:*
> *Then flying to the neighbouring Grove,*
> *She left the tender Flock to rove,*
> *And to the Winds did breathe her Love.*
>     *She sought in vain*
>     *To ease her pain:*
> *The heedless winds did fan her fire:*
>     *Venting her grief*
>     *Gave no relief;*
> *But rather did encrease desire.*
> *Then sitting with her arms across,*
>    *Her sorrows streaming from each eye;*
> *She fix'd her thoughts upon her loss,*
>    *And in despair resolv'd to die.*    (21, 22)

As might be expected, however, such pastoralism does not go unchallenged. The last wistful notes of the song have scarcely died away when Palmer replaces the ladies on the stage and proceeds to sing a series of rollicking and irreverent tavern songs. He is, appropriately, disguised at this point as a merry country-man of whom Wheadle later remarks: "he dares not to go into the Field, without it be among his sheep" (29), and who himself refers to Sir Nicholas as "the Sheep that I must fleece "(30). The pastoral has been undercut with a vengeance, and Act II ends on a note of high good spirits with Palmer riotously singing a ribald song about a "buxome Girl" and her "delight in sporting." Sex and laughter are taking the place of love and despair, and down-to-earth idiomatic speech has shown up the prettified pastoral clichés for what they are.

And in Act III Sir Frederick carries on the high-spirited, antipastoral mood as he leads his forces in the "assault" on the Widow's lodgings. Being Lord Bevill's sister, the Widow clearly belongs to the romantic world of the high plot, and in wooing her Sir Frederick makes ironic use of the rhymed couplets of Lord Bevill's sphere to carry his own "free humour" into a hitherto closed-off circle. And the song he sings plainly parodies the romantic and pastoral modes:

> You Widow, that do sleep dog-sleep
> And now for your dead Husband weep,
> Perceiving well what want you have
> Of that poor worm has eat in Grave;
> Rise out of Bed, and ope the door;
> Here's that will all your joys restore.
> Good-morrow, my Mistress dear, Good-morrow.
> Good-morrow, Widow.    (30)

The song at once identifies the Widow with the "faithful shepherdess" of the pastoral tradition weeping eternally over the grave of her dead lover and summarizes in the space of eight lines the central juxtaposition in the play between death and life, sorrow and joy. Metaphorically, Sir Frederick suggests that he is on the point of joyfully entering the Widow's house—as a breath of fresh air might blow in to clear the staleness from a closed room. "Rise out of Bed, and ope the door" is essentially the motto by which he lives and virtually defines his role in the play, for into the oversophisticated, courtly, pastoral atmosphere he proposes to carry his own "green world" of continual striving—the world in which we find "motion and pleasure and appetite ever producing more motion and pleasure and appetite."

Comedy offers here a continual challenge to a dead world by a living one, and although there is more to Sir Frederick than mere buffoon, Mrs. Langer's definition of that figure serves very well to characterize Sir Frederick in this particular connection: "the indomitable living creature fending for itself . . . getting into scrape after scrape and getting out again, with or without a thrashing. He is the personified élan vital; his chance adventures and misadventures . . . in fact his whole improvised existence has the rhythm of primitive, savage, if not animalian life, coping with a world that is forever taking new uncalculated turns, frustrating but exciting. . . . his energy is really unimpaired and each failure prepares the situation for a new fantastic move."[15]

With virtually inexhaustible energy and inventiveness, Sir Frederick proceeds from triumph to triumph through the play—always the complete showman. Clearly he is creative in an artistic as well as a sexual sense. This is *his* world to do with as he will. In contrast to all the sighing about Heaven's decrees in the high plot, he takes his luck as he finds it and then makes the most of it. The difference between him and Etherege's later comic heroes, Courtall and Dorimant, is largely a question of refinement or polish. After *The Comical Revenge* the farcical element which constitutes such an important part of Sir Frederick's role largely disappears so far as the comic hero is concerned. Or rather, it takes a different form, physical giving way to verbal aggressiveness and trickery. Many commentators on Etheregean comedy have pronounced Sir Frederick to be less witty and more wild than his rake-hero successors, and indeed there is very little genuine wit to be found in the play. His aggressiveness takes the form of physical violence: the breaking of windows and heads, midnight bellringing in the streets, pounding on doors to force an entrance. But are his successors in reality any less wild and aggressive? Is it not rather that their assaults become, for the most part, verbal rather than physical (a case of wit as verbal farce)— that they knock an opponent down or trap him or beat him over the head with a well-turned phrase instead of a club or a fist or a pie in the eye? Indeed Freud has explicitly recognized wit as a "weapon of attack" used by the "refined and cultured" in the cause of giving vent to our "aggressive tendencies," both "lewd and hostile."[16]

If Sir Frederick has no female counterpart possessed of an artistry and aggressiveness to equal and challenge his own, it is presumably because of the kind of boisterous comic hero he is. Unlike a Courtall or a Dorimant, he has not, as the play opens, become an accepted member of the polite world but rather, as already suggested, is seen in the process of claiming a place in that world for both himself and his kind of elemental vitality. Thus he still speaks for the most part the language of the tavern, and hence the Widow, being the "lady" that she is, cannot match him thrust for thrust. Instead she must often pull him up short and self-righteously scold him for sounding "rude" and "lewd." And there is a related difficulty in the fact that so long as Sir Frederick elects to stage his attack on the level of low comedy, as he does more often than not, the Widow is hardly in a position to deliver a counterblow in kind. She can only bar the door or be on her guard against future trickery.

With typical comic audacity Sir Frederick never doubts, of course, that he will triumph in his encounter with the Widow. "What?" he exclaims with customary self-satisfaction, "the Widow has some kind thoughts of my body?" (8) He delights in thinking of himself as one of the "vain idle Fellows" of the town, and at one point the Widow challenges him sarcastically: "I did not imagine you were so foolishly conceited; is it your Wit or your Person, Sir, that is so taking?" (14) A consummate egotist, he laughs off his early rebuffs at her hands with a so-much-the-worse-for-you attitude and is a terrible gloater in victory. "Pish, Widow," he taunts her, when his trickery has finally worked, "why so much out of humour? 'Tis no shame to love such a likely young Fellow" (71). His "glorying" clearly rests on his awareness of his "own power and ability . . . grounded upon the experience of his own former actions."

Yet it must be insisted that for all his unrefined antics, Sir Frederick is no less an artist than his successors, and it is surely a part of the importance of the minor comic characters in the play that they serve as foils to him—as one of the means of defining his successful nature-art synthesis. Dufoy, for example, would seem to supply a representation of nature without art, and Sir Nicholas Cully, one of art without nature. There is no doubt as to Dufoy's earthiness (he is, so to speak, nature in the raw), but his is a vitality without controlling form. His swordsmanship amounts to nothing more than a wild, undirected flailing about, and in his affairs with women he is easily made a fool—either by contracting the "foul disease" or by being effectively "boxed in."

Sir Nicholas is, of course, equally unsuccessful in his wooing and is equally easy to manipulate, but he is a fool of a different kind: "one that has a vain-glorious humour to gain a reputation amongst the Gentry, by feigning good nature, and an affection to the King and his Party" (7). Is not the distinction between Sir Nicholas and Sir Frederick, in fact, just that which Hobbes makes between "glorying" and "Vaine-glory"? Sir Nicholas' aspiring to enter the upper level of the plot will net him, if Wheadle has his way, not Graciana but just plain Grace, and finally does net him Sir Frederick's cast-off mistress. In dressing up as Sir Frederick and imitating his actions, he reveals the essential emptiness of form without content. "*Wheadle,*" he crows, "and what think you of this Habit? is it not very modish? . . . I defie Sir *Frederick;* I am as fine as he, and will be as mad as he" (48). But as we might have expected, "he over-acts the Part" (51) and ends by first making a great chaotic clamor and then falling into a deep sleep brought on by an over-indulgence in wine. The primitive energies which belong to Sir Frederick are no part of the sound and fury of poor foolish Sir Nicholas.

Wheadle and Palmer are no doubt a good deal closer to Sir Frederick in their combination of energy and artistry. Not only do they reveal the same propensities for drinking and gambling, but they also share his delight in trickery and in disguise and dissimulation. "Nay, I should have made an excellent Jugler, 'faith," says Palmer (9). Thus they are, in some sense, the "minor Vices" circling in Sir Frederick's orbit, the important distinction being that they lack the subtlety to carry their devilish spirit effectively beyond their own circumscribed sphere. Palmer, masquerading as Lord Bevill, is at first ludicrous and finally a pitiful flop. And his marriage to Jenny, like Wheadle's to Grace, results because, "excellent Jugler" though he be, he is at last out-juggled by a better artist than himself.

As for Sir Frederick, whether staging a mock assault, a mock funeral, or a mock arrest, he remains always the controlling force of the play; and, like earlier and later comic protagonists, he is always quite insufferable—the impudence of youth and high spirits incarnate—but still a charming scoundrel. "Bedlamé, Mad-cape, diable de matré . . . Villain," we hear Dufoy shouting as the play begins. But his subsequent words soon reveal Sir Frederick's devilish fascination: "Begar you vil never keepé de good Serviteur, had no me love you ver vel." Sir Frederick knows himself for a sinner and accepts the fact with his usual equanimity, not to say pride: "I am of opinion that drunkenness is not so damnable a sin to me as 'tis to many. Sorrow and Repentance are sure to be my first Work the next morning; 'Slid, I have known some so lucky at this recreation, that, whereas 'tis familiar to forget what we do in drink, have even lost the memory, after sleep, of being drunk. Now do I feel more qualms than a young woman in breeding." (Always the fertility suggestion.)

Drinking is indeed in Sir Frederick's world a form of *re-creation*, and it is perhaps further significant that he lives more by night than by day. He belongs to the milieu of Ordinaries, of gaming and drinking and singing lewd and rowdy songs, for that milieu represents the very source of life and is just the kind of Dionysian, Aristophanic world of which Couat has written so persuasively:

> Le vin et l'amour vont ensemble, l'un prépare à l'autre; sous leur influence les hommes redeviennent de simples animaux, innocents et immondes. Au temps de la vendange, hommes et femmes, grisés par la liqueur divine qui fermente dans leurs veines, se livrent à l'amour. C'est pour cela que les comédies acienne, conformément à la tradition antique, se termine par une orgie; l'ivress explique et excuse la lubricité. . . . Les Athéniens ont l'imagination plus licencieuse que les moeurs. Ils aiment, le jour de la réprésentation, à se croire ramenés par la puissance de la poésie, à l'état de nature; a sentir brûler en eux la vie grossiére et ardente des faunes et des satyres qui hantent les gorges du Parnès et du Cithéron. Ils n'y mettent aucune pudeur ni aucune mauvaise pensée; ils rient en enfants de ces choses naturelles dont ils n'ont pas appris à rougir.[17]

For Sir Frederick all of life is a feast of pleasure, and we as audience experience with him his vital and vigorous enjoyment of it.

What Jocelyn Powell says of him and his function can, in this connection, scarcely be improved upon:

> Enjoyment is one of the essential qualities of comic writing, for it is the foundation for the best type of laughter, the laughter of sympathy. This laughter is based on a sense of relationship between the man who is laughing and the man with whom he laughs, and through the laughter there is asserted the value and goodness of the experience that causes the laughter. It is the enjoyment by one human being of the life and vitality of another. The spirit of the man who laughs is broadened and stimulated by the energy of the man who makes the laughter; together they share their joy in life.[18]

Powell goes on to suggest that *The Comical Revenge* should not be read as a comedy of manners that has failed, but as a "comedy ballet," and the suggestion is especially valuable as a means of countering those critics who have insisted on seeing Etheregean comedy as lacking in spontaneity and vigor, as well as those who have argued that the libertine and Machiavellian drives of Sir Frederick are covered over by a polished veneer, for Sir Frederick's life-style actually *expresses* both the freeing of the natural man from the kind of artificial restraints depicted in the high plot and the creative formalizing of that naturalness in the pulsing rhythms of song and dance. As Powell points out:

> Sir Frederick himself is a magnificent blend of freedom and ceremony, elegance and animal spirits, and this tension between the controlled and the abandoned is particularly suited to expression in the dance. By centring the scenes of his wooing of the Widow Rich round a series of midnight masquerades and musical disguises Etherege makes full use of these possibilities. He gives his hero a band of fiddlers that accompany him upon his escapades, ready to give the impetus of music wherever it is needed . . . moving at his pleasure, so that they become extensions of their master, and spread his vigorous personality all over the stage.[19]

Only on rare occasion in this early play does this same "tension between the controlled and the abandoned" also characterize the verbal exchanges between Sir Frederick and the Widow. On such occasions the rhythm of language parallels the rhythm of song and dance, and Etherege achieves a telling contrast between the pretentious diction and predictable rhythm and rhyme patterns of the "ceremonious" lovers and the precariously obtained balances of those combative lovers for whom antagonism is the very breath of life and whose final goal is a creative unity. "In order to form and make up a . . . creative Unity," Isak Dinesen once wrote, "the individual components must needs be of different nature, they should even be in a sense contrasts. . . . A quartet is a Unity because it is made up of dissimilar instruments. . . . In a fight the adversaries become one, and the two duellists make up a Unity."[20]

The final scene of *The Comical Revenge* surely supplies a dramatic confirmation of that view. The concluding marriages and reconciliations of the high plot are referred to by the participants themselves in terms of exhaustion and weariness:

> BRUCE. Come all into my Arms before I rest;
> Let's breathe our Joys into each others breast;
> Thus mariners rejoyce when winds decrease
> And falling waves seem wearied into Peace.     (82)

But Sir Frederick and the Widow, "adversaries" to the end, are destined for a more creative unity. According to Etherege's stage directions, Sir Frederick and Dufoy enter *"at one door, and the* Widow *and* Betty *at another."* The contrasted worlds are thus seen symbolically coming together, with Sir Frederick entering Lord Bevill's house for the first time in the company of Dufoy. "Now I have receiv'd you into my Family," says the Widow (83). Is it then to be assumed that Sir Frederick has "fallen," that he has been reformed? Nearly every detail of the concluding scene demands the denial of any such conclusion. He has, quite literally, brought the primitive vitality of his own lower world along with him. "Day be all at de dooré, begar," announces Dufoy, who has been sent as summoner, "every man vid his pret Metres, Brid, Whore" (84). And Lord Bevill remarks significantly to Sir Frederick: "I shou'd have blam'd you, Sir, if you had restrain'd your humour here./These must needs be pleasant Matches that are of his making" (83). And then, as the play draws to its end:

> Sir *Frederick,* you shall command my House this day;
> Make all those welcom that are pleas'd to stay.     (85)

In short, he has become master of the revels in the upper sphere as well as the lower.

Whether or not we choose to take with a grain of salt Sir Frederick's resolve expressed to the Widow "to lead a virtuous life, and keep house altogether with thee" (84) does not really matter very much. What does matter is that the question of his sincerity does come to mind and that Sir Frederick is the same egotistical, naturalistic, lewd madcap at the end of the play as at the beginning. "Nay, if thou once art acquainted with my Constitution," he confidently advises the Widow, "thou't never let me go" (83). It might well be finally argued that Sir Frederick actually *re-forms* marriage rather than being reformed by it. He and the Widow go on teasing and defying and insulting each other even as they join hands; and when Sir Frederick concludes, "Widow, for all these bloody preparations, there will be no great massacre of Maiden-heads among us," he sounds once more the keynote of his function—that of bringing harmony and fertility out of dissonance and destruction. And finally he leaves the play with four marriages to his credit, one of them his own, and in the concluding dance of his devising he is one of the dancers.

## She wou'd if she cou'd

THREE YEARS LATER (1667) the aristocratic audience at the Duke's Theatre was applauding the spirited doings of another Etheregean rake-hero who could dominate his stage with as much facility as Sir Frederick had dominated his but whose world resembled their own far more closely. As the title of this second play may suggest, it is centrally concerned with oppositions and balances between (and in some instances within) the various characters involved, and in much the manner of his first play, although with a greater degree of subtlety, two worlds are being contrasted, one confined within a house and a family, the other free to "take the air" of the Mulberry-Garden and the Exchange. Indeed the simple list of dramatis personæ suggests a good deal about what Etherege's chief preoccupations are to be, contrived as it is to make up a series of pairs: *"Two Country Knights . . . Two honest Gentlemen of the Town . . . Two young Ladies . . . Two Exchange-women."*
Only one of the major characters stands alone on the list, un-

bracketed with anyone, and that is Lady Cockwood, whose actions have the effect of isolating her further and further from the rest of the world and at the same time of dividing her more and more irrevocably against herself. It is largely by virtue of her loneliness that she stands in the play at the ultimate negative position on the axis, and if the actions of the comic hero are to be fully comprehended, it is necessary first to understand her nature, since it represents the epitome of the force against which he must triumph. Again, as in *The Comical Revenge,* he must invade an alien realm, but in this case it is not one having claims to a higher level of refinement, but rather one involving certain repressive aspects of that social stratum to which he himself belongs. Within that realm the female counterpart of his own comic species is imprisoned, and a part of the action has to do with the respective efforts of hero and heroine to break in and to break out.

Lady Cockwood's home is her castle, or more accurately her fortress, and Courtall and Freeman must gain access to it in order to carry away Gatty and Ariana. As Courtall says, "advantage may be hereafter made, by my admission into the Family" (105).[21] In some sense (certainly in a Freudian one) the fortress represents the person of Lady Cockwood herself, and at its door her "gentlewoman," appropriately named Sentry, unsleepingly stands guard. When Lady Cockwood ventures into the larger world, she "dare not go without" Sentry by her side. "My Maid!" she exclaims to Courtall, "for Heavens sake, what do you mean, Sir? do I ever use to go abroad without her?" (122)

What Etherege has done, in his characterizations of both Lady Cockwood and her husband Sir Oliver, is to present the logical consequences of subscribing in youth to the *précieux* mode of defining male-female relationships—a mode which proves in the outcome hopelessly unnatural. By deifying the lady in the case and placing her on a pedestal of honor and virtue, with her lover a devotee at her feet, the mode, Etherege suggests, actually denies the recalcitrant facts of human nature in two ways: first, and more important, it ignores the realities of physical, appetitive man, and second, it places the female in an unnatural position of dominance over the male. And in this second play Etherege has relentlessly dramatized the consequences of both kinds of restriction, setting in opposition to them the free self-realization of the youthful lovers.

In the case of Lady Cockwood, the fortress of honor has become so impregnable that, even though it has been of her own construction, she herself can no longer break out of it. She is thus no mere oversimplified caricature of a woman who pretends to virtue while seeking sexual gratification. Rather, she is a complex portrait of a divided personality with a self-righteousness so deeply ingrained that it manages to ignore the naturalistic instincts boiling vigorously underneath. So effectively is she self-deceived that she is wholly unconscious of the self-contradictory nature of her own words and actions. "What a strange thing is this!" she rails at Sentry, who has discreetly left her alone with Courtall: "will you never take warning but still be leaving me alone on these suspicious occasions? . . . What may Mr. *Courtall* think of my innocent intentions? I protest if you serve me so agen, I shall be strangely angry: you should have more regard to your Lady's Honour." The outburst may at first appear to be an attempt to save face before a servant—but only until we remember that Sentry, in her role as pimp, has been thoroughly acquainted all along with her lady's "innocent intentions." Thereafter we can only conclude that Lady Cockwood is actually saving face before herself and that she is, as always, remarkably successful—a fact which Sentry confirms in her remark: "If I stay in the room, she will not speak kindly to me in a week after; and if I go out, she always chides me thus: this is a strange infirmity she has, but I must bear with it; for on my conscience, custom has made it so natural, she cannot help it" (113).

The same "infirmity" continually reveals itself in Lady Cockwood's peculiar responses to Courtall. He knows, quite obviously, what she is after, what "mutual happiness" she has in mind. But she can simultaneously both acknowledge and deny it, and with her it is not, as with Courtall, simply a game in which both are saying one thing and meaning another. She fully expects from Courtall, as from Sentry, a belief in her virtue and honor to match her own. Having plotted in detail a future meeting at the New Exchange, she manages, when Courtall is at hand, to play out their little intrigue as if neither he nor she had anticipated any of it in advance. "O Heaven! you must excuse me, dear Sir, for I shall deny my self the sweetest recreations in the world, rather than yield to any thing that may bring a blemish upon my spotless Honour" (122). For whose benefit need she make such protestations? The only witnesses to them, as she is well aware, are Courtall and Sentry, both of whom know all about her "spotless Honour." Clearly she is playing the part for her own benefit and makes up a gullible audience of one. " 'Sdeath, Madam," says Courtall, "if you had made no Ceremony, but stept into the Coach presently, we had escap'd this mischief" (123). Lady Cockwood has denied herself more irrevocably than she knows. "My over-tenderness of my honour, has blasted all my hopes of happiness," she complains, and so indeed it has. She is finally her own sentry—with her own needs effectively blocked off from expression. "She wou'd if she cou'd," but she cannot, and the fault is not really Courtall's.

Yet his lack of interest in joining her in her "recreations" points to another difficulty in the way of her sexual satisfaction, and that is the blatantly aggressive way in which she chooses to pursue her ends. As Courtall says, "she is the very spirit of impertinence, so foolishly fond and troublesom, that no man above sixteen is able to endure her" (98). Her excessively demanding sexual nature presumably has to do in part with the extent of the repression to which she has subjected it: "she would by her good will give her Lover no more rest, than a young Squire that has newly set up a Coach, does his only pair of Horses" (98). But the comparison also suggests her open and unnatural aggressiveness. In the world of the four young lovers—the natural world—the men are the pursuers and the ladies are clever enough to act the part of the pursued. Ariana speaks of Courtall and Freeman as "two men of War that are cruising here, to watch for Prizes" (106), and there are constant references both here and elsewhere to the love game as a chase. "Now art thou as mad upon this trail, as if we were upon a hot scent," says Courtall to Freeman (104). Lady Cockwood, however, is compared not only to a squire driving his horses, but also to a bird of prey, a "long-wing'd Devil": "Why, this ravenous Kite is upon wing already, is fetching a little compass, and will be here within this half hour to swoop me away" (120).

It is against her alternately repressive and blatantly aggressive world—a world devoid of free and creative vitality—that the new,

playful world of Courtall and Freeman, Gatty and Ariana, is opposed. Significantly, Lady Cockwood arraigns as "faithless and
inconstant" (143) an Age which Courtall has earlier characterized
as "warm and ripening" (141), and the difference largely defines
the nature of the opposing worlds. In a play which is centrally
concerned with the ways in which a social framework fails or succeeds in giving expression to natural desires, the youthful characters
are dedicated to the cause of getting what they want from the game
of life by working out a new set of rules.

By the end of Act I the strategy of the youthful protagonists, both
male and female, has been largely mapped out. In the first scene
Courtall instructs the less skilled and disciplined Freeman (who is
at once his confidant and his pupil in the art of living) on how the
game they are setting up must be played. (It is strange that Courtall
and Freeman have seldom if ever been regarded as distinguishable
from each other, when the distinction is so firmly and unmistakably
made from the first.) Setting out eagerly on the trail of some "lucky
Adventure," the two young men at once reveal the significance of
their respective names, and it is clearly Courtall—the audacious
but artful comic hero—who is to assume control. Sly fellow that
he is, he knows just how the courting maneuvers must be contrived and reassures the too-impetuous Freeman while shoving
him precipitately into the closet: "On my life thou shalt have fair
play, and go halfs, if it be a purchase that may with honour be
divided; you may over-hear all: but for decency sake, in, in man"
(92). And when Freeman finally emerges from his "hole," he has
to acknowledge Courtall's skill: "the Scene was very pleasant; but
above all, I admire thy impudence, I could never have had the face
to have wheadl'd the poor Knight so" (97). Clearly Courtall has
a good deal of Sir Frederick's self-confident talent for duplicity,
and the result of the "Scene" which he has so artfully staged has
been to acquaint the young men with the double challenge that
confronts them: Lady Cockwood on the one hand, Ariana and
Gatty on the other; and Courtall, as always, has a plan of attack:
"'twill be very necessary to carry on my business with the old one,
that we may the better have an opportunity of being acquainted
with them" (98).

Freeman, however, proves subsequently to be in need of further instruction. His closing expression of impatience at the end of scene i ("Come along, come along") has its echo in the opening scene of Act II: "What do we here idling in the Mulberry-Garden? Why do not we make this visit then?... Since we know the bush, why do we not start the Game?" Hence Courtall must admonish him: "Gently, good *Franck;* first know that the laws of Honour pre-scrib'd in such nice cases, will not allow me to carry thee along with me; and next, hast thou so little wit to think, that a discreet Lady that has had the experience of so much humane frailty, can have so good an opinion of the constancy of her Servant, as to lead him into temptation?" (104) Courtall knows his woman, and by the mid point in Act II Freeman is quite ready to follow his lead: "Well! what Counter-plot? what hopes of disappointing the old, and of seeing the young Ladies? I am ready to receive your Orders" (121).

The language used by the two young men in their dialogue at the opening of Act II itself expresses the tension which exists in the entire play between the promptings of free-ranging, youthful high spirits on the one hand and the formalized *précieux* dictates on the other, animal imagery being continually alternated with religious terminology and a kind of racy coarseness with a stiff mock-formality of diction. Thus Courtall speaks one minute of the "Pray-ers and Tears" with which Sir Oliver is "forc'd to feign a bitter repentance" and the next minute is exclaiming to Freeman: "Now art thou as mad upon this trail, as if we were upon a hot scent." And immediately following his declarations concerning "con-stancy" and being led "into temptation" he is heard protesting: "Thou may'st reasonably expect that an old Rook should bring a young Snap acquainted with his Bubble" (104, 105). The vulgarities constantly attack, by implication, the falseness of the *précieux* ap-proach to sex, just as Lady Cockwood's own madness on "a hot scent" undercuts her "honourable" pretensions; and Courtall's use of the alternating modes of speech constitutes, in Freudian terms, his witty "weapon of attack." Like Sir Frederick, moreover, he makes use of the "enemy's" language at once as parody and as a handy ticket of entry. And further, in Freeman's final expression of his willingness to take "Orders," surely we are meant to recognize a tension created by the twofold meaning (religious and military) of the word.

Meanwhile, within Lady Cockwood's fortress Gatty and Ariana have laid out their own course of action, and the natural leader of the ladies' team has emerged. Obviously Ariana has as much to learn from Gatty as does Freeman from Courtall, the former's peculiarly feminine problem being not too much impetuosity but too much pastoral sentimentality or romanticism:

GATTY . . . my dear *Ariana,* how glad am I we are in this Town agen.

ARIA. But we have left the benefit of the fresh Air, and the delight of wandring in the pleasant Groves.

GATTY. Very pretty things for a young Gentlewoman to bemoan the loss of indeed, that's newly come to a relish of the good things of this world.

ARIA. Very good, Sister!

GATTY. Why, hast not thou promis'd me a thousand times to leave off this demureness?

ARIA. But you are so quick.

GATTY. Why, wou'd it not make any one mad to hear thee bewail the loss of the Country? speak but one grave word more, and it shall be my daily Prayers thou may'st have a jealous Husband, and then you'le have enough of it I warrant you.

ARIA. It may be, if your tongue be not altogether so nimble, I may be conformable; But I hope you do not intend we shall play such mad Reaks as we did last Summer?

GATTY. 'Slife, do'st thou think we come here to be mew'd up, and take only the liberty of going from our Chamber to the Dining-Room, and from the Dining-Room to our Chamber again? and like a Bird in a Cage, with two Perches only, to hop up and down, up and down?

ARIA. Well, thou art a mad Wench.

GATTY. Would'st thou never have us go to a Play but with our grave Relations, never take the air but with our grave Relations? to feed their pride, and make the world believe it is in their power to afford some Gallant or other a good bargain?

ARIA. But I am afraid we shall be known again.

GATTY. Pish! the men were only acquainted with our Vizards and our Petticoats, and they are wore out long since: how I envy that

Sex! we cannot plague 'em enough when we have it in our power for those priviledges which custom has allow'd 'em above us.

ARIA. The truth is, they can run and ramble here, and there, and every where, and we poor Fools rather think the better of 'em.

GATTY. From one Play-house, to the other Play-house, and if they like neither the Play nor the Women, they seldom stay any longer than the combing of their Perriwigs, or a whisper or two with a Friend; and then they cock their Caps, and out they strut again.

ARIA. But whatsoever we do, prithee now let us resolve to be mighty honest.

GATTY. There I agree with thee.

ARIA. And if we find the Gallants like lawless Subjects, who the more their Princes grant, the more they impudently crave—

GATTY. We'll become absolute Tyrants, and deprive 'em of all the priviledges we gave 'em—

ARIA. Upon these conditions I am contented to trail a Pike under thee—march along, Girl.   (102–104)

Again, as in the Courtall-Freeman exchanges, the imagery establishes a tension between freedom and confinement. The word "mad" is used three times with reference to the irrepressible Gatty and the word "grave," with an obvious double meaning, to characterize the conservative, old-fashioned attitude against which she is in rebellion. (Gatty's use of the word in describing her "relations" anticipates Harriet's impudent reference to "their gravities" in *The Man of Mode*.) Gatty demands to be allowed to enjoy, to "relish" life, and the rather sensuously suggestive word clashes sharply with Ariana's blandly abstract "delight of wandring in the pleasant Groves."

Gatty is, in short, a tough-minded realist who knows exactly the kind of world with which she has to deal, and no vestige of sentimentality will be allowed to weaken her position. The "Town" in her speeches becomes a metaphor for freedom and life—again the "green world" with all its possibilities for self-assertion and renewal —and she rejects out of hand the confinement of both country and family (including a future "jealous Husband"). Certainly she has no scruples about doing verbal violence to the "household gods." Lady Cockwood's kind of household—in which she and Ariana are confined—will supply no satisfactions for so free a spirit as hers. Like Sir Frederick Frollick, she is (and is repeatedly called by Sir Joslin) a "Mad-cap," and the mere "up and down, up and down" rhythm of a caged bird suggests a mode of living of monotonous unimaginativeness for which she refuses to settle. (The image again looks forward to *The Man of Mode* and Harriet's "three or four Melancholy Birds.")

Recognizing that the greater freedom allowed to the male gives him a clear advantage in the sex contest which she anticipates, and determined not to be regarded as a commodity to be bought and sold ("a good bargain"), she resolves to pit her own power against his. But in contrast to Lady Cockwood, her proposed tyranny is a part of a good-natured, give-and-take power game in which she will ask no quarter and give none. It will represent no repressive measure but an imaginative counter-move in a vital contest, where the best defense is a good offense. Thus, as the scene ends, the military metaphor reappears. The lines of battle have been drawn, and the structure of the Act as a whole has suggested what the nature of that battle is to be. Its two scenes perfectly balance and at the same time perfectly oppose each other, and within each a marching order has been established, with Courtall and Gatty leading the way by right of their superior wit and Freeman and Ariana following along as their lieutenants.

Once the escape from Lady Cockwood has been achieved, the next step must be, of course, the encounter between the fully armed and prepared young protagonists, and when the first such clash comes, it proves one of the most effectively staged in all of Restoration comedy. Picking up again from his first play the comic scheme of warring instincts being satisfied in an exuberant game, from which the combatants will emerge "to fight another day," the playwright sets the participants to wielding their words like well-honed weapons of attack, with one witty thrust succeeding another in the effort to take the opposition by surprise and throw them off balance. The scene, moreover, is magnificently contrived in terms of action, with a series of swift exits and entrances to suggest first a chase and then a battle. Ariana and Gatty first cross and recross the stage followed by Freeman and Courtall, and then both sides abruptly shift their tactics. Upon their second exit, *"The Women go out, and go about behind the Scenes to the other Door,"* and Courtall and Freeman re-enter to stand briefly alone on the stage. " 'Sdeath," says Freeman, "how fleet they are! whatsoever faults they have, they cannot be broken-winded." Whereupon they exit once again, the women re-enter, and finally *"after 'em* Courtal *at the lower Door, and* Free. *at the upper on the contrary side."*

Once the ladies are "engag'd" in battle, words begin to fly back and forth with a speed which keeps the scene hurtling forward even while physical motion is at an end, and both sides are very much on the offensive. " 'Slife, their tongues are as nimble as their heels," exclaims Freeman. If, as Underwood suggests, Courtall's stratagem with Lady Cockwood represents a "flight-in-pursuit,"[22] the young ladies' stratagem here is just as plainly a "pursuit-in-flight." Courtall and Freeman have, for once, met their match:

COUR. Can you have so little good nature to dash a couple of bashful young men out of countenance, who came out of pure love to tender you their service?

GATTY. 'Twere pity to baulk 'em, Sister.

ARIA. Indeed methinks they look as if they never had been slip'd before.

FREE. Yes faith, we have had many a fair course in this Paddock, have been very well flesh'd, and dare boldly fasten.

*[They kiss their hands with a little force.*

ARIA. Well, I am not the first unfortunate woman that has been forc'd to give her hand, where she never intends to bestow her heart.

GATTY. Now, do you think 'tis a bargain already?

COUR. Faith, would there were some lusty earnest given, for fear we should unluckily break off again.

FREE. Are you so wild that you must be hooded thus?

COUR. Fy, fy, put off these scandals to all good Faces.

GATTY. For your reputations sake we shall keep 'em on: 'slife we should be taken for your Relations, if we durst shew our Faces with you thus publickly.

ARIA. And what a shame that would be to a couple of young Gallants! methinks you should blush to think on't.

COUR. These were pretty toys, invented, first, meerly for the good of us poor Lovers to deceive the jealous, and to blind the malicious; but the proper use is so wickedly perverted, that it makes all honest men hate the fashion mortally.

FREE. A good Face is as seldom cover'd with a Vizard-Mask, as a good Hat with an oyl'd Case: and yet on my Conscience, you are both Handsome.

[ 66 ]

Cour. Do but remove 'em a little, to satisfie a foolish Scruple.

Aria. This is a just punishment you have brought upon your selves, by that unpardonable Sin of talking.

Gatty. You can only brag now of your acquaintance with a Farendon Gown, and a piece of black Velvet.

Cour. The truth is, there are some vain fellows whose loose behaviour of late has given great discouragement to the honourable proceedings of all vertuous Ladies.

Free. But I hope you have more charity, than to believe us of the number of the wicked.

Aria. There's not a man of you to be trusted.

Gatty. What a shame is it to your whole Sex, that a Woman is more fit to be a Privy-Councellour, than a young Gallant a Lover?

(107, 108)

The whole religious vocabulary of the *précieux* mode is brought into play before the scene is over. Not only does Courtall talk glibly of "pure love" and "service," of "a foolish Scruple," of "honourable proceedings" and "vertuous Ladies," and the ladies themselves of "just punishment" and "unpardonable Sin," but the exchange draws to a close sounding first the note of "despair" and then resorting to an "Oath" of constancy to be taken by the young men. "But are you troubl'd with that foolish scruple of keeping an Oath?" demands Gatty, ironically throwing back Courtall's own phrase. And Freeman quickly reassures her, "O most religiously" (109). Such language, however, far from suggesting an endorsement of the *précieux* mode and an effort to live within it, obviously constitutes a deliberate mockery. Courtall and Freeman do not really expect to be taken seriously, and their metaphorical references to themselves as horses undercut their own protestations from the outset. All four protagonists have, in fact, appropriated the religious terms to their own playful ends of keeping their opponents guessing—and often of denying what they mean to affirm and affirming what they mean to deny. Freeman and Courtall, for example, are all too eager to be regarded as "wicked"—a fact Gatty tacitly recognizes in expressing her mock concern for their "reputations." And Ariana, in a later retort, follows Gatty's lead in neatly turning the courtly implications inside out: "we are very unwilling to have the sin to answer for, of ruining a couple of such hopeful young men" (108). Having already at this point been witness to Lady

[67]

Cockwood's outspoken concern for her "reputation," and having heard her exclaim, "I'm ruined—undone for ever!" we are in a position to respond to Gatty's and Ariana's comic inversions with a full awareness of what they are doing. By making fun of the whole convention, all four young people are at once proclaiming their freedom from it and defining their own self-assertive and combative mode of life.

A game of disguise and deception theirs may be, but because all the members of the youthful quartet remain continually aware that they are "only playing" and because they control and are not controlled by the language and concepts they use, they remain always true to their essential natures. It is a part of the game that the men and women involved not admit the genuine attraction they feel toward one another. Such an admission would at once put either side at the mercy of the other in the power game. Thus at the same time that Freeman and Courtall profess their love, their use of courtly terminology maintains the requisite undercurrent of wry mockery. Yet the witty exchanges, here as always at their best in Restoration comedy, draw their vitality from the emotional and sexual charge which lies not very far below the surface. It is the same paradox, now more fully developed, that we have already encountered in *The Comical Revenge*—the paradox in which a "creative unity" exists by virtue of the oppositions it contains. "A quartet is a Unity because it is made up of dissimilar instruments."

The song Gatty sings toward the end of the play and her subsequent dialogue with Ariana reveal her complete awareness of the tensions which inform her kind of game:

> *How long I shall love him, I can no more tell,*
> *Then had I a Fever, when I shou'd be well.*
> *My passion shall kill me before I will show it,*
> *And yet I wou'd give all the world he did know it;*
> *But oh how I sigh, when I think shou'd he woo me,*
> *I cannot deny what I know wou'd undo me!*

ARIA. Fy, Sister, thou art so wanton.

GATTY. I hate to dissemble when I need not; 'twou'd look as affected in us to be reserv'd now w'are alone, as for a Player to maintain the Character she acts in the Tyring-room.

ARIA. Prithee sing a good Song.

[68]

GATTY. Now art thou for a melancholy Madrigal, compos'd by some amorous Coxcomb, who swears in all Companies he loves his Mistress so well, that he wou'd not do her the injury, were she willing to grant him the favour, and it may be is Sot enough to believe he wou'd oblige her in keeping his Oath too.

ARIA. Well, I will reach thee thy Guitar out of the Closet, to take thee off of this subject.

GATTY. I'de rather be a Nun, then a Lover at thy rate; devotion is not able to make me half so serious as Love has made thee already.    (169, 170)

There is no evidence here of a divided personality. Gatty herself knows she is acting a "Character" when she plays hard to get with Courtall, but the part she plays is prompted by her own clear-headed recognition of the loss of freedom she risks by committing herself irrevocably to a love which her own knowledge of changeable human nature tells her may not last. Thus, even offstage she remains a skeptic about love, and, like Harriet, she knows the perils of taking it too seriously. Hence the "right understanding" at which she finally arrives with Courtall involves no sentimental flinging of herself into his arms but a continuing use of her arsenal of verbal weapons.

And for all their opposition, Courtall and Gatty are essentially at one in the ways in which they respond to and shape their worlds. Both are rebels, troublemakers, madcaps, aggressors, who laugh in the face of repressive custom and take a childlike joy in either a good ramble in the open air or a good fight. Both are at once artists and participants in the dramatic scenes of their own devising. Both seek to wield power over their world that it may not wield its power over them. Both know and accept themselves and each other for what they are and play life as a game, the rules for which grow out of the raw materials at hand. And their business is always pleasure.

The point at which they differ from Sir Frederick, however, suggests to what extent farcical actions have now been replaced by the subtler aggressions and trickery of verbal farce. While the element of horseplay has not entirely disappeared from the physical doings on the stage (there are still vestiges of it in the frantic hustling of people into closets and under tables), the physical aggressiveness of Sir Frederick, where his wooing was concerned, has been almost wholly converted into the verbal aggressiveness of wit combat—a field where female can meet male on an equal footing. Courtall and Gatty have in effect "civilized" the challenges of the comic spirit, one of the marks of civilized laughter being, as one critic suggests, the improvement of the "humour of the body into the humour of the mind."[23] The transition of the comic spirit from the boisterous, Falstaffian tavern world to the sophisticated world of park and drawing room has been almost wholly effected.

Almost, but not quite, for there is still Sir Joslin Jolley. "He is," as Jocelyn Powell perceptively points out, "imported directly from *Love in a Tub,* and brings all Sir Frederick's animal spirits with him, as well as Sir Frederick's apparatus of music, song, and dance. His lewd ballads provide the answer of instinct to the play's title."[24] At the beginning of Act II, Freeman remarks of Sir Oliver and Sir Joslin, "They are Harp and Violin, Nature has so tun'd 'em, as if she intended they should always play the Fool in Consort." It is, in fact, Sir Joslin who releases Sir Oliver from the repressive world of Lady Cockwood( "seduces" him) and leads him into the rollicking tavern world. And Freeman's remark establishes the two "Country Knights" as one of the balanced pairs of the play and hence one of the creative oppositions to the sterile singleness of Lady Cockwood. At one point the two even successfully invade her fortress:

> Sir Oliv. Now the Enemy's march'd out—
> Sir Josl. Then the Castle's our own, Boys—Hey.
>> *And here and there I had her,*
>> *And every where I had her,*
>>> *Her toy was such, that every touch*
>> *Would make a lover madder.*    (118)

Sir Joslin is a "Fool" in the clown or buffoon sense, and thus he duplicates a role from Greek comedy of which Cornford says: "If the hero . . . is more *eiron* than Buffoon, or at least both at once, buffoonery pure and simple is the role of a subordinate character, in some way attached to the hero as friend or attendant. . . . He is a mere delegate on whom this side of the hero's role is devolved in situations where the hero himself has to keep up a less farcical character."[25] In *She wou'd if she cou'd* Sir Joslin is a kind of subordinate "master of the revels" to Courtall, and as such he almost literally dances his way through the play, leading along now Sir Oliver, now Ariana and Gatty. The latter's association with him is firmly underlined when she gaily dances a jig under his supervision: "this is a clean Limb'd wench, and has neither spavin, Splinter, nor Wind-gall; tune her a Jig, and play't roundly, you shall see her bounce it away like a nimble Frigot before a fresh gale— Hey, methinks I see her under Sail already. . . . Hey my little Madcap—here's a Girl of the true breed of the *Jollies,* i'faith" (117). The fact that the same metaphors have been picked up here which appeared in the first sparkling encounter between the young men and women reinforces Sir Joslin's tie with their world. He is the eternal fertility spirit, the Dionysian reveler, who belongs to the tavern environment of wine, women, and song, and who symbolically leads the marriage procession at the end of the play: "Never trouble your heads further; since I perceive you are all agreed on the Matter, let me alone to hasten the Ceremony: come, Gentlemen, lead 'em to their Chambers" (178, 179).

It is Courtall, however—rake, libertine, and skeptic—who really dominates the play and who is finally the master-manipulator of the action. Like all of his comic counterparts, he triumphantly makes use of every element of the world around him to serve his own ends of entertainment and adventure. Delighting in his own superiority and in his own wickedness, he throws himself eagerly into every new challenge, declaring, "I find it a meer folly to forswear any thing, it does but make the Devil the more earnest in his temptation" (106). More completely the conscious artist than Sir Frederick, he is always concerned with a perfection of "design." Thus he complains at one point to Freeman: "Faith, things are not so well contriv'd as I could have wish'd 'em . . . that which troubles me most, is, we lost the hopes of variety, and a single intrigue in Love is as dull as a single Plot in a Play, and will tire a Lover worse, than t'other does an Audience." With Freeman as confidant, lieutenant, and appreciative observer, we watch him contriving and executing plot after plot, sometimes on the spur of the moment, as in the opening scene, where he neatly disposes of first Freeman and then Sentry in furtherance of his ultimate design on Lady Cockwood, but more often with careful forethought, as in his staging of the Exchange encounter, with Mrs. Gazet lined up to play her part in his plot, and later in his magnificently handled masquerade at the tavern. Indeed there is scarcely a major scene in the play which does not reflect the finely-shaping imagination of the clearheaded, ingenious Courtall.

Pitted against him finally in a struggle for dominance, Lady Cockwood herself proves a plotter and designer of no mean ability —as cunning and ruthless as her opponent. One is as much of a "Matchiavil" as the other, and the central themes of the play finally come to focus on their opposition. Against her passionate destructiveness (she would seem to reflect the "vicious" aspect of the old vice-figure and to anticipate both a Mrs. Loveit and a Mrs. Marwood), the controlled, creative artistry of Courtall achieves its clearest definition. Significantly, Lady Cockwood's lines in the latter half of the play are filled with references to "poyson," "killing," and "murdering." Of Courtall's inconstancy she declares: "this has incens'd me so, that I could kill him. I am glad these Girls are gone to the Spring-Garden, it helps my design; the Letters I have counterfeited, have appointed *Courtall* and *Freeman* to meet them there, they will produce 'em, and confirm all I have said: I will daily poyson these Girls with such lyes as shall make their quarrel to *Courtall* irreconcileable" (148).

Within her own "Family," holding as she does her position as "virtuous" and "loving" Lady, she maintains for the most part "an absolute dominion." "Hang her, *Ned*," cries the drunken and hence temporarily defiant Sir Oliver, "by wicked Policy she would usurp my Empire, and in her heart is a very *Pharaoh;* for every night she's a putting me upon making Brick without straw" (115). His courage, however, is short-lived, and having been caught in the act of rebellion at the Bear, he reverts to the role of obedient worshipper. "Dear Madam, do but look up a little, Sir *Oliver* lyes at your feet an humble Penitent," says Sentry, to which Ariana adds: "How bitterly he weeps! how sadly he sighs!" (140) and Sir Oliver finally pulls himself together sufficiently to deny any "disloyal action": "Here's my Brother *Jolly* too can witness the loyalty of my Heart, and that I did not intend any treasonable practice against your Ladiship in the least" (141).

Etherege is doing something rather pointed here with the kind

of imagery he uses in connection with Sir Oliver. His name in itself
has a decided suggestiveness, and his actions are continually being
referred to in political terms. When, for example, Courtall says
to Sir Oliver in the scene at the Bear: "Take my advice, Sir *Oliver,*
do not in your rage deprive your self of your only hope of an ac-
commodation with your lady," he retorts, again with the courage
of drunkenness upon him: "I had rather have a perpetual civil
War, then purchase Peace at such a dishonourable rate" (137). And
later in the same scene, when Sir Oliver repentantly begs Sentry to
"stab me with thy Bodkin rather, that I may here dye a Sacrifice at
her feet, for all my disloyal actions," Sentry makes the rejoinder:
"No live, live, to be a reproach and a shame to all rebellious Husbands; ah, that she had but my Heart! but thou hast bewitch'd her
affections; thou shouldst then dearly smart for this abominable
Treason" (139).

The implication would seem to be that in the family as in the
state an absolute monarchy that is repressive in its measures,
whether in the religious or social sphere, will inevitably breed rebellion, treason, disloyalty. But when poor Sir Oliver tries to assert
his freedom and ventures abroad to seek satisfaction for his natural
appetites, his Lady retaliates by decreeing for him a "day of Humil-
iation," during which he is confined to the house with only his
"penitential suit" to wear, Sentry having "lock'd up" his finery and
by implication his animal desires along with it. But those desires
are not to be denied, and even in his penitential suit Sir Oliver is
driven again to go "a ranging." His acceptance of a "religion" casting him in the role of humble worshipper at his wife's feet and of
a social system requiring him to play the humble subject in a do-
mestic totalitarianism leaves too much of his nature out of account.

He can, however, never finally break out of the confining house
in which he lives, since he has accepted and committed himself
to a confining mode of existence. It seldom occurs to him to question the validity of the system by which he is trapped, however
bitterly he may resent it. "I was married to her when I was young,
*Ned,* with a design to be baulk'd, as they tye Whelps to the Bell-
weather; where I have been so butted, 'twere enough to frighten
me, were I not pure mettle, from ever running at sheep again"
(137). His animal imagery supplies commentary enough on the

falseness of the system; yet complain as he may, he remains blind to any shortcomings of his lady where her "virtue" is concerned and can, therefore, be as easily manipulated by her as she by Courtall. Never questioning the "devotion" he owes to her, he joins her in orgies of sentimentality ("My Dearest"—"My Dearest Dear") of whose falsity he apparently has no conception; and he rises to her challenges to his "Honour" and "Duty" with a smug confidence in his own valor: "Death, and Hell, and Furies, I will have my Pumps, and long Sword!"—and accepts the doubleness of his world without even recognizing it: "Was ever man bless'd with such a vertuous Lady! yet cannot I forbear going a ranging agen" (146).

For all his bluster he has actually been demasculinized by his commitment to the sentimental, unreal, "honourable" mode, and his attempts to play the rake seldom lead him far. A stanza from a Wycherley poem rather accurately defines his plight:

> Such Sighing, Weeping, but discover
> Effeminacy i'th' Male Lover,
>   Which does the Proud, tho' Soft Sex, move,
> But less to Pity, than Disdain,
>   To more Aversion, turns that Love,
> By which, Soft Fools, Hard Hearts wou'd gain.[26]

Sir Oliver and Lady Cockwood are caught within a vicious circle. The thought of love as "duty" effectively kills any physical desire that Sir Oliver might have felt for his wife—"the very sight of that face makes me more impotent then an Eunuch" (114)—and his failure to satisfy her physical desires drives her to seek satisfaction "abroad," but at the same time requires that she keep him deluded as to her virtue in order that she may "take her freedom." And his being driven outside marriage to find satisfaction has the result of further subjecting him to her dominion when he is caught. Only when they have both broken out of their circle for a brief interval does any union become possible—for only then, in the free atmosphere of the appropriately named Bear Tavern, does Sir Oliver find his wife (masked and unrecognized by him) a seductive "shape," "so exact and tempting, 'twould perswade a man to be an implicite sinner, and take her face upon credit" (138). But of course his desire to "turne and winde and fegue thy body" evaporates quickly enough when she reveals her true identity and turns upon him with all her self-righteousness ready at command, and he reverts automatically to the role of craven husband. Each remains in the outcome a "Cockwood," who "wou'd" but alas cannot become, like Sir Joslin, "a true Cock of the Game" (101).

In the later Acts of the play Lady Cockwood becomes passionately determined to impose on her world the same dividedness from which she herself suffers, and for a moment she seems almost to succeed. The "passions" that "spin the plot" are for the moment hers. As a result of her machinations Sir Oliver draws his sword against Courtall, Courtall and Freeman are set at odds, and Gatty and Ariana are turned indignantly against their lovers. Nearly every balance of the play seems to have been upset, every creative possibility destroyed. When Lady Cockwood says to Freeman after luring him into her domain: "I was so distracted with my fears, that I cannot well remember how we parted at the Spring-Garden," Freeman replies with what sounds like a deliberate underlining of her success: "We all divided, Madam" (162).

As the single scene of Act V unfolds, we begin to recognize a deliberate parallel and contrast to the first scene of Act I. Again Freeman is thrust unceremoniously into a closet, and again, upon the approach of Sir Oliver, a second hiding place must be found for a second visitor, this time Courtall. There has been a reversal of roles, with Lady Cockwood as manipulator of the scene and Courtall, instead of Sentry, in hiding. But her management of the complicated deceptions results in a hopelessly confused melee in the darkness. With Sentry's dropping of the candle, Lady Cockwood loses control of her own fortress, and the balances and unities have begun to be restored at the moment when Courtall is directed toward the same closet where Freeman already stands hidden.

Once Courtall has emerged from his "repression" in the closet, he takes charge of affairs with his customary skill and wholly dominates Lady Cockwood's world as he has always been able to dominate his own; and he and Gatty again become allies, aided by Freeman and Ariana. Untangling one by one all the destructive intrigues in which Lady Cockwood has embroiled the various members of her circle, he delivers an extemporaneous performance which positively dazzles by its ingenuity and facility of response, and the play ends with his world of creative balances wholly victorious. This is not to say, however, that any of the oppositions have been resolved. When Lady Cockwood declares her intention "to give over the great bus'ness of this Town, and hereafter modestly confine my self to the humble Affairs of my own Family," she suggests that she is shutting herself off from life, and Courtall's response hints at the direction in which her own nature will inevitably lead her: " 'Tis a very pious resolution, Madam, and the better to confirm you in it, pray entertain an able Chaplain" (178). And when Sir Oliver talks of "Perfect concord," and repeats his simpleminded belief, "Never man was so happy in a vertuous and a loving Lady!" (176) the sentimentality sounds all too familiar, and the easy assumption as to future peace actually assures a continuing state of chaos and division.

But there is a more positive and reassuring ring about the terms by which the quartet of young lovers seek to come to a "right understanding." Courtall's assertion to Sir Joslin that "Mr. *Freeman* and I have vow'd our selves humble Servants to these Ladies" is greeted by the Ladies themselves with the same skepticism with which they have responded to Courtall's and Freeman's earlier "vows" and "oaths," and Gatty, in her turn, reintroduces the warfare metaphor: "if after a months experience of your good behaviour, upon serious thoughts, you have courage enough to ingage further, we will accept of the Challenge, and believe you men of Honour" (176). The dialogue at this point, shot through as it is with "ifs" and with words of ambiguous meaning like "Honour," maintains the same atmosphere of creative uncertainties, oppositions, and tensions which have characterized the earlier scene. The ladies may indeed be, as Sir Joslin says, "two powerful Rivals" to women of Rampant's kind of charms, but they are clearly not going to take their power for granted, and the final words of all four protagonists constitute a full comic recognition that "the world that presents all obstacles also supplies the zest of life." And in the last analysis the very structure of the play grows out of and confirms the central theme, with the two balanced and opposing scenes of Act I melting into the precarious unity of the single long, lively scene which ends the play.

# [ IV ]

# *The Man of Mode, or Sir Fopling Flutter*

---

FASHION, n. A despot whom the wise ridicule and obey.
REASON, v.i. To weigh probabilities in the scales of desire.

—AMBROSE BIERCE, *The Devil's Dictionary*

IF ETHEREGE'S THIRD AND LAST PLAY (1676) IS BY COMMON CONSENT his best, it is also his most insistently tough-minded and unremittingly open-eyed and honest. The comic challenge which the chief protagonists Dorimant and Harriet hurl at their self-consciously polished, rule-bound world is one which draws its vitality from a full awareness of their own deeper, more demonic natures and from their absolute refusal of all illusions. Knowing and accepting themselves for what they are, they *will* be free to be themselves; and they will play the game of life with the bravado and the ruthless skill of born gamblers. The gaiety and zest for life of Etherege's earlier protagonists is still theirs, but they suffer fools less gladly, and they both pursue their Hobbesian "power and pleasure and appetite" with aggressive artistry.

In a more than superficial sense the theme of *The Man of Mode* is, as its title indicates, fashion or "modishness," and the world in which Dorimant and Harriet move is one of "modes"—both of behavior and dress. A man or woman of "quality" (a term which occurs again and again in the play) acts and dresses by the rules—rules sufficiently solidified so that books of instructions have appeared. Asked by Emilia about "any new Wit come forth, Songs or Novels?" Medley replies: "there is the Art of affectation, written by a late beauty of Quality, teaching you how to draw up your Breasts, stretch up your neck, to throw out your Breech, to play with your Head, to toss up your Nose, to bite your Lips, to turn up your Eyes, to speak in a silly soft tone of a Voice, and use all the Foolish French Words that will infallibly make your person and conversation charming, with a short apologie at the latter end, in the behalf of young Ladies, who notoriously wash, and paint, though they have naturally good Complexions." The deeper suggestion here is that the "new Wit" is a far cry from the imaginative expansiveness to be expected from "Songs or Novels"; and indeed "rules" and "modishness" become in the play the central metaphor used to define artificiality, effeteness, sterility as these qualities stand opposed to the natural, the robust, the creative possibilities exemplified by Dorimant and Harriet. Again, as in Etherege's earlier comedies, a dead world is being exposed by juxtaposition to a living one.

At the center of the world of artificiality and so-called wit stands that walking rule-book for social and sartorial affectations Sir Fopling Flutter. If Dorimant is "the Prince of all the Devils in the Town" (237), Sir Fopling enjoys an equally supreme status as "the very Cock-fool of all those Fools" (217). Both are "men of Mode," but with a significant difference that is repeatedly underlined by the dialogue of the play. Being himself made up of "Pantaloon," "Gloves . . . well fring'd," and "Perriwig," Sir Fopling is never happier than when characterized as a "shape" that "Ladies doat on" (231), and the only fault he can find with Dorimant is in the matter of "Crevats": *"Dorimant,* thou art a pretty fellow and wear'st thy cloaths well," he cries condescendingly, "but I never saw thee have a handsom Crevat. Were they made up like mine, they'd give another Aire to thy face. Prithee let me send my man to dress thee but one day. By Heav'ns an English man cannot tye a Ribbon" (261).

For their part neither Dorimant nor Harriet is indifferent to fashion and neither is lacking in his share of vanity, but both reject impatiently Sir Fopling's brand of artifice. "Varnish'd over with good breeding," says Harriet, "many a blockhead makes a tolerable show" (220). For her as for Dorimant the morning toilet is a necessary preliminary to the adventure of living, but clothes do not "make the man." Rather, they must be made to fit him. Thus Dorimant's complaint about his "Shooe" that it "Sits with more wrinkles than there are in an Angry Bullies Forehead" is stoutly denied by the shoemaker (who clearly knows his customer): " 'Zbud, as smooth as your Mistresses skin does upon her" (198). But both Dorimant and Harriet firmly refuse to allow themselves to be turned into manikins. "Leave your unnecessary fidling;" Dorimant says testily to Handy, "a Wasp that's buzzing about a Mans Nose at Dinner, is not more troublesome than thou art" (199). And Harriet exclaims to Busy, "How do I daily suffer under thy Officious Fingers!" (219) Both hero and heroine have planted themselves in indignant opposition to the empty modishness of the world in which they live. "That Women should set up for beauty as much in spite of nature, as some men have done for Wit!" deplores Harriet. "That a man's excellency should lie in neatly tying of a Ribbond, or a Crevat!" protests Dorimant.

Clearly the difference between Dorimant and Harriet on the one hand and Sir Fopling on the other has to do in part with style as a manifestation of self. For Dorimant and Harriet style *expresses* the natural man. For Sir Fopling style *replaces* nature. Or, to put the matter another way, Dorimant and Harriet control and determine their own modes of dress and behavior according to their own individualities, while every piece of clothing donned by Sir Fopling and every move he makes is dictated by his conception of what polite society demands. Sir Fopling's comicality, in fact, may be regarded as an instance of the Bergsonian "covered" having turned into the "covering."[1] Hopelessly bound by social rules, he has no real *life*, no "living suppleness" left. He has acted the part of the "Compleat Gentleman" for so long that no vestige of spontaneity has survived; every motion is made by the book, and the imitation has stifled and obliterated the reality. As Medley says, "He has been, as the sparkish word is, Brisk upon the Ladies already; he was yesterday at my Aunt *Townleys,* and gave Mrs. *Loveit* a Catalogue of his good Qualities, under the Character of a Compleat Gentleman, who according to Sir *Fopling,* ought to dress well, Dance well, Fence well, have a genius for Love Letters, an agreeable voice for a Chamber, be very Amorous, something discreet, but not over Constant" (200, 201).[2]

Sir Fopling, in short, invariably behaves as the rules say he "ought to," and in this respect he is clearly identified with that other slave to form and model of rigidity, Lady Woodvil. If she is "a great admirer of the Forms and Civility of the last Age" (193), Sir Fopling is just as irrevocably committed to the forms and rules of the new age. And if she is an egregious social snob in her constant concern for "women of quality," he is equally snobbish in his desire to parade himself as a "man of Quality" (268)—"in imitation of the people of Quality of France." "It might be said," remarks Bergson, in an observation which is peculiarly applicable to both Lady Woodvil and Sir Fopling, "that ceremonies are to the social body what clothing is to the individual body. . . . For any ceremony, then, to become comic, it is enough that our attention be fixed on the ceremonial element in it, and that we neglect its matter . . . and think only of its form."[3]

Significantly Dorimant has occasion in the course of the action to play the fop in both Lady Woodvil's and Sir Fopling's senses and thus to supply a fully conscious parody of both kinds of empty affectation. For the old lady's benefit he appears as Mr. Courtage— "That foppish admirer of Quality, who flatters the very meat at honourable Tables, and never offers love to a Woman below a Lady-Grandmother!" (244) "You know the Character you are to act, I see!" comments Medley, and not even the guarded Harriet can deny that he delivers a convincing performance: "He fits my Mothers humor so well, a little more and she'l dance a Kissing dance with him anon" (245). But the contrast between a Mr. Courtage and Dorimant himself is later underlined heavily:

> HAR. Lord! how you admire this man!
> L. WOOD. What have you to except against him?
> HAR. He's a Fopp.
> L. WOOD. He's not a *Dorimant,* a wild extravagant Fellow of the Times.
> HAR. He's a man made up of forms and common places, suckt out of the remaining Lees of the last age.     (254)

And subsequently the difference between Dorimant and Sir Fopling is made equally plain in the brief and angry exchange between Dorimant and Loveit:

> Dor. Now for a touch of Sir *Fopling* to begin with. Hey—Page—Give positive order that none of my People stir—Let the Canaile wait as they should do—Since noise and nonsense have such pow'rful charms,
>
> *I, that I may successful prove,*
> *Transform my self to what you love.*
>
> Lov. If that would do, you need not change from what you are; you can be vain and lewd enough.
>
> Dor. But not with so good a grace as Sir *Fopling*. Hey, *Hampshire* —Oh—that sound, that sound becomes the mouth of a man of Quality.   (267, 268)

Several years had elapsed between Etherege's second play and his third, and during that period he had, it would seem, recognized the emergence of a fresh challenge for the comic spirit. In effect, Sir Fopling's modishness represents to the younger aristocratic generation a new kind of affectation which was replacing the *précieux* mode of an earlier time and which had gradually developed to the point where it was, in its own way, equally far removed from the realities of human experience. The trouble with Sir Fopling is that he has taken over a social mode which had originally grown out of the emancipating libertine convictions of Charles II's courtiers and out of the needs of the Hobbesian "natural man," and he has turned it into a social pretense quite lacking its original life-giving force and hence as empty of meaning as Lady Woodvil's *précieux* mode. Oscar Wilde remarks in one of his essays that "Costume is a growth, an evolution, and a most important, perhaps the most important, sign of the manners, customs, and mode of life of each century."[4] But it is a truism to observe that both manners and costume can easily become hollow externals when the real human needs that originally inspired them are lost or forgotten, and it is then that "a man's excellency" comes to "lie in neatly tying of a Ribbond, or a Crevat."

In Dorimant's and Harriet's world the mode has spread so far down the social scale as to include even Tom the Shoemaker (significantly a dealer in "costume"), who prefers the word "Tope" to the word "drunk" and who exclaims: " 'Zbud, there's never a man i'the Town lives more like a Gentleman, with his Wife, than I do. I never mind her motions, she never inquires into mine; we speak to one another Civilly, hate one another heartily, and because 'tis vulgar to lie and soak together, we have each of us our several Settlebed" (198). Artificiality and sterility have extended even into Tom's world. Yet it is the real function of this entire little scene to emphasize, with a kind of sly comic inversion, that for all their affectations there is no essential difference between a Sir Fopling and a Tom nor, for that matter, between a "vulgar" and illiterate "Molly" and a "woman of quality" like Lady Woodvil or Mrs. Loveit. Thus when simple Molly writes to Dorimant: *I have no money and am very Mallicolly; pray send me a Guynie to see the Operies,"* Medley remarks, "Pray let the Whore have a favourable answer, that she may spark it in a Box, and do honour to her profession." And Dorimant assures him "She shall; and perk up i'the face of quality" (204).

To define Young Bellair and Emilia as the "golden mean" in this modish society, as does Norman Holland, is not only to make use of a term which has no validity in the Etheregean comic world unless as a standard to be rejected, but also to ignore the patent tendency of both characters to sentimentality and to what the play repeatedly defines as "unreasonable" behavior and to overlook their commitment to the courtly tradition of love and honor. Bellair, as measured against the positive standards of daring and defiance established by Etherege, emerges as a conservative nonentity. It is he who warns Harriet against the "Mail" as a rather dangerous place for nice young ladies; and earlier Medley has recognized his own and Dorimant's company as equally dangerous for nice young men like Bellair: "how will you answer this visit to your honourable Mistress?" he demands tauntingly, " 'tis not her interest you shou'd keep Company with men of sence, who will be talking reason" (198).

The most Dorimant can say of Bellair is that "He's Handsome, well bred, and by much the most tolerable of all the young men that do not abound in wit," a judgment reinforced by Medley's subsequent characterization: "Ever well dress'd, always complaisant, and seldom impertinent . . ." (201, 202). In Lady Townley's gay social groups, he fades rather colorlessly into the background, and although he is not quite so much in love with Emilia as to marry her while there is a serious risk of losing his inheritance (he is "reasonable" enough about money if not about love) and is not above a contrivance with Harriet "to deceive the grave people," he inspires in Harriet herself nothing more than the lukewarm approbation: "I think I might be brought to endure him" (220). Lacking Dorimant's ruthless aggressiveness, he is also lacking in the vitality, virility, and excitement which contribute to making Dorimant the overwhelmingly dominant figure that he is, and he represents finally only a more subtle foil than Sir Fopling in bringing out the fact of the hero's evident superiority.

Much the same can be said also of the role of Emilia vis-à-vis Harriet, and again it is Medley—serving at once as Dorimant's confidant and as the chorus of the play—who sums her up: "her Carriage is unaffected, her discourse modest, not at all censorious, nor pretending like the Counterfeits of the Age" (202). There is, moreover, a special irony in Dorimant's marking her out as a likely prospect for a future conquest ("I have known many Women make a difficulty of losing a Maidenhead, who have afterwards made none of making a cuckold"), since he is thereby not only underscoring his own skeptical attitude toward every "discreet Maid," but in the process suggesting that the pedestal on which she stands is more than a little precarious and that she is, in her elemental nature, no more civilized and no less appetitive than a Mrs. Loveit, a Bellinda, or a Molly.

On more than one occasion, in fact, Etherege seems to be pointedly asking us to recognize in Emilia something of the same overrefined preciousness that belongs to Sir Fopling. When, for example, Lady Townley says in talking of Dorimant and Mrs. Loveit: "We heard of a pleasant Serenade he gave her t'other Night," and Medley describes it as "A Danish Serenade with Kettle Drums, and Trumpets," Emilia exclaims, "Oh, Barbarous!" and Medley chides, "What, you are of the number of the Ladies whose Ears are grown so delicate since our Operas, you can be charm'd with nothing but Flute doux, and French Hoboys?" (208, 209) And in the next Act Lady Townley feels prompted to tax Emilia with being "a little too delicate" after she has remarked stuffily: "Company is a very good thing, Madam, but I wonder you do not love it a little more Chosen" (228, 229).

Neither exchange by itself may seem to possess much importance, but when placed in juxtaposition with certain of Sir Fopling's scenes, an evolving theme becomes apparent, and it is one which has had its roots in the opening scene of the play. Thus to Sir Fopling's question, "Have you taken notice of the Gallesh I brought over?" Medley replies, "O yes! 't has quite another Air, than th'English makes" and Dorimant adds, "Truly there is a bell-air in Galleshes as well as men." Whereupon Sir Fopling responds approvingly, "But there are few so delicate to observe it" (230, 231). Dorimant and Medley are, of course, playing with Sir Fopling, and their delicacy is only make-believe. The word "delicate," however, has at this point already been used twice about Emilia, and Dorimant's choice of the word "bell-air" is certainly suggestive. In the following scene Sir Fopling makes another statement reminiscent of Emilia when he declares, in response to Bellinda's observation about "all the rabble of the Town" gathered in the Mail, " 'Tis pity there's not an order made, that none but the Beau Monde should walk here" (240). A few lines later we hear him exclaiming, "there's nothing so barbarous as the names of our English Servants" (242). And finally, in the fourth act, Sir Fopling invades Lady Townley's drawing room with a group of masqueraders whom he describes as "A set of Balladins, whom I pickt out of the best in *France* and brought over, with a Flutes deux or two" (253).

In effect, then, two life styles are being repeatedly contrasted with each other throughout the play—a contrast variously expressed in terms of the "barberous" versus the "delicate," the English versus the French, the inclusive versus the exclusive, Dorimant versus Sir Fopling. Sir Fopling, as the embodiment of an effete society which has cut itself off almost wholly from its life-giving roots, defines a mode of life which threatens to overtake Emilia as well. His snobbishness and exclusiveness—"I was well receiv'd in a dozen families, where all the Women of quality us'd to visit" (251)—is set against the "universal taste" which Lady Townley advocates. Her house, representing along with the "Mail" the "green world" of the play, is described as "the general rendevouze, and next to the Play-house is the Common Refuge of all the Young idle people." It is itself, indeed, a kind of "play-house" and "new world," and Dorimant, in his role as Mr. Courtage, succinctly defines its difference from the old for the benefit of Lady Woodvil: "All people mingle now a days, Madam. And in publick places Women of Quality have the least respect show'd 'em. . . . Forms and Ceremonies, the only things that uphold Quality and greatness, are now shamefully laid aside and neglected" (244, 245). And Lady Woodvil goes on to sum-marize the case more accurately than she knows in lamenting: "Lewdness is the business now, Love was the bus'ness in my Time," for in the terms of the play love has become an empty word and "lewdness" a vital reality (and precisely the quality in which Sir Fopling and his ilk are deplorably lacking).

In Sir Fopling's world every judgment as to a man's "excellency" is made in terms of modishness. Strolling in the Mail with Mrs. Loveit, Sir Fopling comments upon the *"four ill-fashioned Fellows"* who have passed singing across their path: "Did you observe, Madam, how their Crevats hung loose an inch from their Neck, and what a frightful Air it gave 'em?" To a man of his refined and "delicate" sensibilities, the smell of such dirty fellows is almost unbearable:

> Lov. Fo! Their Perriwigs are scented with Tobacco so strong—
> Sir Fop. It overcomes our pulvilio—Methinks I smell the Coffee-house they come from.
>                    · · · · ·
> Sir Fop. I sat near one of 'em at a Play to day, and was almost poison'd with a pair of Cordivant Gloves he wears—
> Lov. Oh! filthy Cordivant, how I hate the smell!     (240, 241)

Sir Fopling's own gloves, of course, are delicately perfumed: "Orangerie! You know the smell, Ladies!" (231) And to an edu-cated nose like his, even a burning candle is "filthy" and scarcely endurable: "How can you breathe in a Room where there's Grease frying!" (252) To such foppery, Dorimant's impatient opposition has been expressed early in the play:

> Hand. Will you use the Essence or Orange Flower Water?
> Dor. I will smell as I do to day, no offence to the Ladies Noses.
>                                                              (199)

Only in the last act of the play, however, does the full thematic significance of this kind of emphasis become apparent. The act opens with a conversation which offers a clear parallel with the opening scene of Act I. Again it is early morning and again the talk is about "Markets" and "Fruit," and the earlier conversation between Dorimant and the Orange-woman as well as that already quoted between Sir Fopling and Mrs. Loveit ought to echo in our ears as Bellinda confronts Mrs. Loveit:

> BELL. Do you not wonder, my Dear, what made me abroad so soon?
> Lov. You do not use to be so.
> BELL. The Country Gentlewomen I told you of (Lord! they have the oddest diversions!) would never let me rest till I promis'd to go with them to the Markets this morning to eat Fruit and buy Nosegays.
> Lov. Are they so fond of a filthy Nosegay?
> BELL. They complain of the stinks of the Town, and are never well but when they have their noses in one.
> Lov. There are Essences and sweet waters.
> BELL. O, they cry out upon perfumes they are unwholsome; one of 'em was falling into a fit with the smell of these narolii.
> Lov. Methinks in Complaisance you shou'd have had a Nosegay too.
> BELL. Do you think, my Dear, I could be so loathsome to trick my self up with Carnations and stock-Gillyflowers? I begg'd their pardon and told them I never wore any thing but Orange Flowers and Tuberose. That which made me willing to go was a strange desire I had to eat some fresh Nectaren's.
> Lov. And had you any?
> BELL. The best I ever tasted.    (265, 266)

If any doubt exists as to the sexual implications of "fruit" in the opening scene of the play, it can scarcely survive now. Since Bellinda has just come from her assignation with Dorimant, the double-entendre of her concluding remarks here becomes obvious and is even more insistently underscored a few lines later as Bellinda pretends illness:

> PERT. She has eaten too much fruit, I warrant you.
> Lov. Not unlikely!

PERT. 'Tis that lyes heavy on her Stomach.

Lov. Have her into my Chamber, give her some Surfeit Water, and let her lye down a little.

PERT. Come, Madam! I was a strange devourer of Fruit when I was young, so ravenous—    (267)

The special irony of the scene lies in the fact that both women are explicitly denying their identity with the "Country Gentle-women" and, in effect, their own physical, appetitive natures at the same time that they implicitly acknowledge them. Throughout the play the gap between artificiality and naturalness is expressed in terms of "Orange Flower Water" or "Orangerie" on the one hand and "oranges" (or "peaches" or "Nectarens") on the other. In the broader context of the play, it is the difference between Sir Fopling and Dorimant, between a suit of clothes and a man, between steril-ity and fertility.

The Orange-woman is, of course, by profession both a seller of fruit and a bawd, and the peach which she offers to Dorimant ("the best Fruit has come to Town t'year") has a clear identity with Har-riet ("a young Gentlewoman lately come to Town"). Dorimant cynically begins by expressing a disbelief in the "freshness" of both, calling the peach the "nasty refuse of your Shop" (190) and the gentlewoman "some awkward ill fashion'd Country Toad" (191), but the description Medley supplies is enough to make Dorimant's mouth water with anticipation. He first describes her as being "in a hopeful way" (192)—a phrase which the Orange-woman chooses to interpret according to her own earthy lights—and then goes on to lyricize:

> MED. What alteration a Twelve-month may have bred in her I know not, but a year ago she was the beautifullest Creature I ever saw; a fine, easie, clean shape, light brown Hair in abundance; her Features regular, her Complexion clear and lively, large wanton Eyes, but above all a mouth that has made me kiss it a thousand times in imagination, Teeth white and even, and pretty pouting Lips, with a little moisture ever hanging on them that look like the Province Rose fresh on the Bush, 'ere the Morning Sun has quite drawn up the dew.

By the time Medley has concluded his eulogy, he has Dorimant ex-claiming: "Flesh and blood cannot hear this, and not long to know her" (193). It is in this connection that Bernard Harris, commenting on Etherege's prose, points out that "his similitudes from the natural life offer a relationship to the human, not a distinction or even a parallel. In *The Man of Mode* . . . there is a persistent relationship effected between the forms of life. . . . The simile is perfectly absorbed and absorbing." [5]

Sir Fopling's senses, however, have, in contrast to Dorimant's, virtually lost touch with flesh-and-blood, sensuous reality. Not only is his nose offended by natural smells but his ears are offended by harsh sounds. Preferring delicate flute notes to Dorimant's "barbarous" trumpets and kettle drums, he also finds the name John Trott "unsufferable" and changes it to the more euphonious (and pretentious) "Hampshire." "The world is generally very grossier here, indeed," he remarks, comparing England to France (231), and Dorimant's vigorous masculinity is continually set off against his preciousness and effeminacy:

> MED. He was Yesterday at the Play, with a pair of Gloves up to his Elbows, and a Periwig more exactly Curl'd then a Ladies head newly dress'd for a Ball.
>
> BELL. What a pretty lisp he has!
>
> DOR. Ho, that he affects in imitation of the people of Quality of *France*.
>
> MED. His head stands for the most part on one side, and his looks are more languishing than a Ladys when she loll's at stretch in her Coach, or leans her head carelessly against the side of a Box i'the Playhouse.    (200)

In a later scene, when the group gathered at Lady Townley's tries to persuade Sir Fopling to dance, Medley remarks: "Like a woman I find you must be struggl'd with before one brings you to what you desire." But there is no persuading Sir Fopling, and when he apologizes to Harriet ("Do not think it want of Complaisance, Madam"), she returns, "You are too well bred to want that, Sir *Fopling*. I believe it want of power." To which he smugly assents: "By Heav'ns and so it is. I have sat up so Damn'd late and drunk so curs'd hard since I came to this lewd Town, that I am fit for nothing but low dancing now, a Corant, a Boreè, or a Minnuét; but St. *André* tells me, if I will but be regular in one Month I shall rise agen. Pox on this Debauchery" (253). Sir Fopling, as it proves, can only "endeavor at a caper" and then be content to dance by proxy—throwing out instructions to his "set of Balladins" from his position seated among the ladies. And his "want of power" turns out to include a strong suggestion of sexual impotence when at the end of the play he is all too easily discouraged from continuing his pursuit of Mrs. Loveit: "An intrigue now would be but a temptation to me to throw away that Vigour on one, which I mean shall shortly make my Court to the whole sex in a Ballet" (285).

Even Old Bellair possesses more animal vigor than does Sir Fopling, and indeed it is he who is the true heir to the role of Sir Joslin Jolley of *She wou'd if she cou'd.* Forever dancing, singing, drinking, and "bepatting" the ladies, he is the high-spirited, irrepressible Dionysian clown at Lady Townley's revels and is always in the forefront of the exuberant country dances, which contrast so sharply in their energetic natural rhythms with the mannered "French air" imposed by Sir Fopling on his own little "equipage." Like Sir Joslin, Old Bellaire seems to be constantly in motion ("You are very active, Sir," says Emilia. He views the male-female relationship in coarsely physical terms and acts as good-natured matchmaker at the end of the play. ("Please you, Sir," he bids the Chaplain, "to Commission a young Couple to go to Bed together a Gods name?")

Dorimant, for all his refinement and ironic detachment, possesses the masculine vigor which identifies him with Old Bellair's rather primitive spontaneity and virility, but Sir Fopling has lost touch almost completely with such earthy, natural behavior. Even his carelessness is studied: "We should not alwaies be in a set dress, 'tis more en Cavalier to appear now and then in a dissabillée" (261). And he writes his love songs, as he does everything else, by the rules so that the end product sounds like something straight out of the heroic plot of *The Comical Revenge*—a pretty pastoral with appropriate references to "my wounded heart" and to sighs and languishings. Boasting of having learned singing from Lambert in Paris, he has to acknowledge: "I have his own fault, a weak voice, and care not to sing out of a ruél," whereupon Dorimant comments: "A ruél is a pretty Cage for a singing Fop, indeed" (262).

Dorimant himself refuses categorically to live like a songbird in a cage. Just as he takes over the form of the pastoral love song and uses it to express what Underwood calls his own "'satanic' posture,"[6] so he takes over the vows and protestations of the *précieux* mode and uses them to his own aggressive ends. Always the comic artist, adapting every form and rule to his particular needs, he sings and versifies his way through the play with supreme confidence in his own superior knowledge of the ways of the world and of the women in it, and Young Bellair pays him the ultimate tribute by remarking: "all he does and says is so easie, and so natural" (234).

To him as to Harriet the first requirement of the game of life is freedom to follow one's own inclinations, however arbitrary they may be. "We are not Masters of our own affections," he says to Mrs. Loveit, sounding like an echo of Courtall, "our inclinations daily alter; now we love pleasure, and anon we shall doat on business; human frailty will have it so, and who can help it?" (214) The greatest enemy to the élan vital is restriction of the kind Mrs. Loveit would impose on Dorimant and Lady Woodvil on her daughter, and Dorimant's defiance of Mrs. Loveit in Act I, scene ii, has its counterpart in Harriet's defiance of her mother in Act II, scene i. Harriet too has her own "inclinations," and she confides to her waiting woman her real objection to marrying Bellair:

> HAR. I think I might be brought to endure him, and that is all a reasonable Woman should expect in a Husband, but there is duty i'the case— and like the Haughty *Merab*, I
> *Find much aversion in my stubborn mind,*
> Which,     *Is bred by being promis'd and design'd.*     (220)

And a few lines later, when Young Bellair asks: "What generous resolution are you making, Madam?" Harriet retorts, "Only to be disobedient, Sir."

In terms of the highly civilized world to which Dorimant and Harriet belong, they are both "barberous" (a word which recurs repeatedly in indignant references to Dorimant)—possessed of no illusions about the "native brass" which lies at the bottom of their own natures. Egotistically cognizant of their own value, they shake off impatiently any attempt to reduce them to a civilized formality. Thus, when Busy pleads with Harriet, "Dear Madam! Let me set that Curl in order," Harriet exclaims, "Let me alone, I will shake 'em all out of order" (219). In short, they are both "sons of the morning"—the time of day when they first appear on stage in all their rebellious individuality—armed for their encounter with the world with the freshness and vigor of free spirits but also with a tough skepticism that will take nothing on faith.

Neither harbors any undue respect for "quality" and both are merciless mockers of both the foppish and the *précieux* affectations which surround them. When, for example, Dorimant taunts Harriet by making a jeering comment about ladies' eyes ("Women indeed have commonly a method of managing those messengers of Love! now they will look as if they would kill, and anon they will look as if they were dying. They point and rebate their glances, the better to invite us"), she promptly retorts: "I like this variety well enough; but hate the set face that always looks as it would say *Come love me*. A woman, who at Playes makes the Deux yeux to a whole Audience, and at home cannot forbear 'em to her Monkey" (248). Both hero and heroine can, like their comic predecessors, play a tongue-in-cheek part in the social game and at the same time detach themselves from it either as highly entertained onlookers or as sardonic commentators.

Possessing flexibility of response and a keen eye for the false and the ridiculous in human behavior, they delight in their own superior ability to control the world around them and are consummate Hobbesian "gloriers." And dissembling represents one of their methods of having their own way with the world and of remaining wild and free in a society bent on reducing its members to a common mold. Toward the end of the play Lady Townley observes that "Men of Mr. *Dorimants* character, always suffer in the general opinion of the world," and Medley corroborates her view: "You can make no judgment of a witty man from common fame, considering the prevailing faction, Madam—" (283). The same might be said of the social response to the comic spirit in any age. Representing as they do the rebellious, freewheeling play spirit dedicated to the art of living well on their own terms, the Dorimants of the world will always find people to brand them as "Devil" and "ingrate" with a wholly negative implication.

Sinner and devil are, of course, the names invariably given by a conventional or Christian society to indulgers of the natural instincts, especially sexual, and to indulgers of the truth-speaking instincts as well. But a comic hero such as Dorimant will always in effect contend with Oscar Wilde, "What is termed sin is an essential element of progress"; and he will thus rejoice in and pride himself on his own sinfulness. Medley, in his opening greeting to Dorimant, calls him "my Life, my Joy, my darling-Sin" (191), and Tom the Shoemaker accuses both men of belonging among those "men of quality" who "wou'd ingross the sins o'the Nation" (197). And in a later passage Medley remarks concerning Mrs. Loveit's jealousy of Dorimant: "She cou'd not have pick'd out a Devil upon Earth so proper to Torment her" (208). In fact the language of the play repeatedly associates "that wicked *Dorimant*, and all the under debauchees of the Town" (246) with both sin and the devil; and Lady Woodvil recognizes Dorimant as an exceedingly dangerous tempter: "Oh! he has a Tongue, they say, would tempt the Angels to a second fall" (237). In short, not only is the comic hero himself a rebel against divine authority, but he has so charming and persuasive a way about him that he threatens to carry some segments of the angelic group along with him.

Closely associated with the devil imagery, moreover, is the religious terminology frequently used by the "devils" themselves as one means of defining their own nature and their irreverent attitude toward both orthodox religion and marriage as a sacred institution. The play opens, for example, with Dorimant complaining of the difficulty of writing a love letter with all passion spent: "It is a Tax upon good nature which I have here been labouring to pay, and have done it, but with as much regret, as ever Fanatick paid the Royal Aid, or Church Duties." And later, when Bellmour is discussing with Medley and Dorimant the subject of his approaching marriage, we witness the following exchange:

> BELL. You wish me in Heaven, but you believe me on my Journey to Hell.
> MED. You have a good strong Faith, and that may contribute much towards your Salvation. I confess I am but of an untoward constitution, apt to have doubts and scruples, and in Love they are no less distracting than in Religion; were I so near Marriage, I shou'd cry out by Fits as I ride in my Coach, Cuckold, Cuckold, with no less fury than the mad Fanatick does Glory in *Bethlem*.
> BELL. Because Religion makes some run mad, must I live an Atheist?

MED. Is it not great indiscretion for a man of Credit, who may have money enough on his Word, to go and deal with Jews; who for little sums make men enter into Bonds, and give Judgments?

BELL. Preach no more on this Text, I am determin'd, and there is no hope of my Conversion.    (199)

Clearly Medley is quite as capable as Dorimant of doing witty violence to the religious view of marriage, and in his talk about "Faith" and "Salvation," "doubts and scruples," as well as his glib mixing of religious and economic metaphors, he is following Dorimant's lead and emphasizing his devilish inclination to regard nothing as sacred.

And Dorimant's dialogues with Mrs. Loveit suggest a similar pattern. Mrs. Loveit belongs wholeheartedly to the world of sacred convention, and it has been argued by more than one critic that Dorimant treats her with such calculating cruelty that in our sympathy with her we lose all admiration for him. But although such may be Bellinda's reaction, it can hardly have been the audience reaction expected or intended by Etherege, and the play can certainly be acted so as to call forth quite a different response. If Sir Fopling's rule-bound modishness is sterile, her uncontrolled passion for dominance is actively destructive, and her relationship with Dorimant is actually very much like Lady Cockwood's with Courtall. She wants to possess him wholly, to make his vows and oaths eternally binding, to deny him all his liberty. In a world of human relationships characterized by power politics, she wants absolute dominance where only a balance of power is tolerable.

Like Lady Cockwood, moreover, she is masculine in her aggressive pursuit of Dorimant and would reduce him to the submissiveness of fools like Sir Fopling who, as she says with satisfaction, "are ever offering us their service, and always waiting on our will" (268). And like Lady Cockwood too, her thirst for power, when frustrated, leads finally to a wholly destructive rage. In her fury she is even more the heroine of melodrama than is Lady Cockwood: "Death! and Eternal darkness! I shall never sleep again. Raging feavours seize the world, and make mankind as restless all as I am" (274). She expresses her destructiveness actively by tearing her fan into shreds and "flinging" chaotically about the stage, while Dorimant remarks with a coolness designed to madden her still further: "I fear this restlessness of the body, Madam, proceeds from an unquietness of the mind" (214).

Yet in the devilish terms of the play and of a Hobbesian world, Dorimant is quite "reasonable" in expecting his freedom once he has discovered his "decay of passion," and Mrs. Loveit is wholly "unreasonable" in her jealous possessiveness. (Both words appear repeatedly in the dialogue and always with these same implications.) When Emilia reminds him sentimentally of "afflictions in Love," he retorts, "You Women make 'em, who are commonly as unreasonable in that as you are at Play; without the Advantage be on your side, a man can never quietly give over when he's weary!" (228) To be "reasonable" in Etherege's comic world is simply to be realistic about the appetitive and inconstant nature of man and to comport oneself accordingly. Thus when Mrs. Loveit accosts Dorimant with: "Is this the constancy you vow'd?" he replies, "Constancy at my years! 'tis not a Vertue in season, you might as well expect the Fruit the Autumn ripens i'the Spring." Again "fruit" and naturalness are identified, and the passion-versus-reason exchange continues:

Lov. Monstrous Principle!
Dor. Youth has a long Journey to go, Madam; shou'd I have set up my rest at the first Inn I lodg'd at, I shou'd never have arriv'd at the happiness I now enjoy.
Lov. Dissembler, damn'd Dissembler!
Dor. I am so, I confess; good nature and good manners corrupt me. I am honest in my inclinations, and wou'd not, wer't not to avoid offence, make a Lady a little in years believe I think her young, wilfully mistake Art for Nature; and seem as fond of a thing I am weary of, as when I doated on't in earnest.
Lov. False Man!
Dor. True Woman!
Lov. Now you begin to show your self!
Dor. Love gilds us over, and makes us show fine things to one another for a time, but soon the Gold wears off, and then again the native brass appears.
Lov. Think on your Oaths, your Vows and Protestations, perjur'd Man!
Dor. I made 'em when I was in love.
Lov. And therefore ought they not to bind? Oh Impious!

Dor. What we swear at such a time may be a certain proof of a present passion, but to say truth, in Love there is no security to be given for the future.

Lov. Horrid and ingrateful, begone, and never see me more!

(216)

Like all his kindred comic protagonists, Dorimant matter-of-factly accepts men for the fallen creatures they are and is quite ready (maddeningly so, in Mrs. Loveit's view) to regard himself as more fallen than most. Thus he blandly accepts her cries of "False" and "Impious" and opposes to such passion his own reasonable and realistic analysis of the human condition. The analysis constitutes a highly effective method of verbal attack, both against Mrs. Loveit herself and against the whole religious-moral-social framework which stands behind her abstractions concerning "Constancy," "Oaths," "Vows," "Protestations." Beneath their innocently logical exterior, Dorimant's remarks are patent insults—insults compounded by the smugly condescending tone in which he coolly sets forth the truths that explain his outrageous behavior. Each lengthy, deliberate speech is clearly designed to enrage further an already angry woman, and each is a little exercise in logic which arraigns by implication her stupidity. Not only is the subject of the dialogue passion as opposed to reason, but so also is the dialogue itself.

Only a Harriet can finally successfully challenge a Dorimant, because only she can meet him on his own ground of controlled reasonableness. As aware as he of the ridiculous posturings of the human animal, she is as ingenious as he in deceits and contrivances which will allow her to have her own way. When her waiting woman reproaches her with eluding her mother ("the Extravagant'st thing that ever you did in your life"), Harriet rejoins, "Hast thou so little wit to think I spoke what I meant when I over-joy'd her in the Country, with a low Courtsy, and *What you please, Madam, I shall ever be obedient?*" And poor, baffled Busy can only answer, "Nay, I know not, you have so many fetches" (220). Harriet—like Dorimant although more ingenuously—is overwhelmingly in love with life—with "this dear Town" and with "the dear pleasure of dissembling" (222). Taking nothing for granted, she stubbornly refuses to be taken for granted herself—or to fit docilely into any predetermined mold. "I am sorry my face does not please you as it is," she says defiantly to Dorimant, "but I shall not be complaisant and change it" (248).

Her hatred of life in the country, which she can "scarce indure . . . in Landskapes and in Hangings" (222), suggests a hatred of repose equal to Dorimant's own, and she is as exuberant a contriver and prankster as he is. At one point Medley explains to Lady Townley the reason for Mrs. Loveit's rage by remarking: "*Dorimant* has plaid her some new prank" (225); and later Dorimant reveals to Medley his reason for acting the part of Mr. Courtage with the words: "This is *Harriets* contrivance" (244). Always a sworn enemy of "gravity," Harriet has "so many fetches" that even Dorimant has a difficult time keeping pace. When she makes him a mock curtsey, he protests: "That demure curt'sy is not amiss in jest, but do not think in earnest it becomes you," and in the ensuing dialogue it is clear that for her the curtsey is tantamount to flinging a challenge:

> HAR. Affectation is catching, I find; from your grave bow I got it.
> DOR. Where had you all that scorn, and coldness in your look?
> HAR. From nature, Sir, pardon my want of art:
> I have not learnt those softnesses and languishings
> Which now in faces are so much in fashion.
> DOR. You need 'em not, you have a sweetness of your own, if you
> would but calm your frowns and let it settle.
> HAR. My Eyes are wild and wandring like my passions,
> And cannot yet be ty'd to rules of charming.     (248)

It is Harriet's wit which dominates here, and she is in effect giving Dorimant a taste of his own medicine. She too can appeal to "Nature" and to her "wild and Wandring Passions," and her witty technique inevitably recalls that which Dorimant himself has used in "handling" Mrs. Loveit. Like Dorimant's words in the earlier scene, hers here are also sweetly reasonable and constitute at once a defense and an attack. While remaining, with her wryly spoken "Sir" and "pardon," ostensibly within the bounds of good manners, she is actually insulting and defying and making fun of Dorimant. Etherege's most brilliant stroke in the language of the passage, however, has to do with the rhythms he here imparts to Harriet's speeches, for at the very moment when she is impudently apologizing for her "want of art," she is speaking in blank verse and thus at once parodying such "art" and suggesting the special quality of her own artistic control, organic to her own essentially poetic nature.

Here, as always, Harriet is an indefatigible player (both of roles and of the exciting and even dangerous game of life) and one who delightedly welcomes any challenge. When the respectable young Bellair, escorting her in the Mail a few minutes earlier, has re-marked: "Most people prefer *High Park* to this place," she has had an instant response ready: "It has the better reputation I confess: but I abominate the dull diversions there, the formal bows, the Affected smiles, the silly by-Words, and amorous Tweers, in pass-ing; here one meets with a little conversation now and then." And to Bellair's warning: "These conversations have been fatal to some of your Sex, Madam," she has replied, "It may be so; because some who want temper have been undone by gaming, must others who have it wholly deny themselves the pleasure of Play?" Upon which the always reasonable Dorimant has sounded the familiar note of approbation: "Trust me, it were unreasonable, Madam" (234, 235).

In our softer, more optimistic moods we may all prefer, as so many critics have preferred, a Bellair to a Dorimant, an Emilia to a Harriet, but the comic spirit at its best has no patience with our softer moods, and if the cruelty of Dorimant has often proved a stumbling block to critical appreciation, it has been due to a con-tinuing propensity to regard him as a romantic rather than a comic hero. English comic laughter has always contained a strong vein of cruelty, and no honest study of laughter and comedy has been able to avoid some acknowledgment of the strain. James Sully defines it as an "unfeeling rejoicing at mishap," to be found "in the laughter of the savage and of the coarser product of civilisation at certain forms of punishment, particularly the administration of a good thrashing to a wife," but he reluctantly admits that even " 'polite society' seems to have a relish for this form of amusement."[7] The fact is that neither Hobbes, nor Etherege following in his footsteps, was willing to recognize any essential difference between the mem-bers of a polite society and those of a primitive or savage one. Pre-sumably man, in either setting, laughed from a feeling of his own superiority in which he "gloried," and such laughter is, more often than not, something less than kind.

In Dorimant's and Harriet's world, as in Hobbes's, life is a struggle for power. In more universal comic terms, it is a game involving a battle for self-assertion and self-definition from which the comic hero emerges victorious because he possesses superior mental agility and because he never deceives himself. He is always a disruptive force, challenging a complacent world which would repress his vigorous individuality in the name of civilization. Dorimant's philosophy in matters of both friendship and love is a hard-headed one of mutual advantages or pleasure to be reaped. To Medley's observations about his having "grown very intimate" with Bellair, he explains reasonably: "It is our mutual interest to be so; it makes the Women think the better of his Understanding, and judge more favourably of my Reputation; it makes him pass upon some for a man of very good sense, and I upon others for a very civil person" (202). And when Bellinda, at the conclusion of her assignation with Dorimant, sighs, "Were it to do again—" he replies, "We should do it, should we not?" (258)

Like most of his comic ilk, he is a charming cad, reveling in his own powers of conquest, and he delights in a spirited fight like that with Mrs. Loveit and even seeks it out because it offers him additional opportunity to display his own superiority. Thriving on trouble and excitement, he declares with customary self-confidence: "next to the coming to a good understanding with a new Mistress, I love a quarrel with an old one; but the Devils in't, there has been such a calm in my affairs of late, I have not had the pleasure of making a Woman so much as break her Fan, to be sullen, or forswear her self these three days" (195). The full import of such a statement can perhaps best be appreciated by setting it against an observation made by Faure: "Is not repose the death of the world?" he asked. "Had not Rousseau and Napoleon precisely the mission of troubling that repose? In another of the profound and almost impersonal sayings that sometimes fell from his lips, Napoleon observed with a still deeper intuition of his own function in the world: 'I love power. But it is as an artist that I love it. I love it as a musician loves his violin, to draw out of it sounds and chords and harmonies. I love it as an artist.' "[8]

Dorimant too finds "repose the death of the world" and loves power "as an artist," and it is precisely because Mrs. Loveit lacks his artistic control that her counterplot against him is foredoomed. Possessing passion without wit, she can only shout "Hell and Furies!" in response to his taunt, "What, dancing the Galloping Nag without a Fiddle?" (214) Much in the manner of Courtall in his struggle with Lady Cockwood, Dorimant is momentarily defeated and has to endure Medley's jibes at his expense, but in the final scene he again gathers all the reins into his own competent hands, and Medley declares: *"Dorimant!* I pronounce thy reputation clear—and henceforward when I would know any thing of woman, I will consult no other Oracle" (286). In a world of power-hungry, passion-driven people, it takes a clearheaded, self-aware, resilient manipulator like Dorimant to keep his balance. And, as already stated, it takes a woman of Harriet's wit and cunning to counter him effectively.

In her own way she is as proud and egotistical as her opponent, and the game they play is one in which she is on the offensive as often as he is. She is, indeed, as Medley once calls her, the "new Woman" (244). Wholly aware of her own power and possessed of both "wit" and "malice," she enters the playground attracted by its perils and ready to take on the very "Prince of all the Devils" himself. In fact Lady Woodvil's attitude creates for her recalcitrant daughter sufficient provocation to drive her precipitately into his arms. "Lord," exclaims the Orange-woman to Dorimant, "how she talks against the wild young men o'the Town; as for your part, she thinks you an arrant Devil; shou'd she see you, on my Conscience she wou'd look if you had not a Cloven foot" (193). Harriet corroborates the statement by explaining to Young Bellair: "She concludes if he does but speak to a Woman she's undone; is on her knees every day to pray Heav'n defend me from him." But when Bellair asks, "You do not apprehend him so much as she does?" Harriet, who is "wild" and "extravagant" enough in her own right, replies confidently, "I never saw any thing in him that was frightful" (233, 234). And the very fact that Dorimant is a man of "no principles" (226) only serves to increase her interest. Rejecting the safety and security of an arranged marriage, she insists on living dangerously, whatever the chances of being "ruined" and "undone."

Both Dorimant and Harriet constantly refer to the love game in terms of fighting and gambling. "These young Women apprehend loving, as much as the young men do fighting, at first;" says Dorimant, "but once enter'd, like them too, they all turn Bullies straight" (201). Mrs. Loveit has, in effect, "turned bully," but Harriet seeks an excitement and adventure in her relationship with Dorimant which is quite opposed to Mrs. Loveit's desire for absolute dominance; and the rules by which she plays the game can be reduced to two: play your cards close to the chest and never trust your opponent even for a minute.

Neither Sir Fopling's rule-bound unimaginativeness nor Bellair's and Emilia's complacency will do for either Dorimant or Harriet. Life is for them a continual conflict, and as spectators we are invited to watch the struggle with a full knowledge of the prevailing tensions. "I love her, and dare not let her know it," mutters Dorimant in an aside. "I fear sh'as an ascendant o're me and may revenge the wrongs I have done her sex" (249). "I feel . . . a change within," says Harriet aside, "but he shall never know it" (235). Their self-control is as complete as their self-awareness, and every witty exchange between them pulsates with the resulting rhythmic energies. Both are artists at the game of life, with a pride in their own imaginative and attractive powers which determines them to challenge each other as a part of their refusal to submit to dull and repressive conventionality. "You were talking of Play, Madam;" remarks Dorimant, "Pray what may be your stint?" "A little harmless discourse in publick walks," comes Harriet's rejoinder, "or at most an appointment in a Box bare-fac'd at the Play-House; you are for Masks, and private meetings, where Women engage for all they are worth, I hear." And the battle is on:

Dor. I have been us'd to deep Play, but I can make one at small Game, when I like my Gamester well.

Har. And be so unconcern'd you'l ha' no pleasure in't.

Dor. Where there is a considerable sum to be won, the hope of drawing people in, makes every trifle considerable.

Har. The sordidness of mens natures, I know, makes 'em willing to flatter and comply with the Rich, though they are sure never to be the better for 'em.

Dor. 'Tis in their power to do us good, and we despair not but at some time or other they may be willing.

HAR. To men who have far'd in this Town like you, 'twould be a great Mortification to live on hope; could you keep a Lent for a Mistriss?

DOR. In expectation of a happy Easter, and though time be very precious, think forty daies well lost, to gain your favour.

HAR. Mr. *Bellair!* let us walk, 'tis time to leave him, men grow dull when they begin to be particular.

DOR. Y'are mistaken, flattery will not ensue, though I know y'are greedy of the praises of the whole Mail.

HAR. You do me wrong.

DOR. I do not; as I follow'd you, I observ'd how you were pleased when the *Fops* cry'd *She's handsome, very handsome, by God she is,* and whisper'd aloud your name; the thousand several forms you put your face into; then, to make your self more agreeable, how wantonly you play'd with your head, flung back your locks, and look'd smilingly over your shoulder at 'em.

HAR. I do not go begging the mens as you do the Ladies Good liking, with a sly softness in your looks, and a gentle slowness in your bows, as you pass by 'em—as thus, Sir—    [*Acts him.* Is not this like you?    (235, 236)

In such a passage, typical of the witty exchanges between the two protagonists, language becomes in Dorimant's case a substitute for a more open aggressiveness and in Harriet's a substitute for that elusive female maneuver involving the "no" which suggests "yes." Words take on a decidedly dramatic quality, with physical activity on the stage giving way to an activity of mind of such intensity that we feel as if we were watching two skilled fencers with mind instead of hand in control. As Harriet repeatedly alters her tactics by a facile change of metaphors (from gaming to the flattery of the rich and thence to religion), Dorimant adjusts his own with scarcely a pause for breath, and the sexual implications are invariably and forcefully present beneath the polite metaphorical surface, whether the reference be to "deep Play," to the "power" of the wealthy "to do us Good," or to the following upon "Lent" of "a happy Easter." And presumably the use of religious terminology in connection with sex suggests again, as in earlier passages and in earlier plays, a defiant irreverence of attitude toward both Christianity and the religious stance of the *précieux* mode. At this point, however, Dorimant breaks the unspoken rules by shifting from the impersonal third person to the "particular" second, and Harriet is quite justified in walking off the playground—pausing only to throw back with good measure at the piqued Dorimant the insult which he has resentfully flung and to restore the comic perspective with her pantomime. But we have only to observe the way the evenness of the back-and-forth exchange has been interrupted to know that the rhythmic balance of the game has been broken. Short, sharp sallies have abruptly given way to Dorimant's diffuseness.

Whatever their rivalry on their own playground, however, they are partners on the larger social playground, both "contriving" to "make a little mirth" (276) by turning their world into a vastly entertaining spectacle, both mocking at "gravity" and "Rules" by means of parody, and both glorying none too kindly in their triumphant superiority. "Mr. *Dorimant* has been your God Almighty long enough," cries Harriet to Mrs. Loveit, " 'tis time to think of another—" (286). Seizing upon the affectations of their mannered world, both Harriet and Dorimant turn them into a spirited comedy of which they are at once the authors and the principal actors. And they play with language as they play with life, controlling it with a masterful skill and putting it to use for their own purposes of challenge and aggression.

In the end Harriet has won. Or has she? And Dorimant has won. Or has he? In the last analysis both have won out against the larger world. Mrs. Loveit has been outplotted; Lady Woodvil has been brought around. But on their own playground neither has finally either won or lost, and the game goes on. Superficially, of course, a bargain has been struck: Harriet's money in exchange for Dorimant's promise of marriage. Yet all the important questions remain unanswered, and all the dangers are as threatening as ever. "Do all men break their words thus?" asks Bellinda of Dorimant in the final scene. And he replies, "Th' extravagant words they speak in love; 'tis as unreasonable to expect we should perform all we promise then, as do all we threaten when we are angry—" And, never one to succumb to the "unreasonable," he adds, "We must meet agen" (283). And to Mrs. Loveit he has testily remarked in the same scene: "I must give up my interest wholly to my Love; had you been a reasonable woman, I might have secur'd 'em both, and been happy—" (282, 283). The exchanges ironically undercut all the "extravagant words" which Dorimant has been speaking to Harriet, and those words thus take on the nature of a dare, which she at once recognizes and proceeds to counter with a dare of her own. Thus when Dorimant declares his delight in the "prospect of such a Heav'n" and promises to "renounce all the joys I have in friendship and in Wine, sacrifice to you all the interest I have in other Women—" Harriet cuts him short with, "Hold—Though I wish you devout, I would not have you turn Fanatick—Could you neglect these a while and make a journey into the Country?" (278, 279) Again she is making insinuatingly irreverent use of religious metaphors as an indication of her distrust of his "Heav'n" references and is thereby rejecting the possibility of sinking into any stultifying orthodoxy of the *précieux* kind. But in effect she is also asking Dorimant, in terms of her own earlier metaphor, to "keep a Lent for a Mistriss."

If it is the Country which is to constitute the ultimate testing-ground of their relationship, it is also love, and Etherege significantly seems to ask us to equate one with the other. Both represent, paradoxically, at once the source of life and the threat of repression and sterility. Harriet, who cannot "indure the Country . . . in Hangings," rejects with equal vehemence the thought of representing "the whole mystery of making love . . . in a suit of Hangings," which has become the subject of one of her last witty rallies with Dorimant:

> Dor. What have we here, the picture of a celebrated Beauty, giving Audience in publick to a declar'd Lover?
> Har. Play the dying Fop and make the piece compleat, Sir.
> Dor. What think you if the Hint were well improv'd? The whole mystery of making love pleasantly design'd and wrought in a suit of Hangings?
> Har. 'Twere needless to execute fools in Effigie who suffer daily in their own persons.     (277)

The passage suggests that what Harriet finally cannot endure is any pressure to reduce her to a formalized pattern of behavior and thus to turn her into just another docile fool. When Dorimant utters his last declaration to the effect that his "soul has quite given up her liberty," she at once seems to associate his words with the sterility suggested both by "the dying Fop" and by "the hateful noise of Rooks" in Hampshire ("Hampshire" being incidentally the sound Sir Fopling has found so pleasing); and she declares, "This is more dismal than the Country!" In short, she turns off the threat of such a death by turning it into yet another challenge, and the play ends with both protagonists still in tense and rhythmic comic motion.

# [ V ]

# *Wycherley's Early Plays*

BRIDE, n. A woman with a fine prospect of happiness behind her.
CYNIC, n. A blackguard, whose faulty vision sees things as
they are, not as they ought to be. Hence the custom among the
Scythians of plucking out a cynic's eyes to improve his vision.

—AMBROSE BIERCE, *The Devil's Dictionary*

TO TURN FROM ETHEREGE'S COMIC WORLD TO THAT OF WYCHERLEY IS
to sense a thickening of the atmosphere and a change in the quality
of the laughter. In contrast to the prevailingly fresh, early-morning
mood of Etherege's plays, Wycherley creates a nighttime world
whose occupants are more frequently preoccupied with bedrooms
than with drawing rooms—a world in which the comic spirit is
alternately farcical, aggressive, and heavily ironic but seldom really
gay. The scenes and costuming may still be those of a polite, sophisticated drawing-room society, but rarely in his plays do we find the
kind of polished wit and graceful charm which we habitually associate with a comedy of manners. As often as not the heroes and
heroines are physically rather than wittily aggressive, and there is
a great deal more frank sexuality in Wycherley than in either
Etherege or Congreve. Whatever Palmer, with his comedy-of-
manners orientation, may say to the contrary, the stage direction
*"throws her down"* is, as earlier suggested, hardly as harmless as if
it had read *"walks left centre."*[1] An insistent emphasis on man as

either a healthy or an unhealthy animal pervades all of Wycherley's plays.

If, however, these plays are not, strictly speaking, comedies of manners, nor, as Fujimura would have it, "comedies of wit," how are they to be categorized? The vast majority of critics from Dryden to the present would call them satires, but were all these critics to confront one another in an open debate, they would discover at once a fundamental disagreement among themselves as to just what Wycherley is satirizing. Was he, as both Dobrée and Palmer suggest, a Puritan in his heart, and hence revolted by man's bestiality? A recent article by M. Auffret convincingly disputes such a classification: "C'est meconnaître l'analyste patient desinteressé du coeur humain, c'est confondre la passion du satirique avec les importements de la conscience malheureuse. Les Puritains de ce siècle ne se complaisent pas à sonder le coeur de l'homme, car selon le môt de Pascal, il 'est creux et plein d'ordure.' "[2] M. Auffret, whose article focuses on the classical influence on Wycherley, concludes that he ought rather to stand with Juvenal, Montaigne, and Gracian among "les grands moralistes," and in this opinion many recent critics would presumably concur.[3]

Two questions, however, immediately demand an answer at this point. First, if Wycherley is a moralist, of what does his morality consist? And second, what evidences can we find of his preoccupation with vice and virtue, good and evil? Both questions look toward a single answer. In terms of any conventional kind of morality, any conventional view of vice and virtue, Wycherley's plays from first to last constitute a puzzle. Certain kinds of duplicity and hypocrisy may be condemned; but others are condoned. Certain lechers are ridiculed and despised; others, almost glorified. Symons goes so far as to suggest that Wycherley was not certain himself of "the attitude from which he worked,"[4] and there may be some truth in the thought. But Fujimura has directed attention to one of the playwright's poems which at least helps a good deal in solving the dilemma—a poem ponderously entitled, *"Upon the Impertinence of* Knowledge, *the Unreasonableness of* Reason, *and the Brutality of* Humanity; *proving the Animal Life the most Reasonable Life since the Most Natural, and most Innocent."* The poem is almost interminable, but even a brief excerpt will suggest its general theme and tone:

> Why shou'd Man's vain Pretence to Reason be,
> From Beast, his just Distinction? whom still we,
> More Guilty, and less Human for it see;
> Who, for his Knowledge, and Humanity,
> Lives, deals with his own Kind, more Brutally,
> As for his Reason, more Unreasonably;
> Who for it, o'er his Passions, has less Pow'r,
> Is more a Beast, as is his Reason more;
> The more his Reason, wou'd his Senses sway,
> Which, spight of Sense, his Senses must obey;
> Man, then, by Want of Reason, shows his Wit,
> When his Sense to his Senses, does think fit,
> And Nature, against Reason, to submit;
> Which he finds from Experience, it must do,
> Whether his Sense, or Knowledge, wou'd or not;
> Since Reason serves us, but to justifie,
> By Reas'ning more its Fallibility,
> When its own Practice does its Proofs deny;[5]

The confusion as to whether Wycherley is or is not writing satire would seem to stem largely from the failure to understand his fundamental view of human nature, which is explicitly presented here and which is always implicit in his plays. Ideally, Wycherley felt, we all ought to be Margery Pinchwifes in character, since the vices of the world originate almost wholly from the basic human misfortune of possessing the capacity to reason and hence a conscience. It is our reason which teaches us shame and thus makes us deny our own essential natures and hide them behind hypocritical fronts. Hence a recurring theme of his plays has to do with the failure of human beings to accept and acknowledge themselves for the natural, physical creatures they are and to live accordingly. Incredible though it may appear, Wycherley seems actually to have been idealist enough to believe that men ought to be capable of living as if they had never fallen—as if they were still in a state of unashamed nakedness and innocence. His morality is therefore not a conventional or Christian (and certainly not a Puritan)[6] one, preaching sin and guilt and self-control. On the contrary, in his view it is our sense of sin and guilt regarding our own natures which is reprehensible, and it is that which gives rise to our *real* sins of hypocrisy and moral self-righteousness. Thus the objects of his satire or ridicule are most often those people who, in setting themselves up as better than they are, become thereby a good deal worse.

These satirized characters, however, occupy only minor positions in Wycherley's plays—much the same ones occupied by, say, Etherege's Lady Cockwood, Lady Woodvil, and Sir Fopling, or Congreve's Captain Bluffe, Brisk, Tattle, and Lady Wishfort. They are in Wycherley such characters as Dapperwit, Lady Flippant, Alderman Gripe in *Love in a Wood,* Monsieur de Paris and Don Diego in *The Gentleman Dancing-Master,* Mrs. Fidget, Sir Jasper, and Pinchwife in *The Country Wife,* Lord Plausible, Novel, and Olivia in *The Plain Dealer.* All of these characters represent one or another variety of affectation, dishonesty, hypocrisy with regard to their own basic natures and all are held up in varying degrees to ridicule.

If Wycherley's ridicule of such figures smacks more of satire than does that of Etherege and Congreve, it is not because the latter harbor more illusions about human shortcomings than does he, but because they are content to take the comic view and to accept them as objects of laughter and amusement, while Wycherley seems always to have been torn between the tolerant comic view and the angry satiric one. "Satire," says W. H. Auden, "is angry and optimistic—it believes that the evil it attacks can be abolished: Comedy is good-tempered and pessimistic—it believes that, however much we may wish we could, we cannot change human nature, and must make the best of a bad job."[7] It may well be that the attraction for Wycherley of Ben Jonson was largely owing to his own propensity toward a satiric outlook. Certainly his minor characters almost invariably reveal the "humours" influence of Jonson. They are, more often than not, one-dimensional types drawn with a coarse brush and supplied with tag phrases in their speeches for easy pigeonholing, their creator being less interested in their humanness than in some aspect of hypocrisy which each embodies. And as in Jonson even the most lightly drawn does not escape some touch of his scorn. That is to say, Wycherley's approach to them frequently suggests the corrective or satiric in accordance with his own peculiar morality.

And in the same satiric vein each of Wycherley's four comedies also postulates, in the midst of all the human frailty, one ideal character. Whether called Christina, Alithea, or Fidelia (*The Gentleman Dancing-Master* is a special case), she probably has her origins in the Shakespearean and Fletcherean romances and may perhaps be regarded as existing on what E. M. W. Tillyard has called, in his study of Shakespeare's last plays, another "plane of reality." A kind of dream figure, she is in Wycherley's scheme of things never able to escape some kind of involvement with earthy reality, but she still holds out to that world a vague hope—the hope (which Wycherley himself seems always to have retained, except in *The Plain Dealer*) of the possibility of an ideal love in which mutual honesty and trust combine to produce a wholly natural, free relationship between man and woman.

Yet this is by no means to conclude out of hand that Wycherley is therefore to be classified exclusively as a satirist and that, by that token, he cannot be placed in the same company with writers of comedy like Etherege and Congreve, for the fact to be insisted on is that a genuine comic stance is always to be discovered in Wycherley existing side by side with the satirical. In order to establish this point, however, the nature of Wycherley's morality of naturalness and "self-honesty" must be clearly kept in mind so that we do not make the mistake of lumping together in the same category a Ranger and a Dapperwit, a Horner and a Lady Fidget on the assumption that because both are in a conventional sense sinners, both must be objects of Wycherley's attack. Such is simply not the case. Ranger is an embryonic and Horner a full-blown comic hero, in much the same sense as in Etherege, and they share with each other and with the comic protagonists in Wycherley's other plays a realistic comic philosophy—a philosophy which accepts men as the dishonest creatures they are and neither hopes for nor expects anything better. Often exposers but never reformers, they possess what one critic has called a "healthy robustness"[8] and accept themselves with total candor in naturalistic terms. Horner, for example, is by no means a hypocrite in the same sense as is a Lady Fidget. His pretense to innocence is not, in fact, really hypocrisy at all but is simply a convenient disguise of which he makes use in getting behind the hypocritical fronts of people like Lord and Lady Fidget in the interests of his own pleasure.

And because of his successful dominance, the prevailing mood of *The Country Wife* is, in spite of the satiric strain, that of earthy comedy, and it is characterized, as are the comic areas of Wycherley's other plays, by the same kind of defiant high spirits expressed in a typical Wycherley drinking song:

> Reason our foe, let us destroy
>> Which still disturbs us, when we drink;
> Which lets us not our selves enjoy,
>> But puts us to the pains to think;
>> . . . . .
> Soldiers, Slaves, Men of Bus'ness, take
>> Your Glass off, if you'd active be;
> For as the Head is made more weak,
>> Man is more busie, bold, and free.

## Love in a Wood, or St. James's Park

DESPITE THEIR PROMISE OF THINGS TO COME, neither of Wycherley's early plays has ever aroused much critical enthusiasm.[9] Of the two, *Love in a Wood* (1671) is probably the better play, being a more ambitious and experimental undertaking than *The Gentleman Dancing-Master* (1672), but it is, nevertheless, of only minor interest to the present study largely because of its lack of comic focus. Wycherley has not at this early point in his career managed, as he was later able to do, to make Jonsonian humours characters and the more realistic comic figures centered about the Restoration libertine work together in carrying out a single unified theme.

In the figure of Ranger we find, as already suggested, the closest approach to the archetypal English comic hero as civilized by Etherege—one who belongs to the polite society world, who has something of Sir Frederick Frollick's roguish vitality, and who "ranges" freely through all the levels of the play with the characteristic attitude: "Now the Lucys have renounced us, hey for the Christinas!" (86)[10] An incorrigible liar and boaster of his triumphs with women, he seems intended to play, along with Vincent, the role of reigning spirit of St. James's Park after dark: "Hang me," he exclaims, "if I am not pleased extremely with this new-fashioned caterwauling, this mid-night coursing in the park." And Vincent adds: "A man may come after supper with his three bottles in his head, reel himself sober, without reproof from his mother, aunt, or grave relation" (32). Together they sound the promises of nighttime wandering in the park: the invitation to be free and natural and to follow one's own bent.

Yet neither Ranger nor Vincent nor even both of them together can really be said to control finally either their own fates or those of the play, and as the action progresses, they prove to be contradictory characters. Vincent is finally little more than a spectator to that action; and given Wycherley's peculiarly divided outlook, he would seem to represent one side with Ranger representing the other. Their juxtaposition, in fact, vaguely looks forward to the debate which takes place in *The Plain Dealer,* with Vincent anticipating Manly in many respects, as Ranger anticipates Freeman. Vincent is the moralist and stern judge, the truth-speaker, the true friend, who resents and condemns Dapperwit's backbiting and with whom Ranger has to plead for comic tolerance: "Prithee, Vincent, Dapperwit did not hinder drinking to-night, though he spake against it; why, then, should you interrupt his sport?—Now, let him talk or anybody. . . . Why should you on all occasions thwart him, contemn him, and maliciously look grave at his jests only?" (33) Like Manly, Vincent is the idealist, who is impatient with human frailty and who becomes finally, in a manner of speaking, a defender of the faith. His belief in the fidelity of Christina may waver but it does not fail, and he it is who promises to prove to Valentine the error of his lack of faith—"to lead you out of the dark and all your trouble" (111). The difficulty is that Wycherley never comes to grips in this play with the contradictory views (romantic idealism versus comic realism) toward life in general and Christina in particular which are represented by Vincent and Ranger, and as a result we are left in some confusion as to just where we are expected to take our stand.

As for Christina herself, she is, like the later Fidelia, one of those Wycherley heroines presenting an ideal of fidelity, whose presence always strikes a rather incongruous note in the plays and whose existence is always made to seem a little precarious. In the present instance she is, as Lady Flippant twice calls her, the "faithful shepherdess" of the piece, but the significant thing about her experience in the play is that the "wood" into which she at last ventures is not a remote, unrealistic, pastoral Thessaly, but St. James's Park after dark; and it is not a place where, as in Fletcher's play, even the roughest satyrs stand transfixed by her goddess-like purity. On the contrary the midnight park is described as "the time and place for freedom"—a place where men and women are revealed in their common humanity. "Joan's as good as my lady in the dark," says Lady Flippant (36); and later Christina remarks to Ranger: "it seems, you mistook me for another, and the night is your excuse, which blots out all distinctions" (46). To the midnight park a man may, in Ranger's words, "bring his bashful wench, and not have her put out of countenance by the impudent honest women of the town. . . . now no woman's modest or proud" (32).

There is considerable question, therefore, as to whether Rose Zimbardo's ingenious reading of the play as a "pastoral romance" can really be justified except in a highly ironic sense. She herself suggests that the "wood" in this case is "so delightfully absurd that it skirts parody";[11] and indeed does not the very title of the play itself suggest the necessity for an ironic reading, since to speak of "love in a wood" is surely to define the pastoral mode in a rather reductive way. It is no doubt true, of course, that Christina represents to Wycherley some kind of ideal. Not only is she, like Alithea and Fidelia, an example of complete faithfulness, but she stands explicitly above the economic motive; "But the surest sign of your madness is, they say," her maid informs her, "because you are desperately resolved (in case my Lord Clerimont should die of his wounds) to transport yourself and fortune into France to Mr. Valentine, a man that has not a groat to return you in exchange" (44). Thus she is contrasted in two ways with the lower-level "nymphs" and "satyrs." But are we really being asked to measure the middle and lower levels against the ideal? And is there even, in fact, any justification for such a schematized pastoral hierarchy as Mrs. Zimbardo makes out?

The first difficulty occurs when we are asked to believe that each of the two lower levels among the "gradations of love" depicted in the play ("natural love, and lust") is measured against the "standard of perfection" ("supersensuous love") represented by Christina,[12] for we are given no real evidence for calling Christina's love "supersensuous"—and in point of fact "supersensuous love" as an ideal is the last thing we should expect from Wycherley, as we shall have occasion to recognize more clearly in later plays.

A similar objection arises, moreover, from our being required to view the characters of the lower level in terms of "lust" and to regard them as "monstrous distortions of ideal human nature." "Their excesses," argues Mrs. Zimbardo, "are measured in the degree to which their crude diction clashes with the allusions to romance that stud it."[13] The problem here is that it is by no means clear that Wycherley is regarding these characters as "monstrous" in their "lust and avarice" and therefore as objects of a savage satirical attack. The only character of whom this is in any sense true is Alderman Gripe, who gives occasional evidence of genuinely villainous characteristics; but even he, for the most part, is only ridiculous, and like the other lower-level characters he is depicted as an object for laughter not because of his lust and avarice per se but because he conceals these instincts behind a cloak of moral self-righteousness.

The area in which the hierarchy theory breaks down most seriously, however, is in the placing of Ranger and Lydia. Mrs. Zimbardo makes a brave attempt to find a slot for them, and having done so she then proceeds to ignore them altogether in her discussion of the "high," "middle," and "low" levels, giving the "middle" level finally to Lady Flippant and Dapperwit. Yet Ranger and Lydia play a role in the action too major to be denied all thematic importance. We have only to note how frequently their names (and especially Ranger's) appear in Mrs. Zimbardo's own plot summary to wonder at their being so patently overlooked in the pastoral analysis. But after all, the reason is fairly obvious—to wit, that they do not belong to the pastoral scheme at all. The nymph and satyr references so insistently used in connection with Lady Flippant and Sir Simon Addleplot (whom, incidentally, Mrs. Zimbardo does not even mention) are never used at all by Wycherley with reference to Ranger and Lydia. And the minute we ask ourselves why not, we are on the way to a discovery of what kind of schematization he was presumably trying to set up.

What we have in the play are indeed, as Mrs. Zimbardo main-

tains, an ideal level of "shadowy abstractions"[14] and a level of hypocritical and decidedly materialistic beings, the two levels clearly
contrasted with each other in pastoral terms. But *between* these two
levels lies the real world of St. James's Park presided over by
Ranger, Vincent, and Lydia; and it is this world with which each
of the pastoral ones must ultimately be confronted. Ranger is, as his
name implies, a free-ranging spirit capable of being drawn upward
into Christina's sphere or downward into that of either a Lady
Flippant or a Lucy Crossbite and of adjusting his attitude accordingly. Mrs. Zimbardo has provided us with admirable analyses of
the ways in which the diction used by upper- and lower-level characters accurately reflects their position, with Christina speaking an
elevated language which is "impeccably romantic" and Lady Flippant resorting to "a confusion of pastoral allusion with Restoration
slang."[15] What she has not given us is any analysis of Ranger's
speech beyond concluding that it accords with "the level of discourse common to the age."[16] And here again she has done him less
than justice, for he is as flexible in his changes of language as in his
changes of role.

In talking of Christina, for example, he not only expresses a romantic sentiment but adopts romantic diction as well. "Faith I am
sorry she is an heiress," he repines, "lest it should bring the scandal
of interest, and the design of lucre, upon my love" (53). Such a
speech contrasts sharply first with the mock-formal, "civil-Gentle-
man" tone which he uses ironically in addressing Lady Flippant:
"Cursed be the man should do so rude a thing as to persuade you to
anything against your inclination! I would not do it for the world,
Madam" (29), and then with the mock sentimentality of his remarks about Lucy Crossbite, which simultaneously constitute a parody of Dapperwit's so-called wit: "Don't speak so loud, you'll break
poor Lucy's heart. Poor creature, she cannot leave you; and rather
than leave her, you would leave writing of lampoons, or sonnets—
almost" (67). The implication is that he is always the good-natured
comic realist who can respond and adapt to any situation in his own
interest and recognize it for what it is. He is constantly playing one
part or another, and the kind of language he uses frequently
amounts to both a commentary and an exposure. And in his own
character he is always the natural man seeking pleasure and satis-

faction. In the last analysis, moreover, the play concludes that it is his world of the midnight park which is the true one.

Into this world the "faithful shepherdess" is drawn in spite of herself. Thinking to be able to shut herself safely away—"I have made a resolution to see the face of no man, till an unfortunate friend of mine, now out of the kingdom, return" (45, 46)—she finds her good intentions rudely shattered by the "intrusion" of the irrepressible Ranger—that rake who sees every woman as a fresh challenge, who is forever improvising himself into holes and out again, and who always refuses to admit defeat. He may recognize Christina as a "glorious creature" and an "angel," but it does not take him long to become convinced that she is nonetheless seduceable. Laying his irreverent hands on everything in sight, he draws from Christina the angry and rather puzzling outburst: "I confess, my visit was intended to a man—a brave man, till you made him use a woman ill; worthy the love of a princess, till you made him censure mine; good as angels, till you made him unjust:—why, in the name of honour, would you do't?" (115)

Just what are the implications here? Are we to see Ranger as Christina sees him—as a wicked seducer of the noble and the good? Or as Vincent describes him: a man who "spares not the innocents in bibs and aprons"? (54) In some sense the answers to both questions must be affirmative, for Ranger would seem intended to represent throughout the play the same devilish challenger whom we already know so well from Etherege—a kind of personification of the libertine, skeptical spirit of the age which bursts through the closed doors of every ideal and brings it to the test of experience. And there is no immunity for a "faithful shepherdess" in the real world which he inhabits. The harsh fact is, Wycherley seems to be saying, that in a world where impudence can be mistaken for innocence (as in the case of Lucy Crossbite), innocence can also be mistaken for impudence (as even Valentine himself mistakes his "angel" for a "common visitant"), and for all of Vincent's faith, it is only by plunging into the dangers and freedom and dark confusions of the park, where all identities are called into question and all false moral and social and romantic pretensions are stripped away, that Christina can establish the truth of her fidelity and innocence.

In short, are we not asked to recognize that in a world where appearances and realities are more often than not far apart, where the realms of romance and of moral righteousness are seldom related to the truths of man's aggressive and appetitive instincts, such an ideal as Christina represents is unlikely to be accepted at its face value even in the rare instances where it exists and is, in fact, almost inevitably drawn into the very deceits which it deplores? And perhaps, after all, those best equipped to thrive in the real world are men and women like Ranger and Lydia, who acknowledge the truth about their own natures and who regard both the ideal and the pretenders to it with a certain comic detachment. Having nothing to do with pastoral romance as either ideal or pretense, their own world remains the wholly natural one of St. James's Park.

Those guilty of pretense, of course, are those Jonsonian "humours" characters who people the lower levels of the pastoral world —the characters whose romantic or moralistic poses are repeatedly belied by their actions. Lady Flippant indicates what the central thematic concern on this level is to be when she declares in the opening line of the play: "Not a husband to be had for money!" and the contrast with Christina is later made clear. For all of the fools of the play, love and marriage are matters to be dealt with in terms of a coldly calculating expediency and usually the expediency has to do with the real or fancied availability of the pound sterling. Theirs is a world where nymphs and satyrs are interested more in attaining pecuniary satisfaction than sexual and where a knight buys his title from a court-laundress and frees a "captive lady" who turns out to be six months pregnant and in desperate need of a husband.

Lady Flippant once refers to herself explicitly as a "nymph" and twice to hoped-for male pursuers as "satyrs." And both of these references seem to carry with them the comic suggestion that nymphs and satyrs are not what they used to be. Always vainly seeking to be pursued, Lady Flippant first observes:

> For now a-nights the jostling nymph is bolder
> Than modern satyr with his cloak o'er shoulder.     (35)

And in her second nighttime foray into the park, she complains: "I have left the herd on purpose to be chased, and have wandered this

hour here; but the Park affords not so much as a satyr for me . . ."
(106). Her "satyr" in the first instance proves to be Sir Simon
Addleplot, who, according to one stage direction, enters *"muffled
in a cloak"* and according to another *"stands still in a cloak and
vizard; but sometimes goes about, peeping, and examining the*
Women's *clothes—"*. But when Lady Flippant finds occasion to
play the "jostling nymph" in earnest to Sir Simon's "satyr" (the
stage direction describes her as *"jogging him"*), Sir Simon's "sa-
tyric" powers turn out to be so unimpressive (or Lady Flippant's
nymph-like capacities so nonexistent) that, as he complains, "all
that I could do to her would not make her squeak" (83).

Here, Wycherley seems to be telling us, is the kind of pastoral
world which exists "now-a-nights," a world in which either the
lusts are largely make-believe or, as with Alderman Gripe, hide
themselves behind a mask of holiness and self-righteousness—and
in which the prevailing lust is a lust for money. (Hence, it would
seem to be the case even with Alderman Gripe that he wants to pay
as little as possible for Lucy's favors, and when she and her mother
neatly blackmail him for five hundred pounds, his desire for her
becomes primarily a desire to get his money's worth. And he finally
marries her chiefly in order to keep his fortune out of Dapperwit's
eager hands—Dapperwit himself having courted Martha with an
eye to a substantial inheritance.)

It is while we are involved with these lower-level characters that
we feel most strongly how different is Wycherley's world from that
of Etherege and Congreve. Not only are we confronted with such
grossly physical facts as Sir Simon's attentions to Lady Flippant and
Alderman Gripe's attempted rape of Lucy—and with such thoroughly unpleasant characters as the Widow Crossbite, who handles
her daughter like a prime commodity—but the tone and texture of
the language possesses a darkness and heaviness, a coarseness which
is peculiar to Wycherley and which no doubt stems from the satirical side of his temperament. In depicting such characters as Lady
Flippant and Alderman Gripe, he often seems unable to hold on to
the amused detachment characteristic of his own most successful
comic heroes. Convinced of the truth of his statement that man "Is
more a Beast, as is his Reason more," he concludes logically that it is
always the self-styled Puritan, the person of moral righteousness

(an Alderman Gripe, a Mrs. Caution) who has the dirtiest mind
and uses the dirtiest language. But any Wycherley character who is
guilty of denying his own basic nature or that of others will invariably, when he is not mouthing platitudes, speak a language of
smutty suggestiveness and coarse physical reference. Thus, we hear
Lady Flippant talking to Mrs. Joyner as the play opens of having
"owned myself (against my stomach) the relict of a citizen," of
having "exposed" herself in "publick marts," and of refusing to be
"as tractable as the wenches that eat oatmeal" (12, 13). And later
we hear her talking to Ranger of being "debauched to beastly matrimony" and of knowing no man "that will not thrust a woman up
into a corner" (28, 29). Examples could be multiplied almost in-
definitely as could similar ones taken from the dialogues in which
Alderman Gripe is involved, as when he says to Mrs. Joyner: "You
are a nursing mother to the saints . . . through you they fructify
and increase" (15) and when he holds his little tête-à-tête with
Lucy, who has been turned out of the same hypocritical mold:

> GRIPE. 'Tis a private lesson, I must teach you, fair.
> LUCY. I don't see your fiddle, sir; where is your little kit? (72)

The controlling spirit of this lower level of mercenary intrigues—
the character who delights in using the whole pack of knaves and
fools to her own advantage—is the redoubtable Mrs. Joyner, who is
significantly a dealer in love to the end of her own profit. She is
kin to those typical Jonsonian combinations of parasite and Vice
such as Brainworm and Face, who live by their wits and who operate with a full knowledge of the folly of the fools and the knavery
of the knaves and with a feeling of conscious superiority toward
them all. Something of a wit in her own right, and possessed of the
requisite sense of showmanship, she toys unmercifully with first one
self-deceiver and then another, attacking them with wittily veiled
truths and letting the audience in on her duplicity with self-satisfied
asides. And she makes her own laws and in opposition to the "con-
scientious" Alderman has her own ideas of justice: "Like the lawyers," she declares, "while my clients endeavour to cheat one
another, I in justice cheat 'em both" (120). Yet master-plotter
though she is, her powers end where the upper plot-levels begin,

and although she may bring her own little world into focus, fully half of the play sprawls out beyond her reach.

In seeking a genuinely unifying force in the play, then, we ought probably to look to the park itself, the real world where Ranger dominates and where the false pretensions of all the various nymphs and satyrs are torn away. It is in the park that poor silly Sir Simon is divested of his knightly airs and recognized for what he is—no better than Jonas and an ass—and that Alderman Gripe ventures to parade openly with his Lucy, "because in the dark, or as it were in the dark, there is no envy nor scandal" (105). And it is there too that Valentine regains his shaken faith in Christina (and is brought "out of the dark" only after going into it). Each of the characters, having been drawn into the midnight park environment, must then settle for a marriage which is "natural" to him, given his particular characteristics. Thus Valentine ends by winning his Christina, and the free-wheeling, gaily deceiving Ranger meets his match in Lydia. And on the lower level Sir Simon wins Lady Flippant, who is a fortune-hunter as destitute as he; Dapperwit is outwitted and trapped by the pregnant and penniless Martha; and moralistic Alderman Gripe wins his Lucy, whose innocence is as false as his own.

It is clear, moreover, that Christina herself does not emerge untouched and that Valentine has also won a partner to fit him, for her closing words, in the wake of her recent experience, sound a new note of wariness. Thus when Valentine suggests marriage as a means of putting "me out of all my fears," Christina rejoins: "I am afraid then you would give me my revenge, and make me jealous of you; and I had rather suspect your faith than you should mine" (123). It is her turn to entertain "fears," and the question is left open as to whether a freedom-denying jealousy or a freedom-assuring faith will finally prevail in their relationship. And it is Ranger who utters the final ironic word on the subject. Refusing to accept the fact that he is about to enter into what Lydia calls "the bondage of marriage," he exclaims to her: "You talk of matrimony as irreverently as my Lady Flippant: the bondage of matrimony! no—

> The end of marriage now is liberty.
> And two are bound—to set each other free." (123)

The double entendre here is obvious. Two alternatives for retaining freedom within marriage are being simultaneously suggested: one the mutual faith of which Valentine and Christina have been talking, the other a mutual faithlessness rather in the Dorimant vein. A defier of conventional morality to the end, Ranger continues to champion the cause of his own freedom and pleasure.

Yet somehow it must finally be acknowledged that he is not wholly satisfactory as a comic hero. For one thing, there is Vincent to detract from his dominance. And for another, he himself is not clever or artistic enough to control his world. Both he and Lydia possess a certain comic tolerance for the fools who surround them; and both, at one time or another in the play, adopt the role of delighted spectator of the vanities and pretensions of people like Dapperwit and Lady Flippant—leading them on and manipulating them for their own entertainment. But both are content to take their world largely as they find it without imposing their own rules and forms, and both are wanting in a truly assertive individuality. They do not always succeed in playing with life, but rather allow life to play with them; and their exchanges with each other lack the aggressive vitality of genuine wit. Perhaps it is because Wycherley has drawn them with a somewhat uncertain hand that they lack the confident egotism of a Horner—a confidence which must lie behind any truly creative challenge.

It must be ultimately concluded, then, that Ranger is simply not a dynamic enough character to make his park world dominate the play. Hence the action, in the last analysis, falls apart into three different and unreconciled tonalities or atmospheres: one of heroic or pastoral romance; a second of realistic but not wholly satisfactory comedy; and a third of "humours" comedy (which is, in accordance with Jonson's own frequent practice, alternately farcical and satirical). Not until *The Country Wife* was Wycherley to succeed in making all three levels cohere into a single dark and yet vibrant comic world—a world in which the qualities and abilities of a Restoration rake like Ranger and a Jonsonian parasite-type like Mrs. Joyner were to merge into one of the most artistic and unscrupulous heroes ever to have his own way on the English comic stage.

## *The Gentleman Dancing-Master*

IN HIS SECOND PLAY Wycherley has moved a good deal closer to *The Country Wife* than has generally been realized, and to examine the thematic concerns of this play is to anticipate many of those to which he devoted his masterpiece. The weakness of *The Gentleman Dancing-Master* is, however, undeniable and may be largely attributed first to a failure of inventiveness which has led the playwright to prolong single scenes unnecessarily and to fall back on the same farcical proceedings again and again, and second to the fatal inconsistency of the central character. Yet for all its shortcomings the play deserves a certain amount of attention, if only for the help it gives in understanding more clearly the directions in which Wycherley's comic vision will henceforth be leading him.

*The Gentleman Dancing-Master* is a far simpler and more unified work than *Love in a Wood,* focusing as it does on a single character and giving more explicit statement to its central themes. Indeed those themes are largely summarized in a song sung early in the play, which we may perhaps forgive its lack of dramatic justification in view of this thematic usefulness:

> Since we poor slavish women know
> >  Our men we cannot pick and choose,
> To him we like why say we no,
> >  And both our time and lover lose?
> With feigned repulses and delays
> >  A lover's appetite we pall;
> And if too long the gallant stays,
> >  His stomach's gone for good and all.
>
> Or our impatient amorous guest
> >  Unknown to us away may steal,
> And rather than stay for a feast,
> >  Take up with some coarse ready meal.
> When opportunity is kind,
> >  Let prudent women be so too;
> And if the man be to your mind,
> >  Till needs you must, ne'er let him go.

The match soon made is happy still,
  For only love has there to do.
Let no one marry 'gainst her will,
  But stand off when her parents woo,
And only to their suits be coy:
  For she whom jointure can obtain,
To let a fop her bed enjoy,
  Is but a lawful wench for gain.    (171, 172)

The play, in short, is to be concerned primarily with the positive considerations of freedom of choice and "seizing the day" and the negative one of marriage as an economic transaction, and the song is, As Hippolita says, "to my purpose now.—"

Among all the comedies here being studied, *The Gentleman Dancing-Master* is the only one to be wholly dominated by a comic heroine. It is Hippolita who makes the rules and devises the intrigues and the challenges, and it is her "healthy robustness" which brings a dead world to vigorous life. "To confine a woman just in her rambling age!" we hear her exclaiming as the play opens, "take away her liberty at the very time she should use it! O barbarous aunt! O unnatural father! to shut up a poor girl at fourteen, and hinder her budding! All things are ripened by the sun . . ." (131). The play, in fact, comes close to sounding at times like a tract in defense of the emancipated woman. Hippolita bursts upon the stage, full of the sense of new horizons, new possibilities for self-realization and freedom of expression. "Courage then, Hippolita!" she tells herself, "make use of the only opportunity thou canst have to enfranchise thyself. Women formerly (they say) never knew how to make use of their time till it was past; but let it not be said so of a young woman of this age" (158).

Clearly Wycherley has chosen her name with full consciousness of its overtones. She is indeed the contemporary Amazon woman, determined to flex her new-found muscles now that she has become aware of her own strength. And she is Wycherley's challenge to the hypocritical prudery he despised in women—a challenge which becomes unmistakable in the Epilogue spoken by Flirt:

Yet lest the merchants' daughters should to-day
Be scandalised, not at our harmless play,
But our Hippolita, since she's like one

Of us bold flirts of t'other end o'th' town;
Our poet sending to you (though unknown)
His best respects by me, does frankly own
The character to be unnatural;
Hippolita is not like you at all:
You, while your lovers court you, still look grum,
And far from wooing, when they woo, cry mum
And if some of you e'er were stol'n away,
Your portion's fault 'twas only, I dare say.

Yet there is a defensive quality to the tone here which we may do
well to pause and consider, since it helps to explain a good deal
about Wycherley's characterization of both Hippolita and later
heroines. In all his plays he draws back from a wholesale endorsement of feminine boldness (even Margery Pinchwife apologizes
for taking the initiative), and the fact seems to be that, for all his
theoretical advocacy of sexual freedom, he could not quite bring
himself to like the thought of the same freedom for women as for
men. He retained in spite of himself an idealism which often tends
to undercut his thematic emphasis. Hippolita is not, after all, "like
one/Of us bold flirts of t'other end o'th' town," and Wycherley has
taken pains to emphasize the difference in the course of the play.
Gerrard remarks at one point that "modesty in a man is as ill as
the want of it in a woman" (188), and one suspects that, even
though he later contradicts himself on this point ("Modesty between lovers is as impertinent as ceremony between friends; and
modesty is now as unseasonable as on the wedding night"), neither
he nor his creator would have much liked Etherege's Gatty and
Harriet or Congreve's Bellinda and Millamant. Hippolita's ratio-
nalization of her own behavior pointedly suggests that Wycherley
ultimately lacks the courage of her original convictions, and the
speech in which it occurs sounds again the defensive note: "I am
thinking if some little, filching, inquisitive poet should get my
story, and represent it to the stage, what those ladies who are never
precise but at a play would say of me now;—that I were a confident,
coming piece, I warrant, and they would damn the poor poet for
libelling the sex. But sure, though I give myself and fortune away
frankly, without the consent of my friends, my confidence is less
than theirs who stand off only for separate maintenance" (226).

Obviously the "separate maintenance" reference is intended to call to mind women like Flounce and Flirt, and presumably a large part of Wycherley's purpose in introducing the rather peculiar scenes in which these "ladies" appear is to underline the distinction between such "tearing midnight ramblers, or huzza women" and our own "naturally modest" Hippolita. "Wat," cries Monsieur de Paris, "do the women hunt out the men so now?" (146) And Don Diego queries: "are they not men in women's clothes?" (232)

The difficulty into which Wycherley's ambivalence leads him, however, only becomes wholly apparent at the point in the play where he decrees that Hippolita must lose her nerve when the very moment of "opportunity . . . to enfranchise" herself is at hand. It is here that we can begin to understand Mrs. Zimbardo's labeling her a "romance heroine," for that is precisely what she has suddenly turned into.[17] "Could all that so natural innocency be dissembled?" demands Gerrard angrily (210), and Hippolita has really no defense except her own willful "humour" and a feeble "I am not ready." The whole heated exchange is probably intended to dramatize the familiar expostulations of a lover with his "coy mistress" and to point back directly to the "feigned repulses and delays" which may "pall" a "lover's appetite." But Hippolita's role here is not one that the character, as hitherto portrayed, should be playing. She is ignoring all the warnings of the song to which she once assentingly listened ("When opportunity is kind,/Let prudent women be so too,") with the result that, as predicted, she risks losing Gerrard altogether (and incidentally, brings on all the chaotic violence of Act V). In terms of the way we have been asked to view her up to this point, she has indeed now proved merely a dissembler of "natural innocency," and has begun to sound like simply one more coy prude.

Yet Wycherley apparently does not want us to reach any such conclusion. Rather, he asks both himself and his audience to let her have it both ways—to be, in effect, a real Lydia and an ideal Christina at the same time. Whether consciously or not, he must have sensed the inconsistency, for in *The Country Wife* Hippolita again divides into two women: Margery Pinchwife on the one hand and Alithea on the other. But at present poor Gerrard is left to cope with a Margery (although a more worldly-wise one) who has before his very eyes turned into an Alithea, and to make him consent, Wycherley has to convert him, in Act V, into a credulous puppet. "The time last night," Hippolita explains to him smugly, "was not so proper for us as now, for reasons I will give you." But the reasons are not forthcoming either now or later, and if Gerrard can swallow her ensuing statement, surely the audience at least must protest. "But besides that, I confess, that I had a mind to try whether your interest did not sway you more than your love; whether the twelve hundred pounds a-year I told you of had not made a greater impression in your heart than Hippolita . . ." (225). Are we to ignore, then, two disturbing details previously given: the first, that it was Hippolita herself who, early in the play, voluntarily threw out the economic lure, and the second, that Gerrard was, at the moment of "opportunity," quite ready to carry her off, with or without benefit of independent income?

What has happened to the fifth act is, in fact, symptomatic of what has happened to Hippolita herself. The play has abruptly divided itself into two levels. Hippolita has become not a comic but a romantic heroine (with a notable adoption of romantic diction accompanying the change) and has become dissociated almost altogether from the lower world of farcical sword-play, with Gerrard left to straddle the gap as best he can. And in much the manner of *Love in a Wood,* we are left with an upper-level concern over fidelity and jealousy questions and a lower-level concern with love as an expedient economic arrangement (in Flirt's "separate maintenance" arrangement with Monsieur de Paris).

Whatever her final character, however, there can be no doubt that Wycherley originally conceived of Hippolita as an embodiment of his conception of "natural innocency" (since her ignorance is "feigned" but not her "shameless" desire for natural fulfillment). Impatient with the conventional view of appetitive indulgence as sin, Wycherley felt that the trouble with man could be boiled down to the fact that he

> Has, for his Reason, more Guilt, Fear, or Blame;
> Whilst Beasts for Want of it, want Fear, Guilt, Shame;
>
> . . . . .
>
> Since nothing in our Nature can be thought,

Our Shame or Blame, if it be not our Fau't;
Who are, or not, as made by Providence,
Whose Act in us, cannot be our Offence;
Our Want of Reason is our Innocence.

And until relatively late in the play Hippolita is presented consistently in these terms. Thus when Don Diego refers to her as a "poor innocent wretch" and when Gerrard praises her for having "not only the beauty, but the innocency of an angel" (157), we are already in a position to recognize the irony of both evaluations, possessing as they do at once falseness in the conventional sense in which they are made and truth in Wycherley's own special sense. The Hippolita to whom we have already been introduced at this point knows her world a good deal better than they think, and she is using the appearance of conventional innocence in a thoroughly Machiavellian way, much as Horner is later to use it: "the mask of simplicity and innocency is as useful to an intriguing woman as the mask of religion to a statesman, they say" (157). What she would assert is her right to live freely and naturally and not to be repressed and restricted by propriety and conscience or to be sold to the highest bidder. Like Margery Pinchwife, she wants to live the spontaneous life of the healthy young animal that she is before it is too late.

Virtually all the thematic emphasis of the play during the early acts leads us, then, to regard her as the champion of life and freedom and pleasure in opposition to the life-denying forces represented by her "barbarous aunt" and her "unnatural father." Mrs. Caution, for example, is plainly a negative character, and she is, as her name implies, the voice of reason or conscience in the play—the "watchful porter" (225) who raises the outraged cry of conventional morality and invariably thinks the worst. In defying her Hippolita sounds the note of audacious comic challenge which always revels in sinfulness ("to be delighted when we wake with a naughtly dream, is a sin, aunt," she taunts, "and I am so very scrupulous, that I would as soon consent to a naughty man as to a naughty dream.") To her as to her comic predecessors it is the town that represents the green world. "I am for going into the throng of temptations," she declares; "And would take all the innocent liberty of the town:—to tattle to your men under a vizard in the playhouses, and meet 'em at night in masquerade" (140). Her use of the word "innocent" here is instructive, and when Mrs. Caution wails, "O, the fatal liberty of this masquerading age! When I was a young woman—" Hippolita breaks in impatiently with: "By what I've heard, 'tis a pleasant, well-bred, complaisant, free, frolic, good-natured, pretty age: and if you do not like it, leave it to us that do" (141). Her only fear in being carried off is the fear of being carried into the country—and hence away from life. ("What young woman of the town could ever say no to a coach and six, unless it were going into the country?")

Her maid Prue is at once her confidante and a coarser, earthier counterpart. She too is determined to "shift for herself," and she too leads a wicked life in her dreams. Longing "to drink a pint of wine with a friend at the Prince in the Sun" (132), she belongs to the plain, vigorous world of sturdy English realists against which both French foppery (Monsieur de Paris) and Spanish gravity (Don Diego) are measured. It is the same robust, honest world to which Gerrard and Martin belong (men who prefer a cheerful glass to a "damned French song" and who, if they sing, choose a good English "catch").

In the kind of commentary here being made on social pretentiousness and foreign affectations, *The Gentleman Dancing-Master* clearly anticipates a similar theme in *The Country Wife,* and both plays would appear to have influenced Etherege's parallel emphasis in *The Man of Mode* (1676). For Wycherley, as for Etherege, either social or moral pretentions constitute a denial of one's basic human nature, and either can turn life into a sterile, empty shell. According to Hippolita, Monsieur de Paris is "not a man . . . but a monsieur," and it is important to note that the two characters in the play to use the word "beastliness" pejoratively in referring to human behavior are Mrs. Caution and the Monsieur (186, 201). Monsieur is a patent forerunner of both Sparkish and Sir Fopling Flutter, anticipating the latter even in the matter of an oversensitive nose: "your Spanish hose are scurvy hose, ugly hose, lousy hose, and stinking hose . . . for how can they choose but stink, since they are so *furieusement* close to your Spanish tail, da?" (179).

In comparing the Monsieur with Sir Fopling, however, we can at once recognize that fundamental difference between Wycherley and Etherege in the matter of tone which we have already felt in the lower-level characters of *Love in a Wood*. The Monsieur has none of the complexity and rather lovably ridiculous individuality of Sir Fopling, or for that matter of Congreve's Tattle and Witwoud. On the contrary, he is an oversimplified "humours" character. His actions more often than not take the form of broad farce (as in his "dancing lesson" for example), and in retrospect we are likely to remember little more than a pair of pantaloons and a rather unimaginatively conceived French accent, just as in the case of Don Diego we are unlikely to think of anything but a stuffy formality. Both are merely talking abstractions, thematically useful but dramatically lifeless.

And further, there is a grossness about the texture of both the Monsieur's own language and the language aimed at him which recalls Alderman Gripe and Lady Flippant and at once marks him as one of those falsifiers of his own basic nature whom Wycherley always singles out as the objects of his particular dislike. His references to Don Diego's "stinking hose" and "Spanish tail" are cases in point, as is his exclamation to Flounce: "ha, ha, ha!—Hark you, madam! can't you fare well, but you must cry roast meat?/ You spoil your trade by bragging of your gains;/The silent sow (madam) does eat most grains" (150). And in a similar vein, Gerrard and Martin, while commenting on his success in the role of Frenchman, advise him to be "more slovenly," "never be clean," and to "be very pocky too" (146).

In confronting the Monsieur with his origins as a beer merchant's son and in taunting him with having learned his French from a French footman, Gerrard underscores the ridiculousness of his social pretensions. And Monsieur, in his turn, revenges himself on Don Diego by undercutting his boastful talk about "the grave, wise, noble, honourable, illustrious, puissant, and right worshipful family of the Formals!" with the timely reminder that his "great, great, great-grandfather´ . . . was a felt-maker, his son a wine-cooper, your father a vintner, and so you came to be a Canary merchant" (230). In the world of Wycherley's plays men who drink off their glass (Vincent, Ranger, Gerrard, Martin) are always men of vigor ,"busie, bold, and free," men approaching, as closely as possible, to the happy "natural" state; and the Monsieur's foppery in declining at once to drink and to acknowledge his brewery origins suggests both emasculation and dehumanization.

And meanwhile Prue keeps reminding us of both her own and everyone else's basic nature. She bemoans the plight of "the poor watchful chambermaid, who sits knocking her heels in the cold, for want of better exercise, in some melancholy lobby or entry, when she could employ her time every whit as well as her mistress, for all her quality, if she were but put to't" (199). Prue, it is apparent, is a companion of quite a different kind from Mrs. Caution; she represents, along with Hippolita, the natural inclinations of youth and of the present, set against the conscience and repression of age and of the past. And she becomes the commentator on one kind of dancing lesson in the play as Mrs. Caution is the commentator on the opposite kind. While Monsieur de Paris is being taught to walk in the Spanish manner by Don Diego's black ("Must I have my dancing-master too?"), Prue's futile attempts to arouse his interest ("I have pinched him, punched him and tickled him; and yet he would never do the like for me") supply an appropriate comic contrast and evaluation. The stiff, self-conscious formality and ceremony of the lesson are continually undercut by Prue's spontaneous and irrepressible "provokings," and the entire scene is placed in ironic juxtaposition to the central dancing lesson of the play which is, of course, of a totally different nature.

That lesson is, as the eternally suspicious Mrs. Caution recognizes clearly enough, a dance of seduction, and the dialogue becomes a tour de force of double meanings which, were it not carried on at such tedious length, would deserve to stand beside the "china" scene of *The Country Wife* as one of Wycherley's supreme comic achievements. The constant references to loss of time which are thrown back and forth between Gerrard and Don Diego always carry with them the *carpe diem* implications of Hippolita's "song against delays in love," and the sexual suggestiveness ("about with her," "fall back," "He does not doubt his reward, father, for his pains") grows heavier with each successive maneuver.

Mrs. Caution, of course, can only see Hippolita's actions as "debauched harlotry" and can only regard Gerrard as a "lewd villain." Puritanical watchdog that she is, the vulgarity of her outlook is predictable, as when she exclaims to Gerrard: "he is no dancing-

master, but some debauched person who will mump you of your
daughter" (206). "I will not go out, I will not go out," she declares,
"my conscience will not suffer me, for I know by experience what
will follow" (87). And Hippolita, who dances freely enough with
her maid for audience, complains of Mrs. Caution: "I cannot dance
while she looks on for my heart, she makes me ashamed and afraid
together" (187). (As in Wycherley's poem, man "Has, for his
Reason, more Guilt, Fear, or Blame,/While Beasts, for Want of it,
want Fear, Guilt, Shame.") Mrs. Caution summarizes her conception of Hippolita's and Gerrard's guilt by characterizing their lesson as "Adam and Eve's dance, or the beginning of the world"
(190), and the description brilliantly captures what may be called
the "guilt as innocence" paradox which runs through the play. In
Wycherley's terms Hippolita's dance is the "shameless" dance in
the Garden—the dance of creative life. Hers is to be a new world:
"here's my hand now in earnest," Hippolita exclaims, "to lead me
a dance as long as I live" (224); and there is a special appropriateness in the fact that they are to make their way past the "watchful
porter" with the help of a group of armed "fiddlers." "So, so:"
warns Mrs. Caution, "he'll fiddle your daughter out of the house.—
Must you have fiddles, with a fiddle faddle?" (217)

The dance performed by Hippolita and Gerrard is to be one of
their own improvising and neither a stylized French "corant," in
the mode of Monsieur de Paris, nor a formal Spanish "saraband"
as decreed by Don Diego. Hippolita insists, above all, on being
free, and the house in which she is "kept up" is to her as "unnatural" as her father. Gerrard, in fact, voices one of Wycherley's recurring preoccupations when he declares: "Well, old Formality,
if you had not kept up your daughter, I am sure I had never cheated
you of her.

> The wary fool is by his care betrayed,
> As cuckolds by their jealousy are made."    (192)

Sir James Formal (alias Don Diego) is alternately referred to as
a "starched fop" and a "eunuch," and the proprieties which he
imposes on his household reflect his own sterility. The word "keeping" in the play always refers to an unnatural and repressive human
relationship, and at one point there is what appears to be a deliber-

ate juxtaposition of two kinds of "keeping." Thus as Act I closes we hear Monsieur de Paris complaining: "How! keep, *jarni!* de whore Englis have notinge but keepe, keepe in dere mouths now-a-days," to which Flirt rejoins threateningly: "Nay, I will be kept, else—". And as Act II opens we hear Don Diego inquiring, "have you kept my daughter close in my absence, as I directed?" And Mrs. Caution protests, "Nay 'tis a hard task to keep up an English-woman." Hippolita has no more intention of being "kept up" by a jealous husband than by a mercenary, straight-laced father, since either status reduces her to a position which is little better than that of a "kept woman."

In her roguish and ebullient high spirits and in her capacity for turning her world into a lively stage, she is (at least for the first several acts of the play) the most Etheregean of Wycherley's comic heroines. "Well, thou art a mad girl," cries Mrs. Caution (141), and so she is in terms of any conventional morality. Mischievously aware of her own wickedness, she is equally aware of her own superior cleverness and takes a special joy in fooling the fools and telling them truths which they fail to recognize as such (or in-sulting them with flattery). "Well, cousin," she says to Monsieur de Paris, "not to make you proud, you are the greatest fool in En-gland, I am sure" (175). In fact, such is her audacity that Prue at one point warns: "Indeed, little mistress, like the young kitten, you see you played with your prey till you had almost lost it" (168).

Alternately chief actress and mistress of the revels, she knows the difference (of which both the Monsieur and Don Diego have lost sight) between playing the fool and being one, and she delights in staging comic confrontations between the real fools of her world. "We shall have sport anon, betwixt these two contraries," she exclaims (178), and the statement at once aligns her with all her kind in comic artistry. Setting fools at odds and exposing them in all their foolishness, she revels in her own mischievously shaping powers; and she manipulates situations as she manipulates words, artistically playing with their variable meanings and deceiving all those incapable of recognizing a double entendre either in word or action when they are faced with one.

If Gerrard is Hippolita's teacher in the art of seduction, it is she who instructs him in the art of intrigue and deception. Capable of

delivering an impromptu performance or carrying off an anticipated scene with equal facility, she handles every challenge of her
would-be repressors with a counter-challenge of her own, and while
Monsieur smugly laughs at the "recreation" he is having "wit dat
coxcomb Gerrard" (173), she is having her own recreation with
the real coxcomb of the piece, until she has Gerrard exclaiming in
admiration: "So much wit and innocency were never together
before."

He is a good deal less delighted, however, when he finds himself
also apparently being used for her "divertisement." "I am become
her sport!" he declares angrily. "Death! hell! and the devil!" (214)
He begins to sound like the villain of a melodrama, and it is at
this point in the play that problems of consistency begin to arise
and that we begin to realize uncomfortably that we have, after all,
a romantic heroine with whom to deal. It is tempting to explain
Hippolita's delaying tactics as simply another move in the game
of power she is playing and to apply to her maneuver Prue's earlier
warning: "you played with your prey till you had almost lost it."
She has, after all, been careful to keep Gerrard guessing all along
and to call into question any assumptions he may have harbored
of an easy victory over her. And the behavior which Gerrard calls
"cruel" might well be regarded, as she herself suggests, as a test
of his love—and also as her way of making sure that she is not, in
a manner of speaking, about to jump out of the frying pan into
the fire, out of one repressive situation into another—since we have
only to consult *The Country Wife* to know that jealousy, in Wycherley's view, can be the greatest threat of all to freedom. And
psychologically we might explain Hippolita's last-minute with-
drawal as a young girl's sudden loss of nerve at the moment of
decision.

The nagging difficulty is, however, not only that the whole
*carpe diem* emphasis has been violated in her unexpected recal-
citrance but that Hippolita has become altogether too earnestly
self-righteous. And we can only finally conclude that it is Wycherley himself who has lost his nerve. The Hippolita of Act V no
longer has the distance from herself which was part of the secret
of her comic power. She has begun to regard herself with utter
seriousness. And the comic tone of raillery and aggressive wit with

which she has hitherto tossed Gerrard's challenges back at him and with which she has parried his efforts at logical persuasion has abruptly disappeared. We are finally left, therefore, without a comic heroine and with a fifth act in which a great deal of noisy farce does not quite cover over the comic void that lies beneath. The armed "fiddlers" are somehow less gay than grim, and Hippolita's final triumphant statement, although thematically appropriate, has a disquieting ring: "So, so, now I could give you my blessing, father; now you are a good complaisant father, indeed" (241). She has won her freedom, but we can allow it to her only grudgingly. In attempting to merge two planes of reality which simply refuse to merge, Wycherley has come close to betraying his comic vision, and we look in vain, as the curtain is about to fall, for the early, delightfully youthful and spontaneous Hippolita who longed to be "ripened by the sun."

# [ V I ]

## *The Country Wife*

---

ABSTAINER, n. A weak person who yields to the temptation of
denying himself a pleasure. A total abstainer is one who
abstains from everything but abstention, and especially from
inactivity in the affairs of others.
MALEFACTOR, n. The chief factor in the progress of the
human race.
—AMBROSE BIERCE, *The Devil's Dictionary*

IN ONLY ONE PLAY DID WYCHERLEY SUCCEED FULLY IN DRAWING
together into a unified whole all the themes which interested him
as a comic dramatist, and that was *The Country Wife* (1673).
Here characters representing the real and the ideal exist within the
same world without seriously contradicting one another, and
Wycherley's ironies, alternately grim and hilarious, play unsparingly over the whole. And if the play is, as Wycherley's French
biographer and critic Charles Perromat would have it, "une pièce
gaie,"[1] it is surely with the dark gaiety which we tend to associate
with Ben Jonson rather than the comparatively sunny gaiety of
an Etherege.

Indeed nowhere in Wycherley is the debt to Jonson so apparent
as here. The overwhelmingly dominant figure in the action is, of
course, Mr. Horner. It is he who has the first word and the last,
and it is his ribald vitality which establishes the prevailing tone.
More than one critic has called him a Restoration Volpone—a

comparison which, if hardly justifiable, at least points in an instructive direction. Certainly the two worlds are similar, and the parallel between Corvino and Pinchwife, both old husbands with young wives whom they jealously lock up and whom they even forbid to stand too near the window, suggests what may even be a direct borrowing on the part of an inveterate borrower. If, moreover, both Volpone and Horner are in some sense "villains," they are so in a predominantly villainous world which deserves nothing better than to be preyed upon. Each in his own way affects a sickness which is designed to take advantage of the sick society in which he lives.

Yet Horner is not finally a villain of the same kind as Volpone, and a closer Jonsonian ancestor, in terms of spiritual kinship, would be Face of *The Alchemist*. Like Face, he would seem to derive some of his characteristics from the parasite of Roman comedy, living as he does in the houses of other men and, in Horner's case, providing entertainment in exchange for hospitality. "Come, come, man," Sir Jasper bids him, "you must e'en fall to visting our wives, eating at our tables, drinking tea with our virtuous relations after dinner, dealing cards to 'em, reading plays and gazettes to 'em, picking fleas out of their smocks for 'em . . . 'tis fit you know your work before you come into your place. And since you are unprovided of a lady to flatter, and a good house to eat at, pray frequent mine . . ." (280, 281).

Considerably more important than the parasite qualities the two men hold in common, however, are the audacious cleverness and the comic and creative resiliency which they share with each other and with all their comic kind. They have none of the cynical destructiveness which makes of Volpone and Mosca villains in the tradition of an Iago, and it is a serious misreading of the spirit of the play to contend, as does Anne Righter for one, that Horner is "wholly negative" and an "agent of destruction" and to base such a judgment on the fact that he is a man who "flays romantic and social ideals"—a fact which, after all, is invariably true of the comic hero whenever such "ideals" become false or hollow.[2] Both Horner and Face are, it is true, unmitigated self-seekers and both shamelessly enjoy their sense of power over men and women whose human fallibilities they know as they know their own. But both, living in worlds almost wholly given over to avarice and pretension, possess an innate and hard-headed *joie de vivre* and practice their craft in the laughing, lively spirit of comedy with which Volpone and Mosca, both of whom *are* essentially agents of destruction have virtually nothing to do.

To compare Horner with Jonson's Face is not, however, tantamount to saying that he consequently belongs to a satiric and not a comic scheme of things. *The Country Wife* undeniably contains elements of satire, but the satire is limited to Wycherley's own attitude toward certain of his minor characters and has nothing to do with either the attitude of the comic protagonist toward his world or the playwright's attitude toward him. Mrs. Zimbardo, for all her satiric bias, comes close to admitting this when she defines Horner as something she calls a "parasite-satirist" and, in comparing him with Manly, concludes "that while the former is lacerated by the sight of vice, the latter is amused by it. . . . The tone . . . is, therefore, always closer to comedy than that of the malcontent satirist."[3] Unfortunately she then goes on to insist, as her own informing thesis requires, that he is nonetheless a part of the "moral decay," "the perverted morality" of the play and "a grotesque exaggeration of the vice we are to watch for."[4]

She is, of course, hardly alone in making such a judgment, even though her descriptive vocabulary may tend toward the extreme. Essentially she is in agreement with Norman Holland's "right way—wrong way" thesis[5] and with Anne Righter's conclusion that Wycherley intends us to judge Horner by the ideal standard supplied by Alithea and Harcourt. In reply to such overwhelming censure, perhaps we can only repeat Lady Townley's comment regarding Dorimant and conclude that "Men of Mr. [Horner's] character, always suffer in the general opinion of the world." But no doubt a more specific defense is in order in view of so formidable an opposition, and it will therefore be a major concern of the present chapter to show that Horner is (and in part by virtue of his very "wickedness") a wholly positive and creative comic hero, and that much of the imagery of the play places him squarely on the side of health, of freedom, and most controversial of all, of honesty.

It is true enough that Horner, in the conventional moral terms used by blind fools like Pinchwife and Sir Jasper, is a "lewd villain" —"a dissembler, a rogue" (357). He is possessed, as Thomas Moore once put it, of "the very esprit du diable."[6] "Now," he mutters in one of his "villainous" asides, "must I wrong one woman for another's sake,—but that's no new thing with me, for in these cases I am still on the criminal's side against the innocent. . . . It must be so. I must be impudent, and try my luck; impudence uses to be too hard for truth" (354). The fact is that Horner, in the tradition of his comic predecessors, belongs to a different scheme of things from Alithea's (she being the innocent woman whom he must "wrong"). If he is the spokesman for vice in opposition to virtue, it is first because in his world, as distinct from Alithea's, virtue is a mere masquerade and second because he interprets good and evil in terms of his own comic oppositions of life and death, reality and pretension, freedom and repression. According to Alithea's standards of truth and rectitude, he is not a "man of honour" but precisely the "lewd villain" that Pinchwife takes him for. But he has very little to do with Alithea's sphere. Hers is a plane of romantic idealism; his, one of comic realism. So far as his unsentimental plans are concerned, innocence will have to take care of itself—a grim irony, perhaps, but an inescapable one when the life and the freedom of the natural man are the values he knows to be at stake. He is no selfless servant of mankind. He is the champion, without illusions, of every individual's right, including his own, to be what he is, and his kind of comic challenge will always be to a great extent antisocial—the challenge of the "criminal" to a society whose laws, both social and moral, are dictated by a Pinchwife, a Sir Jasper, a Lady Fidget. "By temperament," says Wylie Sypher, "the comedian is often a fifth columnist in social life."[7]

Yet Alithea, whose very name signifies *truth* (presumably in Wycherley's usual senses of both honesty and "fidelity"), remains as always a possibility in Wycherley's vision, and even skeptical libertines like Horner, who see their world with unvarnished clarity, believe in and respect her kind of honesty and innocence. But it cannot be too strongly insisted that she does *not* exist in the play as a standard against which we are to measure the "infamies" of a Horner. There is not much question, it is true, that like

Christina she does represent some sort of ideal standard in the play. But it is an ideal that cannot hope to stand unchallenged above the fray, and if Horner must wrong Alithea, it is for much the same reason that Ranger must wrong Christina. The relationships are quite similar, and in each case there is the implication of reality's breaking in upon the ideal and bringing it to the test of experience.

In order to understand Alithea's particular role with accuracy, however, we must begin by determining Wycherley's central thematic concern in *The Country Wife*. The title of the play offers the opening clue, and by the end of the first act it has become clear that attention is to be focused on various kinds of wives and husbands and on the whole question of repression or tyranny as opposed to freedom in marital relationships. To Wycherley, convinced as he was at least in theory that at bottom women as well as men were by nature healthy animals, the only sin—or sickness—in male-female relationships was finally the denial of freedom in the name of morality or of civilized respectability or in the cause of a jealous possessiveness. Ideally, he felt, as the terms of Alithea's marriage to Harcourt make clear, that a "matrimonial love" based on mutual honesty and trust could lead to a mutual freedom that did not entail sexual promiscuity. But where (as almost everywhere) trust is lacking or where men and women deny their own basic natures and hide them behind false social and moral façades, there will always be the need for an irrepressible Horner to cuckold tyrannical husbands and to challenge dishonesties. Where lying and deception have become the only path to freedom, the world has become ripe for comedy, and it will take a master deceiver like Horner to bring the world back to life.

The entire marital dilemma, as Wycherley sees it, is summarized by the concluding scene of the play:

> ALITH. Come, brother, your wife is yet innocent, you see; but have a care of too strong an imagination, lest, like an over-concerned timorous gamester, by fancying an unlucky cast, it should come. Women and fortune are truest still to those that trust 'em.
>
> LUCY. And any wild thing grows but the more fierce and hungry for being kept up and more dangerous to the keeper.
>
> ALITH. There's doctrine for all husbands, Mr. Harcourt.

Har. I edify, madam, so much, that I am impatient till I am one.
Dor. And I edify so much by example, I will never be one.
Spark. And because I will not disparage my parts, I'll ne'er be one.
Horn. And I, alas! can't be one.
Pinch. But I must be one—against my will to a country wife, with
a country murrain to me!
Mrs. Pinch. And I must be a country wife still too, I find; for I
can't, like a city one, be rid of my musty husband, and do what I
list.    (359)

Margery, for all her innate honesty and innocence, and indeed by
virtue of it, has been trapped into marriage with Pinchwife and
hence has been caught within a world in which she cannot "do
what she lists" and in which, as she quickly learns, she will always
be required for survival to "tell more lies." And her kind of marriage, in which she is "kept up," is set against the ideal marriage
involving trust and freedom.

Alithea, however, has not easily achieved the ideal, and what
the play reveals, before this final scene can be reached, is that where
the question of marriage is concerned, naiveté is a dangerous quality
—that its possessors are always subject to being tricked and trapped,
through ignorance of reality, by the world of hypocrisies and repressions. There is always the danger that innocence will misplace
its trust. And in this connection it becomes apparent that Margery
and Alithea are actually parallel characters in spite of the fact that
one belongs to the world of reality and the other to that of the
potential ideal. Both are natural, honest women who, like Hippolita, ask only to be allowed to "take the innocent liberty of the
town" (266). Alithea's innocence may be of a different kind from
the simple naiveté of a Margery, but it is a form of naiveté nonetheless. In the name of her own abstract ideals of "honour" and
"justice" and of her naive assumptions about love—"Love proceeds
from esteem; he cannot distrust my virtue: besides, he loves me,
or he would not marry me" (272),—she proposes to enter "freely"
into a marriage in which the very freedom she cherishes will be
denied her—a marriage in which she will indeed be "as one gone
into a monastery, that is, dead to the world" (270). Her own
ignorance of the ways of the world will then have trapped her in
very much the same way that Margery has been trapped. In seeking

to live according to an honorable ideal, she is thrown perilously off guard.

In short, Alithea's kind of unyielding idealism can prove in the real world of vain, mercenary, and possessive men a dangerous blindness, and by the end of the play the idealist has been thoroughly educated regarding her own folly. And meanwhile Wycherley has by no means exempted her from his irony. If she does not finally walk into the trap of her own setting, the action of the play makes it quite clear that her escape comes through no plan of her own. It is her earthy, high-spirited, realistic maid Lucy who finally saves her, and it is Lucy, "robust creature" that she is (304), who tells her the real truth. Accusing her mistress of "rigid honour," she declares indignantly: "But what a devil is this honour! 'tis sure a disease in the head, like the megrim or falling-sickness, that always hurries people away to do themselves mischief. Men lose their lives by it; women, what's dearer to 'em, their love, the life of life" (308).

Lucy, who is to *The Country Wife* what Prue is to *The Gentleman Dancing-Master,* belongs to the coarse, common-sense, pleasure-oriented world of which Horner is the guiding spirit, seeing human beings for what they are and challenging misguided complacency in the interest of life. As Harcourt turns to Horner for instruction ("I am in love with Sparkish's mistress, whom he is to marry to-morrow: now how shall I get her?"), Alithea, as well as Margery, depends on Lucy; and the methods which Horner advises bear a close resemblance to those by which Lucy also achieves her ends. According to Horner, "a foolish rival and a jealous husband assist their rival's designs; for they are sure to make their women hate them, which is the first step to their love for another man . . . fools are most easily cheated when they themselves are accessaries" (289). And it is with just this same sure instinct for manipulating fools to her own ends that Lucy devises, move by move, her plan wherein Pinchwife docilely arranges for his own cuckolding and Sparkish eventually reveals himself before Alithea for the unfeeling, mercenary fop that he is. Horner, in fact, has very little to do with his successful seduction of Margery. It is Lucy, considerably better endowed with plain common sense than the over-wise Alithea, who triumphantly stages the single ingenious action which at once frees both "innocents" from their present or theatening prisons.

The association being made in the play between the current plight of Margery and the prospective one of Alithea becomes still clearer upon a closer look at the verbal parallels and the developing ironies. Pinchwife of course is repeatedly characterized as Margery's "guardian" or "keeper" and is forever being portrayed in the process of locking her up; and by the beginning of Act III, Margery has begun to think of herself as "a poor lonely sullen bird in a cage," in contrast to women like Alithea who "took their flight themselves early, and are hopping abroad in the open air" (284). What Pinchwife recognizes from the outset is that to "keep" his wife successfully, he must "keep her in ignorance" of what he calls "town-documents" (267). As Alithea puts it, "Jealousy in a husband . . . begets a thousand plagues to a poor woman, the loss of her honour, her quiet . . . nay, her life sometimes; and what's as bad almost, the loss of this town; that is, she is sent into the country . . ." (309). The statement contains heavy ironic overtones, however, for at the same time that Margery is moving toward a release from the prison of the country and of her husband's jealousy and hence toward at least a temporary life, Alithea is, in her ignorance, moving toward the very kind of imprisonment which she most fears and is about to marry a man whom Lucy likens by implication to "a London jailer."

That Sparkish offers no better prospect for freedom than Pinchwife should, of course, have been obvious to Alithea all along had she not had her eye fixed so exclusively on the ideal as to fail to see the reality, for Sparkish has shown, as clearly as Pinchwife, that he is capable of treating a woman as little more than a piece of property. If Pinchwife thinks of Margery as his "freehold" (275) and of all women as "fit for slaves" (314), Sparkish regards Alithea as something to be shown off to feed his own vanity. "Tell me, I say, Harcourt," he says smugly, "how dost thou like her?" (270) And again, "go with her into a corner, and try if she has wit" (271). And Alithea finally has to protest, "Sir, you dispose of me a little before your time—." Love to both men is ultimately just another business transaction. "I must give Sparkish to-morrow five thousand pounds to lie with my sister," complains Pinchwife early in the play (260), and later: "our sisters and daughters, like usurers' money, are safest when put out" (342). And toward the end of the closing act Sparkish proclaims to Alithea with all the nastiness of injured vanity,"I never had any passion for you till now, for now I hate you. 'Tis true, I might have married your portion, as other men of parts of the town do sometimes: and so, your servant" (345).

Lucy is not far wrong in seeing Alithea's kind of "honour" (which could prescribe for any woman marriage to such a man) as a killing disease—"a disease in the head, like the megrim or falling-sickness"—and her simile futher reinforces the parallel that Wycherley is establishing between the binding effects of jealousy and of an unrealistic code of honor. The play is filled, in fact, with references to sickness and disease, all of which in one way or another suggest the health-destroying results of some particular human folly in connection with love. Thus Horner defines jealousy, at the close of Act I, as "The worst disease that love and wenching breeds," and Pinchwife's curses over and over again suggest the diseased mind which spawns them: "Ten thousand ulcers gnaw away their lips," he cries when Horner and his cronies kiss Margery (302, 303)—and again, "An eternal canker seize it, for a dog!" (314)—with reference to Horner's impudent tongue. Meanwhile Alithea has compared jealousy to "plagues," and later Pinchwife closes Act IV with:

> Hows'e'er the kind wife's belly comes to swell,
> The husband breeds for her, and first is ill.   (335)

At one point, indeed, Wycherley seems plainly to be implying that the playwright who sees human beings realistically will see them as diseased. "Don't you give money to painters to draw you like?" Dorilant asks Sparkish, "and are you afraid of your pictures at length in a playhouse, where all your mistresses may see you?" And Sparkish replies: "A pox! painters don't draw the small-pox or pimples in one's face" (291).

More specifically, the persistent disease imagery usually associates itself with some form of repression of natural instinct. "I have not been well," Margery informs her husband, "since you told me there was a gallant at the play in love with me." And the dialogue continues:

> Pinch. Nay, if you are not well, but are so concerned, because a lewd fellow chanced to lie, and say he liked you, you'll make me sick too.
>
> Mrs. Pinch. Of what sickness?
>
> Pinch. O, of that which is worse than the plague, jealousy.
>
> (285)

Significantly, one of the longest of Margery's speeches in the play is centrally concerned with this same theme and may be taken to constitute a kind of summary statement:

> Well, 'tis e'en so, I have got the London disease they call love; I am sick of my husband, and for my gallant. I have heard this distemper called a fever, but methinks 'tis like an ague; for when I think of my husband, I tremble, and am in a cold sweat, and have inclinations to vomit; but when I think of my gallant, dear Mr. Horner, my hot fit comes, and I am all in a fever indeed; and, as in other fevers, my own chamber is tedious to me, and I would fain be removed to his, and then methinks I should be well. Ah, poor Mr. Horner! Well, I cannot, will not stay here; therefore I'll make an end of my letter to him, which shall be a finer letter than my last, because I have studied it like anything. Oh sick, sick!     (333)

It is one of the overarching ironies of the play that if Horner is to live and love freely in the diseased society to which he belongs, he can only do so by feigning disease himself. He must, in short, get behind the defenses of "the city husbands, and old fumbling keepers" (249). "You told 'em," he asks the doctor, whom he has commissioned to spread the word of his impotence, "it was by an English-French disaster, and an English-French chirurgeon, who has given me at once not only a cure, but an antidote for the future against that damned malady, and that worse distemper, love, and all other women's evils?" (250) What Horner's real role is to be, however, has been made clear in his opening lines: "A quack is as fit for a pimp, as a midwife for a bawd; they are still but in their way, both helpers of nature." In other words, Horner has given the doctor what might be termed a fertility function, and with his aid, Horner himself will play the part for which nature intended him. "Nay, now you shall be the doctor;" says the Quack, "and your process is so new that we do not know but it may succeed. . . . Well, I wish you luck, and many patients, whilst I go to mine" (254). Horner is to be the health-giver, the curer of the disease of stifled sexuality. (In Mr. Horner's chamber, says Margery, "methinks I should be well.")

It is a part of Horner's shrewdness, however, that he recognizes the necessity among women not so innocent as Margery, not only of putting their jealous husbands off their guard, but also of insinuating himself behind the defenses of "honour" and "reputation" which the women themselves have set up. With Margery he has only to "help her over the pale out of the briars" (333), to "help" a nature which still remains wholly natural to express itself. But with women like Lady Fidget, Mrs. Dainty, and Mrs. Squeamish, the challenge, as their names indicate, becomes a good deal more complicated. And it marks the special ingeniousness of his "eunuch" strategy that it at once puts the various jealous or morality-bound "keepers" off their guards and protects the "honourable" façade of the ladies. "But, poor gentleman," exclaims Lady Fidget, "could you be so generous, so truly a man of honour, as for the sakes of us women of honour, to cause yourself to be reported no man?" (282).

This is not to suggest, of course, that their kind of honor is to be compared with Alithea's. They are, in Horner's own words, mere "pretenders to honour, as critics to wit, only by censuring others," and are to be distinguished from ladies (like Alithea presumably) "of as great honour as quality" (278). It is not, after all, the genuineness of Alithea's sense of honor which is called into question but ironically the wisdom of adhering to it too idealistically in a world that is far from ideal. But Lady Fidget's honor means only reputation and consists in a self-righteous moralizing and a social pretentiousness which constitute a denial of the pretender's own nature. In contrast to Alithea, who is the spokesman for "innocent liberty" and for the privilege of following freely and honestly one's own inclinations, Lady Fidget and her friends are scarcely even willing to admit to having natural inclinations, and all behavior is a matter of surfaces. In their world, as Horner points out, "honour, like beauty now, only depends on the opinion of others"

(352). As self-styled "women of quality," they sneer at "common women" (348), and a dialogue like the following is typical:

> LADY FID. Foh! 'tis a nasty world.
>
> MRS. SQUEAM. That men of parts, great acquaintance, and quality, should take up with and spend themselves and fortunes in keeping little playhouse creatures, foh!
>
> LADY FID. Nay, that women of understanding, great acquaintance, and good quality, should fall a-keeping too of little creatures, foh!
>
> MRS. SQUEAM. Why, 'tis the men of quality's fault; they never visit women of honour and reputation as they used to do; and have not so much as common civility for ladies of our rank, but use us with the same indifferency and ill-breeding as if we were all married to 'em.
>
> LADY FID. She says true; 'tis an arrant shame women of quality should be so slighted; methinks birth—birth should go for something; I have known men admired, courted, and followed for their titles only.
>
> MRS SQUEAM. Ay, one would think men of honour should not love, no more than marry, out of their own rank.
>
> MRS. DAIN. Fy, fy, upon 'em! They are come to think cross breeding for themselves best, as well as for their dogs and horses.
>
> LADY FID. They are dogs and horses for't.     (276)

Such women have, in effect, lost their innocence by failing to accept it as such; they make their world "wicked" by seeing it so. And their language, in consequence, reveals the same grossness in the use of physical and animal imagery as that of a Lady Flippant or an Alderman Gripe, a Monsieur de Paris or a Mrs. Caution. "I would as soon look upon a picture of Adam and Eve, without fig-leaves, as any of you, if I could help it;" Mrs. Squeamish declares to Horner and Dorilant; "therefore keep off, and do not make us sick" (278). And when Sir Jasper refers to "the naked truth—" Lady Fidget squeals, "Fy, Sir Jasper! do not use that word naked" (278). For Lady Fidget to speak truly means the same thing as "to speak obscenely," for to her all truth is "obscene." In the words of Wycherley's poem, she is one of those "Who, for his Knowledge, and Humanity/Lives, deals with his own Kind, more Brutally,/As for his Reason more Unreasonably." While pretending to "de-mureness, coyness, and modesty" (350), she, like Mrs. Squeamish and Mrs. Dainty, has become herself "lewd," "filthy," "obscene." By virtue of her "reason," she is one who "O'er his Passions has less Pow'r,/Is more a Beast, as is his Reason more." And what Horner says of Sparkish and his ilk applies equally well to all these "ladies": "A pox on 'em, and all that force nature, and would be still what she forbids 'em! Affection is her greatest monster" (257).

In such a diseased world the final unnaturalness, already hinted at in *The Gentleman Dancing-Master* and in Etherege's plays as well, would seem to be a reversal of sexual roles. It is the ladies who drink down their "two bottles" and sing a rowdy, ribald drinking song. "But do civil persons and women of honour drink, and sing bawdy songs?" asks the doctor incredulously (320). These, ironically, are the women of whom the dull-witted Sir Jasper says to Horner: "Come, come, man; what, avoid the sweet society of womankind? that sweet, soft, gentle, tame, noble creature, woman, made for man's companion—" (279). Sparkish, on the other hand, is an "affected, dull, tea-drinking, arithmetical fop" (278), who "cannot drink" (256). And if Horner is to gain admission to this unnatural society for his own ends, he can only do so by himself adopting an unnatural role—by affecting impotence, by railing at women as they rail at "filthy men" (calling them "fawning spaniels" and "monsters" as they call men "dogs and horses"), and by drinking with the women, a practice which, as Dorilant says, "is as unnatural as scolding with 'em" (288).

Nowhere does it become clearer than in *The Country Wife* that Wycherley was no Puritan and that if he was a moralist at all, the morality that he espoused was one of naturalness and honesty. Here, as elsewhere in his writings, it is not animal appetite that he condemns but the hypocritical man or woman who, by claiming "o'er Brute Beasts, Pow'r, or Sway," becomes "more a Beast than they." In this regard an even worse offender than the Lady Fidgets of the world is a man like Pinchwife, who sees women as "dough-baked, senseless, indocile animals" (334), who calls Alithea a "jillflirt, a gadder, a magpie . . . a mere notorious town-woman" (266), and who rails constantly against the "wicked town-life" and against "lewd libertines" like Horner. The only innocence he believes in or values in a wicked world is Margery's simple ignorance, which he counts on to keep her his exclusive property. To him love is a "little monster" which he proposes to "strangle" (314). And as if to confirm the unnaturalness of the repression he imposes on Margery, he dresses her as a boy before allowing her out into the town. While hysterically accusing virtually everyone he sees of "beastliness," he emerges as little better than a "wild beast" himself— "D'ye mock me, sir? a cuckold is a kind of a wild beast; have a care, sir" (356)—and proves capable of treating his wife with utter brutality: "Write as I bid you," he shouts, "or I will write whore with this penknife in your face. . . . I will stab out those eyes that cause my mischief" (316).

Into a world peopled by moralizing hypocrites like her husband and Lady Fidget, Margery with her simple honesty and innocence enters like a breath of health-giving air, and it is astounding to discover how many critics, even in our own supposedly liberated century, have seen her as simply another object of Wycherley's moral condemnation, as one more example of immorality in an immoral world. The mistake, of course, originates invariably from a failure to perceive the defiant unconventionality of Wycherley's moral stand. There does exist a "right-way—wrong-way" dichotomy in the play, as Norman Holland suggests, but he has drawn the line on the wrong premises (his own and not Wycherley's) and in the wrong place. Both Margery and Horner, in Wycherley's comic framework, belong in a "right-way" category. They are the comic hero and heroine of the piece (although Margery has to depend rather heavily on Lucy in working out her "designs") and each in his own way challenges the morality, the tyranny, and the hypocrisy of the world to which he belongs. Theirs, however, is the "right way" not in a conventional moral context but in a comic one and not because they are good or virtuous but because they are on the side of the instincts and of freedom, life, and health. Both see life as a pleasurable game to be played. As Sypher has pointed out, "comedy is a process of safe-guarding pleasure against the denials of reason, which is wary of pleasure. Man cannot live by reason alone or forever under the rod of moral obligation."[8] Thus when Alithea expresses surprise at Margery's new restlessness, Margery rejoins: "I confess I was quiet enough till my husband told me what pure lives the London ladies live abroad, with their dancing, meetings, and junketings, and dressed every day in their best gowns; and I warrant you, play at nine-pins every day of the week, so they do" (284).

Margery's challenge, however, is, at least at first, largely inadvertent. That is, she challenges not by conscious commentary or direct action but by example. The simplicity and openness of her language supplies an implicit contrast to the high-flown phrases of the pretentious "ladies" of the play, and of her letter Horner remarks: "'tis the first love-letter that ever was without flames, darts, fates, destinies, lying and dissembling in't" (331). Greeting every new town experience with open-hearted delight, she is the complete child of nature, with no nagging "reason" to tell her that she ought not to follow wherever her inclinations may lead her. Wholly free of inhibitions, she is also free of any feeling of guilt or recognition of the necessity for it. But it is the irony of her situation that, before she has even become aware of the full possibilities for "hopping abroad in the open air," she has in spite of herself already been trapped and restricted. As Mrs. Caution is the conscience of Hippolita's world, so is Pinchwife of hers, teaching her both guilt and fear and also the need for deception. To her the words "nauseous" and "loathed" are themselves "filthy" and not the "kisses and embraces" of Horner to which Pinchwife would have her apply them. "Nay, why should I say so?" she demands. "You know I told you he had a sweet breath" (316). Having once learned the words, however, she later gives them their proper application in another letter in which she defines her feelings toward her tyrannical, nasty-minded husband.

It is one of Wycherley's most impressive achievements in the play that he has filled Margery's innocent speeches with heavily ironic double meanings of which the speaker herself is wholly unaware, thus developing on the verbal level as well as on the level of action the theme of innocence mistaken for guilt. And the speeches further present a standard against which to measure exchanges such as those in the famous "china" scene, where the double entendre is wholly conscious on the part of the speakers and where the lascivious references are accepted by gullible fools like Sir Jasper as mere innocent small talk. Margery's remarks are of the type classified by Freud as "naive wit," and what he has to say on the subject is peculiarly applicable here:

> The naive originates when one puts himself completely outside of inhibition, because it does not exist for him; that is, if he seems to overcome it without any effort. What conditions the function of the naive is the fact that we are aware that the person does not possess this inhibition, otherwise we should not call it naive but impudent, and instead of laughing we should be indignant. . . . In view of the understanding about the genesis of inhibitions which we obtained while tracing the development of play into wit, it will not surprise us to learn that the naive is mostly found in children, although it may also be observed in uneducated adults, whom we look on as children as far as their intellectual development is concerned.[9]

Whether Margery is expressing a natural enthusiasm, giving vent to a childish petulance, or asking a well-meaning question, she is forever stumbling into some "guilty" suggestiveness all too readily recognized by those who knows the ways of the world better than she. Of her husband, for example, she complains to Alithea: "He says he won't let me go abroad for fear of catching the pox" (266), to which the adult Alithea replies, "Fy! the small-pox you should say." And a few lines later she inquires of her husband: "do the town-women love the playermen too?" and concerning Horner: "but if he loves me, why should he ruin me? answer me, that. Methinks he should not, I would do him no harm." During her walk in the Exchange she exclaims delightedly to the squirming Pinchwife, "Lord, what a power of brave signs are here! stay—the Bull's-Head, the Rams'-Head, and the Stag's-Head, dear—" (294), and upon returning from her brief sortie with Horner, she reports, "The fine gentleman has given me better things yet" (305).

But Margery's kind of free and ingenuous honesty of language is finally as impossible as her free pursuit of pleasure and her simple assumption that she may set aside her unsatisfactory first husband in favor of a more attractive second; and this she recognizes soon enough. She quickly learns the necessity for deceit in order to be free in a repressive society. In short, her trip from country to city becomes a trip from innocence to experience, a growing up. As in Freud's analysis, her kind of naive self-expression gives way in a civilized, adult, morality-bound society (in Wycherley's terms a fallen world, where guilt and shame are felt) to the kind of self-expression which can find an outlet only by pretending to be something it is not (as, on the level of action, Margery pretends to be Alithea).

Meanwhile, however, Horner is dealing with the social pro-scription upon the open expression of instincts in a way which ingeniously parallels Margery's, for he frees himself from social repressions and achieves his satisfactions by *masquerading* as an innocent—"He's an innocent man now, you know," says Sir Jasper (253); and again: "Sister cuz, I have provided an innocent play-fellow for you there" (282). For him as for Hippolita the mask of innocence gives him the child's privilege of both doing and saying whatever he likes. When, for example, Lady Fidget says indignantly, "How, you saucy fellow! would you wrong my hon-our?" Horner replies with a cutting sarcasm of which she is quite unaware: "If I could" (252). Safe behind his own mask, he pulls off the masks of everyone around him and exposes each for the righteous fool or the vain hypocrite that he is. And like Hippolita too he plays with words as he plays with situations, veiling his meanings behind the mask of their innocent surface appearance in order that he may voice the truths which civilized society forbids his saying openly. And such is his ingenuity that he can often man-age to play two games at once, as in the following dialogue:

> LADY FID. . . . but, indeed, sir, as perfectly, perfectly the same man as before your going into France, sir? as perfectly, perfectly, sir?
> HORN. As perfectly, perfectly, madam. Nay, I scorn you should take my word; I desire to be tried only, madam.
> LADY FID. Well, that's spoken again like a man of honour: all men of honour desire to come to the test. But, indeed, generally you men report such things of yourselves, one does not know how or whom to believe; and it is come to that pass, we dare not take your words no more than your tailor's, without some staid servant of yours be bound with you. But I have so strong a faith in your honour, dear, dear, noble sir, that I'd forfeit mine for yours, at any time, dear sir.
> HORN. No, madam, you should not need to forfeit it for me; I have given you security already to save you harmless, my late reputation being so well known in the world, madam.    (282)

So far as Lady Fidget knows, Horner is playing the same game that she herself is playing—using courtly love terminology, as "china" terminology is later used, with an obvious double reference. But he is actually playing with her in another sense as well, for by acting the gallant lover to her "woman of honour" he turns the whole scene into a comic parody of affectations.

The complex ironies of which Wycherley is master become still more apparent in Horner's dialogues with Sir Jasper. Described by Horner as a "formal fool" (251), Sir Jasper is much the same as Don Diego in *The Gentleman Dancing-Master,* although with an added dimension. While he is smugly planning to "play the wag with" Horner and while he complacently assures Mrs. Squeamish that Horner "is good enough to play at cards, blindman's-buff, or the fool with, sometimes!" (282), he is unwittingly playing just the role which Horner has mapped out for him and is himself the real fool of the piece. Contentedly offering an "innocent diversion" to his wife, he declares to her: "here's a gamester for you," and to Horner: "you shall have your liberty with her . . . Ay, ay, ay, all sorts of freedom thou canst take" (281). Again the irony is double. Most obviously Sir Jasper is blind and misguided, and in his own terms what he takes for an innocent game is a blatantly "guilty" one. But in Wycherley's and Horner's terms he is also giving expression to the real truth by establishing the connection between "freedom" and "liberty" on the one hand and innocence on the other. In an unfallen world sex *is* an "innocent diversion"—a pleasure to be freely and shamelessly indulged.

But to Sir Jasper, himself a "grave man of business," pleasure means simply effeminate frivolity or "unlawful" self-indulgence. Always in a hurry to keep some important appointment, we hear him at the opening of the play exclaiming: "'Tis, let me see, a quarter and half quarter of a minute past eleven. The council will be sat; I must away. Business must be preferred always before love and ceremony with the wise, Mr. Horner." To which Horner adds slyly, "And the impotent, Sir Jasper" (252, 253). As always Horner, while seeming to make a joke at his own expense, is actually supplying an ironic assessment of the values of his world. By implication it is Sir Jasper who is the "impotent," and at one point in his career the poet Wycherley found occasion to provide his own direct commentary on the subject in a poem entitled *"Upon the Idleness of Business. A* SATYR; *To one, who said,* A man show'd his Sense, Spirit, Industry, and Parts, by his Love of Business":

> Your man of Bus'ness, is your idlest Ass,
> Doing most, what he least can bring to pass;
> To satisfie vain Aims, at Wealth, Praise, Pow'r.
> Which but augment, by their Additions, more;
> Whose Bus'ness is, to gain himself more Ease,
> Whilst that his pains, his Labours but increase.
> His Aim at Rest, becomes his Restlessness;
> Since his Desires, with his Success, augment,
> Till his Success does his Desires prevent,
> The more he gains, to have but less Content;
> • • • • •
> So Bus'ness is the Bane of Active Life,
> Which shou'd procure our Ease, maintains our Strife,
> Which, wears out Life, whilst Life it shou'd sustain,
> Till our Death, by our Livelihood, we gain,
> Who Life, in quest of Sustenance, destroy,
> Our Lives so, but against our Lives, employ,
> For Bus'ness lets none, Wealth it brings, enjoy;[10]

Within the play Horner's fellow-libertine Dorilant expresses a similar view when he observes: "we they call spendthrifts, are only wealthy, who lay out his [the usurer's] money upon daily new purchases of pleasure" (257). And Lady Fidget supplies her own footnote on the question by remarking:

> Who for his business from his wife will run,
> Takes the best care to have her business done.    (283)

The fools who regard women as property are equally convinced that time is money (there is repeated emphasis on their being in a hurry), and in the cause of acquisitiveness they eschew life. "I have business at Whitehall, and cannot go to the play with you," says Sir Jasper (278). And again, "go, go to your business, I say, pleasure, whilst I go to my pleasure, business" (283). Pinchwife sounds much like an echo as he later proclaims to Horner in a tone of superior virtue: "I have business, sir, and must mind it; your business is pleasure, therefore you and I must go different ways" (300). And meanwhile the foppish Sparkish hides from Alithea when he sees her at the Exchange, with the explanation: "'Tis time to go to Whitehall, and I must not fail the drawing-room. . . . I know my interest, sir" (292).

Lady Fidget, Mrs. Squeamish, and Mrs. Dainty, it is clear, have also sacrificed pleasure to acquisitiveness in their own way, and Horner finds occasion to explain to them that it was not only their "reputation" that "deterred" him but also the fact they they are "so expensive":

> HORN. That I was afraid of losing my little money, as well as my little time, both which my other pleasures required.
>
> L. FID. Money! foh! you talk like a little fellow now: do such as we expect money?
>
> HORN. I beg your pardon, madam, I must confess, I have heard that great ladies, like great merchants, set but the higher prices upon what they have, because they are not in necessity of taking the first offer.
>
> MRS. DAIN. Such as we make sale of our hearts?
>
> MRS. SQUEAM. We bribed for our love? foh!
>
> HORN. With your pardon, ladies, I know, like great men in offices, you seem to exact flattery and attendance only from your followers; but you have receivers about you, and such fees to pay, a man is afraid to pass your grants. Besides, we must let you win at cards, or we lose your hearts; and if you make an assignation, 'tis at a gold-smith's, jeweller's, or china-house; where for your honour you deposit to him, he must pawn his to the punctual cit, and so paying for what you take up, pays for what he takes up.
>
> MRS. DAIN. Would you not have us assured of our gallants' love?
>
> MRS. SQUEAM. For love is better known by liberality than by jealousy.     (350, 351)

All the characters in the play who are on the side of life and freedom, including Alithea, are also on the side of pleasure and of "seizing the day," and all of them, unlike these ladies, know enough "Gold to despise, for Freedom, Pleasure, Ease./Best Ends of Wealth, and Proofs of Happiness."[11] As the crucial dialogue between Lucy and Alithea in Act IV brings out, loss of liberty means not only loss of honor but loss of pleasure and even of "life" (309), and both Lucy and Horner know that if people are not to be enslaved and controlled by their moral, pretentious, acquisitive world, they must continually pit their cleverness against the enslaving forces and devise ever new means of making them cater to their own ends.

"I am a Machiavel in love," proclaims Horner (321), and like Lucy he is always to be seen in the background of his sphere of action, complimenting himself on the success of his "designs." Thus when the doctor questions him: "Well, sir, how fadges the new design? have you not the luck of all your brother projectors, to deceive only yourself at last?" he replies confidently, "No, good domine doctor, I deceive you, it seems, and others too . . ." (319). And Lucy, witnessing Sparkish in the process of giving himself away to Alithea, comments with satisfaction, "So, 'twill work, I see" (344). Together Horner and Lucy finally triumph by pooling their resources. "I'll fetch you off, and her too," Lucy assures Horner, "if she will but hold her tongue" (357), and when with his help she has been as good as her word, Horner queries, "Well, doctor, is not this a good design, that carries a man on unsuspected, and brings him off safe?" In the last analysis both are liars, paradoxically, in the cause of truth to human nature. Always exposing themselves to the accusation of "impudence," they are themselves exposers and plotters against all of the characters within their overlapping spheres whose vanities and hypocrisies threaten to destroy the "life of life."

Horner's machinations, however, are far less disinterested than Lucy's. Not content with a mere behind-the-scenes role, he self-assertively dominates every scene of which he is a part. Whether playing the gallant lover with Lady Fidget, the charming rake with Margery, or the cynical realist with Harcourt and Dorilant, he flaunts his own superiority and remains the undeceived deceiver. He is, as Perromat puts it, "un fanfaron de vice,"[12] and he delights in thinking of himself as being in league with the devil. "To talk of honour in the mysteries of love," he informs Lady Fidget, "is like talking of Heaven or the Deity in an operation of witchcraft, just when you are employing the devil: it makes the charm impotent" (321). And he is forever exclaiming, "the devil take me."

With his talent for playing first one part and then another, he turns his world into a comic stage on which he is actor and director at once. His taunting and tormenting of Pinchwife ("Harcourt,

Dorilant, let us torment this jealous rogue a little"), his open insulting of Sparkish (always too much of a fool even to know he is being
insulted), and his out-pretending of the pretentious "ladies"—all
are carried on for his own entertainment and that of the audience
of whose presence he is always conscious. Aided by his fellow libertines Harcourt and Dorilant, he exposes Sparkish for just the "fool
upon the stage," (291) that he is, most notably in his perpetual desire to show himself off: "I have to show fine cloths at a play-house,
the first day, and count money before poor rogues" (299). Like Sir
Jasper, Sparkish smugly assumes that all the world is laughing with
him at Horner—"Well, faith, Harry, I must rally thee a little, ha!
ha! ha!" (258)—while in reality, of course, Horner has arranged the
situation the other way around.

But while he is playing unscrupulously with every fool who ventures into his arena, Horner prides himself on being the master
player of them all in the comic scenes of his own creating. Thus
when Harcourt comments on his "appearance at the play yesterday," Horner demands, "Did I not bear it bravely?" And Dorilant
confirms his success: "With a most theatrical impudence, nay, more
than the orange-wenches show there, or a drunken vizard-mask, or
a great-bellied actress" (254, 255). Lady Fidget and her friends can
always count on him to play his deceptive part with dramatic and
imaginative ingenuity and, when surprised, to improvise with
consummate dexterity, as he does with such genius in the "china"
scene. "I thought you had been at the china-house," says Sir Jasper
to his lady upon discovering her with Horner, whereupon Horner
mutters aside, "China-house! that's my cue, I must take it," and in
an instant, a new scene of hilarity has been launched.

For the most part, however, he counts on being able to play his
game as the "innocent playfellow "of a prepared script—discovering, through his "stratagem," any who "love the sport" of love as
much as he (254). He is a "gamester" who knows that in love as in
cards "old rooks, are not to be cheated but by a new unpractised
trick" (250). In Alithea's sphere mutual trust in affairs of love may
be the ideal path to mutual freedom, but Horner moves in a gam-
bler's world where no one trusts anyone else and hence where freedom is to be gained only by the cleverest of tricksters. It is a sphere
in which "women are least masked when they have the velvet

vizard on" and of which Lady Fidget says: "Lord, why should you not think that we women make use of our reputation, as you men of yours, only to deceive the world with less suspicion? Our virtue is like the statesman's religion, the quaker's word, the gamester's oath, and the great man's honour; but to cheat those who trust us" (349, 350).

In this kind of world the dance of life derives its rhythmic tensions, in effect, from the struggle of wild things to be free. As the challenger to repression and the freer of locked up passions, Horner with his irrepressible élan vital becomes the focal point for the new sense of awakened life. It is his lodging which is to provide the setting for the final "frolick," and Sir Jasper informs him that "my lady, and the whole knot of the virtuous gang . . . would come to no man's ball but yours" (343). It is to be, of course, an "innocent" ball. Glasses go round, masks are thrown off, along with inhibitions, and "innocence" is vindicated on all sides. We are witnessing, in fact, a banquet which represents at once the most complete and yet the most ironic enactment of a fertility rite to be found among the major comedies of the Restoration. "Now, sir," cries Horner, the deceiver to the end, "I must pronounce your wife innocent, though I blush whilst I do it; and I am the only man by her now exposed to shame, which I will straight drown in wine, as you shall your suspicion; and the ladies troubles we'll divert with a ballad.—Doctor, where are your maskers?" (359) It is symbolically appropriate that the doctor, the curer of disease, should be called upon by Horner to lead the dance. And if this concluding "dance of cuckolds" is imaginatively staged, Horner will stand at the vital center of the circling dancers—the phallic symbol incarnate—and will draw each of the ladies in turn into the center with him to dance a turn, for he represents, in all his impudence, the life force triumphant.

# [VII]

# The Plain Dealer

ABSENT, adj. Peculiarly exposed to the tooth of detraction;
vilified; hopelessly in the wrong; superseded in the consideration
and affection of another.
IMMORAL, adj. Inexpedient. Whatever in the long run and with
regard to the greatest number of instances men find to be
generally inexpedient comes to be considered wrong,
wicked, immoral.

—AMBROSE BIERCE, *The Devil's Dictionary*

AMONG WYCHERLEY'S COMEDIES *The Plain Dealer* HAS PROBABLY
been the most controversial; and the recurring question has been
whether it is, in fact, a comedy at all. Not only does it contain disquieting elements of romance and melodrama, but the "plain
dealer" himself, who stands unmistakably at the center of the action,
seems to belong more to a tragic or a tragicomic scene and certainly
to a satiric one. It is his persistent misanthropy which gives to the
play most of the murkiness of atmosphere that sets it off sharply
even from the comparative darkness of Wycherley's other plays;
and clearly we must look elsewhere in the play if we are to discover
a comic hero.

But meanwhile what are we to make of Manly and of the complex and seemingly contradictory play in which he occupies the central position? Is *The Plain Dealer* a satire, with Manly as "satiric

spokesman" in the Thersites tradition?[1] Or is Manly "an object of ridicule" or "a dupe"?[2] Norman Holland has supplied us with a useful summary of the diverse and confusing critical reactions that Wycherley's play has inspired over the years and has gone on to set forth an interpretation of his own which is, in spite of the occasionally puzzling handling of Manly, often convincing and certainly provocative. The interpretation, in effect, follows up a suggestion put forward by Thomas Fujimura that the key to the play may well lie in its Horatian motto: "Ridicule commonly decides great matters more forcibly and better than severity."[3] It will be the major purpose of this chapter to pursue the same suggestion in a rather different direction[4]—to argue that, if all of Wycherley's complex preoccupations in the play really center upon this ridicule-severity opposition, the opposition may be still more meaningfully defined in terms of a comedy-satire confrontation, and that if Manly is the "satiric spokesman," then Freeman is the "comic spokesman" with the two men actually playing the role of "adversarius" to each other.[5]

Throughout the play the "merry lieutenant" sets himself in opposition to the "surly captain." It is quite true, as Mrs. Zimbardo argues, that Freeman "plays the role of devil's advocate" and that he "is not on the side of virtue"—that he hopes, in effect, "to reason the satirist to the side of unreason." But in his comic framework, to be on the side of "vice" and "unreason" means, as it has meant to Horner and to Etherege's rake-heroes, to be on the side of life—of freedom and pleasure. And further, it seems obvious that the debate works both ways and that Manly, in his turn, tries to reason his lieutenant to the side of his own particular morality of "truth" as the word is always used by Wycherley in the two senses of fidelity and honesty.

Thus the play is actually *about* both comedy and satire, as well as about realism and idealism. It weighs each mode against the other, not merely as offering a method of viewing the world but as supplying a pattern of life for its particular champion. In short, we are witnessing throughout the play a comedy-satire *debate* in which each spokesman alternately gives a conscious defense of his position and then reveals through his actions the way of life to which such a position leads. Wycherley was writing, after all, at a time in history when skepticism was widespread and hence a time when the debate was a highly popular literary form, as witness Dryden's use of it. And certainly the form must have had a particular attraction for a writer with the kind of inner conflict which we have seen to have existed in Wycherley.

In some sense what he has done within the debate framework is to set Molière's Alceste (in whom, given his latent idealistic tendencies, he must have felt a definite interest) against his own Ranger-Horner type of comic hero in order to examine the merits and characteristics of each position. And to understand what each position entails, we may turn once again to Auden's succinct definition:

> The goal of satire is reform, the goal of comedy acceptance. Satire attempts to show that the behavior of an individual or a group within society violates the laws of ethics or common sense, on the assumption that, once the majority are aware of the facts, they will become morally indignant and either compel the violators to mend theirs ways or render them socially and politically impotent. Comedy, on the other hand, is concerned with the illusions and self-deceptions which all men indulge in as to what they and the world they live in are really like, and cannot, so long as they remain human, help being. . . . Satire is angry and optimistic—it believes that the evil it attacks can be abolished: Comedy is good-tempered and pessimistic —it believes that, however much we may wish we could, we cannot change human nature, and must make the best of a bad job.[6]

It is this difference Wycherley is dramatizing, and he begins, as often noted, by establishing clear parallels and contrasts between Freeman and Manly. As the play opens, both are "just come from sea" (424), and all through the play both are repeatedly associated with the "sea world." If Manly's role as "sea-captain" is to be given significance, so also must be Freeman's role as "sea-lieutenant."[7] Both belong to the natural world, and both approach the shore as outsiders. Their modes of life at sea, however, have apparently been as different as their modes of life ashore. To Manly the sea represents two things: first, a path of escape for one "a-weary of this side of the world here" and with "a mind to go live and bask himself on the sunny side of the globe" (379), and second, a place for giving vent to his quarrelsome, destructive instincts. "I never saw him pleased but in the fight;" remarks one of his sailors, ". . . there's no more dealing with him, than with the land in a storm." To which a second sailor adds: "he's like the Bay of Biscay, rough and angry, let the wind blow where 'twill." It is the angry satirist's intention to abandon the world altogether ("he was resolved never to return again for England"), and thus it must fall to Freeman—to the comic realist—to command the homeward voyage ("our merry lieutenant was to succeed him in his commission for the ship back").

The difference between Freeman's philosophy of life and Manly's has interesting and instructive analogies with a distinction made, in a recent psychological study of childhood, "between behavior that *copes* with the requirements of a problem and behavior that is designed to defend against entry into the problem." Significantly, the study continues: "It is the distinction one might make between playing tennis on the one hand and fighting like fury to stay off the tennis court altogether on the other."[8] In Huizinga's terms and in those of the "play" world, Manly is in effect a "spoil-sport."[9] In those of Northrop Frye he is the "refuser of festivity."[10]

To Manly his own sailors are as alien as are the members of the shore society, and he treats them with the same suspicion and the same physical and verbal violence. " 'Tis a hurry-durry blade," says one of his sailors. "Dost thou remember after we had tugged hard the old leaky long-boat to save his life, when I welcomed him ashore, he gave me a box on the ear, and called me fawning water-dog?" (379) Trusting in his sailors' sincerity as little as in anyone else's, he continually calls them "rascals," "slaves," "Rogue," "dog," and responds to their good-natured jesting by kicking them out the door. It remains for Freeman to state the case for comic tolerance: "Nay let the poor rogues have their forecastle jests: they cannot help 'em in a fight, scarce when a ship's sinking" (381). Like Freeman, the sailors are on the side of life and laughter, both of which Manly rejects by rejecting them. Thus when they roguishly suggest that as sentries at the door they cannot surely be intended to exclude women as well as men, they are rewarded for their good intentions by the usual angry outburst: "Would you be pimping? sea-pimp is the strangest monster she has." Blinded by his own misanthropy, he cannot see that the sailors are simply accepting themselves honestly as natural men with natural desires: " 'twill be hard for us to deny a woman anything, since we are so newly come on shore" (380).

The same sentiment is later echoed by Freeman when, in response to Widow Blackacre's sardonic comment—"so you want women, and would have me your bawd to procure 'em for you"—he replies, "Faith, if you had any good acquaintance, widow, 'twould be civilly done of thee; for I am just come from sea" (424).

It is important to emphasize in this particular context, however, that Manly is himself at no time being satirized by Wycherley and that when the response to him among the other characters in the play is negative, it is because, having been an extreme and unreasonable idealist, he has logically become, when disillusioned, an extreme misanthropist, completely and unreasonably intolerant and hence quite intolerable. In this he is, of course, much like his original in Molière, and the conclusion about the misanthropist in each of the two plays is much the same—to wit that, to cite Norman Holland's statement regarding Manly, "his ideal of sincerity makes him unfit for civilized living."[11] What Holland does not acknowledge, however, is that in presenting the character of Manly to us, Wycherley is asking not for our acknowledgment of his folly (except in a very special sense to be discussed) but for our understanding. We often cannot sympathize with his actions and tirades any more than can his own sailors, but we can be asked to comprehend the reasons for the extremist behavior to which, as idealist and satirist, he is driven. To be an idealist is not, in Wycherley's view, to be a fool. To him, to the extent that he was himself an idealist, the world *ought* to be and *could* be a place where people can live naturally and honestly—where the truths of man's basic nature need not, in Freudian terms, be disguised in order to find acceptance and where love and justice need not be perverted in the interest of economic gain.

Yet there is no doubt that, given the world as it is, the comic pessimist emerges in the play as, paradoxically, the happier man, and over and over again in the course of the play Freeman's laughingly tolerant responses to worldly folly are juxtaposed to Manly's uncompromising severity. His laughter, in which he repeatedly and always unsuccessfully invites Manly to join, can draw him into the very world at which he laughs, since it carries with it an ability to accept both himself and others for what they are—an ability which the lonely satirist cannot share. To him all of life is a comedy which men, in their natural gregariousness, join together to enjoy. "Faith, I am sorry you would let the fop go," he says to Manly, after Lord Plausible has been shoved unceremoniously out the door. "I intended to have had some sport with him." And the dialogue continues:

> MAN. Sport with him! A pox! then, why did you not stay? You should have enjoyed your coxcomb, and had him to yourself for me.
> FREE. No, I should not have cared for him without you neither; for the pleasure which fops afford is like that of drinking, only good when 'tis shared; and a fool, like a bottle, which would make you merry in company, will make you dull alone.    (380)

Always Freeman is the showman, and always Manly is the refuser of festivity, who cannot be persuaded to watch the show, "Nay, pray stay," Freeman is still begging him three acts later, as Widow Black-acre and Major Oldfox are announced: "the scene between us will not be so tedious to you as you think. Besides, you shall see how I rigged my 'squire out, with the remains of my shipwrecked ward-robe; he is under your sea valet-de-chambre's hands, and by this time dressed, and will be worth your seeing. Stay, and I'll fetch my fool." But Manly makes the predictable refusal: "No; you know I cannot easily laugh" (459).

To the satirist, seeing things as he does in terms of absolutes, laughter either is one more form of false flattery or suggests the condoning of a world which simply cannot be condoned, and he prides himself on his lonely, unlaughing isolation. "I'll have no leading-strings;" says Manly defiantly, "I can walk alone; I hate a harness, and will not tug on in a faction, kissing my leader behind, that another slave may do the like to me." And when Lord Plausi-ble exclaims, "What, will you be singular then, like nobody? follow, love, and esteem nobody?" Manly retorts, "Rather than be general, like you" (375). Hence, in his continuing debate with Freeman he refuses the role of parasite as insistently as he rejects laughter— seeing the false flattery of a hoped-for patron in the same light as "laughing at his dull no-jest" (390).

What Freeman keeps pointing out to Manly is the fact that his kind of courageous honesty can only be self-destructive in the civil-ized world. "Why, don't you know, good captain, that telling truth is a quality as prejudicial to a man that would thrive in the world, as square play to a cheat, or true love to a whore? Would you have a man speak truth to his ruin? You are severer than the law, which requires no man to swear against himself" (383). But for all the evidences he can muster to testify that truth-telling only serves to get a man hanged, ruined, cashiered, mauled, and hated, Manly remains intractable and produces his own logical rebuttal, point by point, with the conclusion: "and in lieu of being mortified, am proud that the world and I think not well of one another." "Well," shrugs Freeman in reply, "doctors differ. You are for plain dealing, I find: but against your particular notions, I have the practice of the whole world" (384).

The debate, however, is by no means at an end. In Act III it is Manly who takes the initiative and marshals his evidence for a new offensive. In effect, he stages a show of his own (a "satire" to counter the "comedy") and triumphantly displays before Freeman at Westminster Hall the passing parade of fawning self-seekers who pretend friendship only for their own economic advantage. "You see now," he crows, "what the mighty friendship of the world is; what all ceremony, embraces, and plentiful professions come to! . . . Why the devil, then, should a man be troubled with the flattery of knaves if he be not a fool or cully; or with the fondness of fools, if he be not a knave or cheat." But Freeman this time has his own expected reply ready: "Only for his pleasure: for there is some in laughing at fools, and disappointing knaves." And the seesaw battle goes on:

> MAN. That's a pleasure, I think, would cost you too dear, as well as marrying your widow to disappoint her. But, for my part, I have no pleasure by 'em but in despising 'em, wheresoe'er I meet 'em; and then the pleasure of hoping so to be rid of 'em. But now my comfort is, I am not worth a shilling in the world, which all the world shall know; and then I'm sure I shall have none of 'em come near me.
>
> FREE. A very pretty comfort, which I think you pay too dear for.
>
> (450)

To Wycherley the civilized world is, so to speak, a sick patient, much as in *The Country Wife*—a patient for whom Manly prescribes a satiric treatment and Freeman a comic, laissez-faire one. "To be able to laugh at evil and error," says Wylie Sypher, "means that we have surmounted them. Comedy may be a philosophic, as well as a psychological compensation. Whenever we become aware that this is not the best of possible worlds, we need the help of the comedian to meet the 'insuperable defects of actuality.' We escape with him into a logical order by laughing at the imperfections of the world about us; the comic artist releases us from the limitations in things as they are."[12] Just such a comic artist is Freeman. Remaining within the boundaries of civilization, he draws sustenance and enjoyment from the follies which surround him and by laughter frees himself to create his own thriving world of pleasure. Freeman's comic achievement might be described as transcendence through acceptance, with his comic rebellion taking the form of subtly turning the follies of the world to his own advantage. A clever knave, he can achieve his own freedom, his own right to live naturally and honestly, by outflattering the flatterers, outrailing the railers, and outwitting the self-styled wits.

But an idealist like Manly, who "cannot easily laugh," lacks the objective distance from himself and his world which makes up so large a part of the requirement for laughing acceptance. Unable to surmount the "evil and error"—and more specifically the dishonesty and avarice—which make the world as it is such a far cry from the world as it ought to be, he lashes out in impotent fury at the men and women around him who fail to live up to the standards of honesty and courage which he himself has set. "Satire," says J. Y. T. Greig in a highly pertinent passage, "is a weapon of offence, used originally for private quarrels. It is a weapon forged by hate." And he continues:

> Hate . . . is ultimately a derivative of love; it grows out of the frustration of love. But it may, on occasion, so possess a man as virtually to obliterate all signs of its connection with love. It is then as nearly whole-hearted as human behavior can ever be. More usually, hate is restrained and modified, on the one hand by fear, and on the other by the reinforcement of its inherent love strain. The hater is then not so cocksure of his intentions; his whole behaviour is or tends to be ambiguous. At some stage in the progressive modification of hate the ambiguity or ambivalence becomes manifest, for the hater begins to laugh at his opponent, instead of setting upon him with unmitigated vigour.[13]

Within the boundaries of society there can be no escape for a man with Manly's passionately held convictions. He can only find his "ease" or "pleasure" among the mass of self-interested, mercenary hypocrites by "despising 'em" and by throwing into their faces his bitter "aversion." With his example before us it is easy enough to see why the satirist was so long thought to derive from the pastoral satyr and why Meredith spoke of *The Plain Dealer* as Molière travestied, with the hoof to his foot, and hair on the pointed tip of his ear."[14] Manly has, in effect, a personal quarrel with the world, and because he is a man of courage, unrestrained by fear, he directs his vituperative satiric attack—his "weapon forged by hate"—with destructive violence. "He rails at all mankind," says Olivia (472). And when his sword of truth can make not even a dent in the smug complacency which he despises, his fury only becomes the greater.

In his revulsion against "decorums, supercilious forms, and slavish ceremonies" (375), he deliberately sets himself outside the world of "pure good manners." He is an "unmannerly sea-fellow" and an "arrant sea-ruffian" and prides himself, satyr-like, on the "rough part" which is to be his in the play. According to Novel, "he never pulls off his hat," and Plausible adds: "he hates good company" (411). "Gads-precious, you hectoring person you, are you wild?" the Alderman asks him (449), and even Freeman suggests to him "that the world thinks you a mad man, a brutal . . ." (383, 384). "Nay, faith," he exclaims later, "you are too curst to be let loose in the world: you should be tied up again in your sea-kennel, called a ship" (443). In such a world the only satisfactory outlet he can find for his aggressive need to strike out is the taking command of a warship, and when such an occasion presents itself, his unleashed fury, so long pent up, seems apt to result in self-destruction. Thus when one of his sailors comments on his being "a-weary of this side of the world here," the other replies, "Ay, or else he would not have bid so fair for a passage into t'other" (379). The only permanent escape, finally, short of destroying himself altogether, is to cut himself off from the shore world physically, as he has already done symbolically—"to go where honest, downright barbarity is professed, where men devour one another like generous hungry lions and tigers, not like crocodiles; where they think the devil white, of our complexion" (394). For him, given as he is to demanding absolutes, there can only be angels on the one hand and devils on the other. "How's this?" he exclaims of Olivia, "Why, she makes love like a devil in a play; and in this darkness, which conceals her angel's face, if I were apt to be afraid, I should think her a devil." The satirist, in short, belongs in some sense to a morality-play scheme of things in which romanticized angels and melodramatic devils fight for a man's soul.[15]

It is a part of Manly's complex psychology, however, that his behavior is not without the ambivalence of which Greig speaks. Even though, when the play opens, his hatred has already become so intense as "virtually to obliterate all signs of its connection with love," he is clearly not quite the wholehearted misanthrope that most of his actions suggest. That his hate is "ultimately a derivative of love" and of an innate idealism is first indicated when he objects to Lord Plausible "that speaking well of all mankind is the worst kind of detraction; for it takes away the reputation of the few good men in the world, by making all alike" (376). And the suggestion is reinforced in Act III when we discover that he has given his last twenty pounds to his boat's crew: "Would you have the poor, honest, brave fellows want?" (450).

But the clearest revelation of his psychology is to be discovered in his altered attitude toward Olivia. His experience with her actually amounts to a reenactment, within the limited confines of the play, of precisely the process by which he has arrived at his outspoken misanthropy. Thinking her a "miracle of a woman" and then having his faith irrevocably shattered, he concentrates on her all the brutal aggressiveness engendered by his extreme disenchantment. And in proportion as his idealistic belief in her has been the more concentrated and intense when so much of the world has already failed him, his reaction is an overreaction in the opposite direction—an intensified brutality, which his own ambivalence makes still more intense. "Her love!—a whore's, a witch's love!—But what, did she not kiss well, sir?—I'm sure I thought her lips—but I must not think of 'em more—but yet they are such I could still kiss—grow to—and then tear off with my teeth, grind 'em into mammocks, and spit 'em into her cuckold's face" (455).

Yet even while caught up in his own ambivalence, he has moments of clarity. "True perfect woman!" he declares with embittered sarcasm. "If I could say anything more injurious to her now, I would; for I could outrail a bilked whore, or a kicked coward; but now I think on't, that were rather to discover my love than hatred" (418). With her, as with the world at large, he is incapable of pretending indifference. He cares too much to pretend not to care. And as in Greig's analysis, the hater's "ambivalence becomes manifest" when he "begins to laugh at his opponent." "Thou wouldst laugh," he tells Vernish, "if thou knewest but all the circumstances of my having her. Come, I'll tell thee" (489). And again, "anon, at supper, we'll laugh at leisure together at Olivia's cuckold" (494).

What Wycherley brilliantly reveals in his characterization of Manly at this point is the terrible irony of the satirist's ambivalent reactions. Having thought that he could wholeheartedly reject the world with which he has become disillusioned and finding himself hopelessly entangled by his own natural desires, he cannot bear the thought of Freeman's scorn, and hence, in order to hide what he can only regard as his shame, he succumbs to the very hypocrisy and cowardice which he has most despised. And thereafter, tormented almost to madness by his own self-contempt and by the intense inner conflict between his desire for Olivia and his hatred of everything she stands for, he is plunged into an irrational darkness, where love and revenge motives are impossibly confused and where he cannot even hear Fidelia's still small voice of reason. Indeed, by being driven to make truth (in the person of Fidelia) pimp for him, he not only defiles his own ideals but exposes Fidelia to the dangers of murder and rape, and he thus comes close to destroying the very honest love which has constituted his dream of perfection.

Yet it must again be insisted that, revolting as we may find Manly's actions and language in these scenes, we are not finally asked to condemn his double dealing or even his brutality but to recognize and understand them as the behavior of a tormented man—and as behavior, the responsibility for which must be laid to the charge of a corrupt, fallen world. Manly's is the heavily ironic fate of the passionate idealist in a far-from-ideal society—a society in which he has sought to preserve, all alone, his standards of absolute honesty and justice: "I that can do a rude thing, rather than an unjust thing" (376). As he sees it, the perverters of love and friendship,

like the perverters of justice, cannot be laughed at but must be
despised and cast off, and it is his inability to cast off Olivia that
leads him—always a violent extremist in his reactions—to an almost
unbearable self-hatred and to brutalized behavior.

Nor does the irony end here, for having become convinced that
friendship, love, and justice in the shore world are all determined
by mercenary self-interest, he even rejects Fidelia, accusing her of
"flattering and lying" (385), and declaring: "thou art a hopeful
youth for the shore only. Here thou wilt live to be cherished by fortune and the great ones, for thou mayst easily come to outflatter a
dull poet, outlie a coffee-house or gazette-writer, outswear a knight
of the post . . . therefore thou'lt do better with the world than with
me, and these are the good courses you must take in the world."
And when Fidelia deplores her friendlessness, he exclaims sardonically: "Friendless; there are half a score friends for thee then.—
[Offers her gold]" (386, 387). His own ironic gesture is, of course,
ironically undercut by the fact that he makes it toward almost the
only person in his sphere who does not deserve it. But again the
fault of failing to recognize truth when he sees it is to be attributed
much less to him than to a world into which, after all, "truth" has
only dared to enter in disguise and which has heretofore given him
ample cause for his distrust. If friendship, love, and justice are only
to be given or received to ends of economic self-aggrandizement,
then he will adjust his actions and his language accordingly, giving
Fidelia coins when she asks for friends and referring to love and justice in deliberately gross terms, as he speaks in the last act of a
"refunding lawyer" and a "refunding wench" (suggesting that
either will be far to seek even in a clear case of the services paid for
not having been rendered).

It is because he sees love, friendship, and justice everywhere perverted in the interest of pecuniary gain that he takes comfort from
the thought of his own poverty. ("I am not worth a shilling in the
world, which all the world shall know; and then I'm sure I shall
have none of 'em come near me.") Yet for all his cynicism he still
retains a lingering idealistic hope that the rewards of the world
have not been so irrevocably misdirected that honesty and honor
are no longer given their due, and when, in reply to his expressing
the possibility of being given another ship, Freeman protests, "Give

you a ship! why, you will not solicit it," Manly asserts, "If I have not solicited it by my services, I know no other way" (487).

Again the dialogue between the two men continues the debate between two ways of regarding the world, with Freeman as always speaking as the hard-headed realist. "I have heard of a thing called grinning honour," he tells Manly, "but never of starving honour . . . nay, then I'm satisfied, I must solicit my widow the closer, and run the desperate fortune of matrimony on shore." Unhampered by Manly's kind of idealistic concern for honesty and justice, he proposes to beat the Widow Blackacre at her own legal game—in short to *use* the apparatus of justice in order to do justice to himself:

> If you litigious widow e'er would gain,
> Sigh not to her, but by the law complain;
> To her, as to a bawd, defendant sue
> With statutes, and make justice pimp for you.     (426)

Freeman, of course, has many fewer illusions about himself and his world than does his idealistic friend. Exclusively concerned with freedom and survival, he is, in the fashion of the typical amoral rake-hero, an unprincipled and cunning plotter, egotistically confident of his own ability to control and enjoy life on his own terms. Money to him is not something to be scorned (his reference to the widow as a "bawd" suggests its creative potential), and to Manly's question, "Would you have the poor, honest, brave fellows want?" he gives the realist's answer: "Rather than you or I" (450). He knows as well as Manly that in the shore world love, friendship, and justice are no longer ends in themselves but have been turned into means of attaining money: "money summons lovers more than beauty," he says on one occasion (393). But he is no reformer, and if such is the way of the world, he will make the most of it. Lawyers, remarks Jerry Blackacre with an obvious reference to Freeman, are like "the unconscionable wooers of widows, who undertake briskly their matrimonial business for their money; but when they have got it once, let who will drudge for them" (435). The statement at once defines the world's standards and Freeman's willingness to make use of them for his own purposes.

Thus he makes love to the widow only with an eye to gaining control of her purse strings; and in effect he *buys* Jerry's friendship and thereafter uses his legal knowledge to further his design. "But come, bully guardian," says Jerry, "we'll go and advise with three attorneys, two proctors, two solicitors, and a shrewd man of White-friars, neither attorney, proctor, nor solicitor, but as pure a pimp to the law as any of 'em: and sure all they will be hard enough for her, for I fear bully-guardian, you are too good a joker to have any law in your head" (464). The difference between Freeman's perversions of love and frienship and justice and those of the shore world in general is that his are fully conscious and are pursued to creative ends. In a society where money is freedom and power, Freeman will be a "Machiavel" in money as Horner was a "Machiavel in love"—and will make love, friendship, and justice "pimp" for him.

The relationship between Freeman and Jerry reveals, in fact, significant parallels to that between Horner and Margery. Both Jerry and Margery are childlike innocents whose "guardians" have deliberately kept them in ignorance in order to further their own selfish ends. Both have been subjected to unnatural repressions, and both have chosen to exchange one guardian (or husband) for another who will help them to enjoy the world as they would. "By my fa—" exclaims Jerry of Freeman, in what sounds like an echo of Margery, "he's a curious fine gentleman!" (439) And later he declares to his mother: "I'll do anything he'll have me, and go all the world over with him; to ordinaries, and bawdy-houses, or anywhere else. . . . Pray hold yourself contented; if I do go where money and wenches are to be had, you may thank yourself; for you used me so unnaturally, you would never let me have a penny to go abroad with; nor so much as come near the garret where your maidens lay; nay, you would not so much as let me play at hotcockles with 'em, nor have any recreation with 'em though one should have kissed you behind, you were so unnatural a mother, so you were" (461).

Dressing him in "red breeches" and giving him the money his mother has denied him, Freeman has freed Jerry and opened up for him a whole new world of pleasure and recreation. (The fertility imagery abounds throughout these dialogues, most notably in the frequent references to "bawdy houses," "wenches," and "breed-ing.") In the true comic spirit Freeman has released Jerry's natural instincts from "the modest seemly garb of gown and cap"—thus "safe-guarding pleasure against the denials of reason, which is wary of pleasure." He has put money to its proper use in the service of *life*: "have I lost all my good inns-of-chancery breeding upon thee then?" the Widow protests, "and thou wilt go a-breeding thyself . . .?" (460) Just as Manly's involvement with Olivia dramatizes the whole experience of the idealist and satirist, so Freeman's scenes with Jerry dramatize the experience of the comic realist. Freeman's freeing of Jerry from the repressions imposed on him by being kept penniless becomes, in effect, a kind of metaphor for his efforts to achieve on his own behalf a similar freedom from a similar repression. There is, however, no more selflessness implied in his extending his hand to Jerry than in the case of Horner and Margery. Like Horner, he is an audaciously unprincipled opportunist who, while he will always do what he can for his friends, is primarily bent on asserting in an unnatural world his right to express his natural self.

He is, as the Widow says of him, a "wild rude person," "an impertinent person." (420), and "an idle fellow" (421), and his "business" with her is aimed at achieving his own pleasure. But like Horner, he finds pleasure also in the challenge itself—in the prospect of outwitting an opponent who is herself well endowed with wit and shrewdness. The very fact that the Widow knows him so well and that she is as cynical a realist as he makes the excitement of the challenge all the greater and the contest he wages with her all the more exhilarating. Twice he confidently assumes a victory and twice the widow seizes the offensive and sends him back to draw further on his resources of ingenuity. Yet in the end he actually wins a double victory—receiving the money into his hands without at the same time having the Widow on them.

For all his comic triumph, however, Freeman does not by any means dominate the play, nor is there any song or dance to contribute a festive air. It is clearly Manly, with his irascible honesty and his violence of temper, who is the more central of the two heroes and it is he who imparts to the play its prevailingly angry tone. That Wycherley himself was in an angry mood when he wrote *The Plain Dealer* seems evident enough from the Prologue, which, unlike the prologues to his other plays, constitutes less a spirited defiance of a hard-to-please audience than an attack on a world wholly given over in his view to affectation and dishonesty. The fifty aggressive lines are, of course, given to Manly to deliver, but much of the attack is directly attributed to Wycherley himself: "Our scribbler therefore bluntly bid me say" (373). And we are thus at the very outset invited to recognize Manly as in some way identified with the playwright. The latter half of the Prologue makes such a conclusion virtually unavoidable:

> Plain dealing is, you'll say, quite out of fashion;
> You'll hate it here, as in a dedication;
> And your fair neighbours, in a limning poet
> No more than in a painter will allow it.
> Pictures too like the ladies will not please;
> They must be drawn too here like goddesses.
> You, as at Lely's too, would truncheon wield,
> And look like heroes in a painted field.
> But the coarse dauber of the coming scenes
> To follow life and nature only means,
> Displays you as you are, makes his fine woman
> A mercenary jilt, and true to no man:
> His men of wit and pleasure of the age
> Are as dull rogues as ever cumber'd stage:
> He draws a friend only to custom just,
> And makes him naturally break his trust.
> I, only, act a part like none of you,
> And yet you'll say, it is a fool's part too:
> An honest man who, like you, never winks
> At faults; but, unlike you, speaks what he thinks:
> The only fool who ne'er found patron yet,
> For truth is now a fault as well as wit.
> And where else, but on stages, do we see
> Truth pleasing, or rewarded honesty?
> Which our bold poet does this day in me.

What Manly is announcing is that *The Plain Dealer* is to be a "plain dealing" play—that "the course dauber of the coming scenes" is going to tell unsparingly the truth about the "fine woman" (Olivia) who is in reality "a mercenary jilt" and the "friend" (Vernish) who will "naturally break his trust." As Manly is a plain dealing character *in* the play, Wycherley is a plain dealing author in *writing* the play.

The very words with which Manly describes the playwright—a scribbler who speaks "bluntly," "a coarse dauber," a "bold poet"—

suggests a definite identification with Manly himself; and the coarsely aggressive expressions which Manly often uses as a way of expressing his hatred by cynically adjusting his tone down to the level of those he hates precisely parallel the kind of language we have seen Wycherley to be capable of using in his angry characterizations of such women as Mrs. Caution and Lady Fidget, who, like Olivia, make sex "filthy" by calling it so and "cheap" by putting a price on it. The identification between Manly and his creator is surely reinforced, moreover, in Act II when Novel refers to the author of *The Country Wife* as a "surly fool" (410), since Manly has been described in the list of dramatis personæ as being of "an honest, surly, nice humor," and since his first entrance is made "surlily."

Like Manly too, Wycherley refuses to resort to false flattery in his own interest and thus pens a "plain dealing" dedication (we may note Manly's reference to just such a "dedication" in the Prologue) to that "great and noble patroness" Mother Bennet, who as a prostitute is honest about her selling of love in exchange for money. And if any additional evidence is required, it can further be pointed out that the objects of Manly's hatred are just those that the earlier plays have shown to be Wycherley's own: self-important men of business, social pretenders, perverters of human values to mercenary ends, and in general all self-deceivers and hypocrites who fail to come to terms honestly with themselves as they are. In Manly's clearest and most detailed statement as to these hatreds, he proclaims: "I would jostle a proud, strutting, over-looking coxcomb, at the head of his sycophants, rather than put out my tongue at him when he were past me; would frown in the arrogant, big, dull face of an over-grown knave of business, rather than vent my spleen against him when his back were turned; would give fawning slaves the lie whilst they embrace or commend me; cowards whilst they brag; call a rascal by no other title, though his father had left him a duke's; laugh at fools aloud before their mistresses" (377).

Both Manly and Wycherley himself are moralists in the same rather special way. Thus it ought to become clear that Dryden knew whereof he spoke when he made reference to " 'Manly' Wycherley" —for Manly's views certainly represent those which the playwright himself held. Through him, then, Wycherley would seem to be saying to his audience: in terms of absolute honesty and justice, here is the kind of plain-spoken, severe dressing-down your dishonesties and mercenary perversions really deserve; but witness the experience in store for a man of genuine honesty and courage and idealism in your kind of world; and witness too the utter fruitlessness of such idealistic and courageous severity in a world where cowardice passes for courage and railing for satire. In short, Wycherley is cagily managing to give expression to his own satiric bent while suggesting at the same time that to be a satirist in such a world can only be both useless and maddeningly frustrating. It is in this sense that Manly's is, indeed, as he suggests in the Prologue, "a fool's part."

In the world as it now is, Wycherley suggests, everything that Manly stands for has become perverted. Not only has morality come to mean prudery instead of honesty, but masculine courage is made the object of raillery and laughter (as in Act II, scene i); a wit has come to mean "a loud-laughing, talking, incorrigible, coxcomb, as bully a roaring hardened coward" (493); and any superficial "railing" passes for "satire" (491)—with even a fop like Major Oldfox parading as a Horatian satirist ("I'll give you a cast of my politics in prose. 'Tis 'a Letter to a Friend in the Country;' which is now the way of all such sober solid persons as myself, when they have a mind to publish their disgust to the times; though perhaps, between you and I, they have no friend in the country" [460]). Even quarreling is no longer honest but has become a matter of policy and self-interest in matters both of love and of justice. Not only is the Widow Blackacre a clear case in point, but Olivia is another: "Well," she says, "we women, like the rest of the cheats of the world, when our cullies or creditors have found us out, and will or can trust no longer, pay debts and satisfy obligations with a quarrel" (413). And of Westminster Hall Manly declares that "now the lawyer only here is fed;/ And, bully-like, by quarrels gets his bread" (451). Olivia herself, of course, besides being a false railer, is simply another and more sinister Lady Fidget who, through her prudish protestations, has denied the naturalness of her own instinct and has become almost masculine in her sexual aggressiveness. Another one of those who regards "truth" as synonymous with "obscenity" (408), she characterizes men like Horner as "filthy creatures" (408) and sets a high price on the favors she grants. In short, she has perverted the very meaning of love, reducing it to a gross, mercenary thing.

In many ways Manly's experience in the world dominated by her kind repeats that of Alithea in *The Country Wife*. In their different ways, both are idealists, and both, by misplacing their trust, ironically subject themselves to being used to satisfy the mercenary ends of the very people to whom they have pledged their constancy. What Olivia says of Manly is almost equally true of Alithea: "he that distrusts most the world, trusts most to himself, and is but the more easily deceived, because he thinks he can't be deceived" (471). Both set up absolute standards of right conduct and then naively accept a counterfeit of that conduct as the genuine article. And in the process both blindly and ironically reject the genuine as counterfeit. Their very constancy, therefore, turns into a misguided faithfulness to their own idealistic illusions, which no amount of talking can persuade them to abandon. "I knew of your engagement to this lady," says Fidelia, "and the constancy of your nature; which nothing could have altered but herself" (504).

In neither case, however, is Wycherley attacking the satirist and idealist. Rather, he is illustrating the pitfalls into which the rigid absolutes of the honest man are all too likely to lead him in a deceitful world. In *The Plain Dealer,* as in *The Country Wife* and *Love in a Wood,* the world is no respecter of idealists. There can be no immunity, and people like Manly and Fidelia who "fain would find a heaven here" (474) will be drawn in spite of themselves into a world of "Darkness everywhere" (468). Inevitably the more extreme the illusion, the more extreme the disillusion. And *The Plain Dealer,* while not precisely the "satiric questioning of satire itself" which Mrs. Zimbardo suggests[16] (the satiric spokesman ultimately proving himself no better than the objects of his attack), *is* a commentary on the futility of satire, along with an assessment of the plight of the satirist in whom the extremes of love and hate produce a violent conflict.

To summarize then, Wycherley, in his portrayal of Manly, is holding his society up for scorn, both directly and indirectly. Most obviously, Manly expresses, in his misanthropic lines, the playwright's own disgust with the hypocrisies he hated. But at the same time Wycherley is dramatizing the fact that the honest man who attempts to live uncompromisingly by his principles—to settle only for an honest love and a true friendship and a perfect justice—will, given the current state of things, only end by being used and mocked; and the disappointed idealist who attacks, with aggressive hatred, a society which hopelessly fails to correspond with his ideal, will find himself involved, by his own ambivalence, in destruction and darkness. As Manly himself says in the Prologue: it is now only on stages that "we see/Truth pleasing or rewarded honesty." And it is only on stages that we can find "ladies . . . like goddesses."

Fidelia, of course, is such a lady, and as many critics including Holland have emphasized, she does not belong to the real world at all but is a figure straight out of romantic pastoral or "a painted field." And does not her very unreality represent Wycherley's ultimate revenge on the women in his own audience? Manly may be able to find at last a true friend in the real world, but a true love exists only as a kind of romantic dream—a Fidelia Grey, who is a shadowy figure "from the north." As with Manly's own blank verse soliloquy, her two poetic soliloquies suggest at once her identification with romance and the inner conflict which results from seeking to find a heaven in the shore world.

Thus, if it is true, as has so often been purported, that she may be regarded as a Restoration Viola, she may perhaps be even more aptly termed a Restoration Perdita—a figure who, as Tillyard says of Shakespeare's heroine, belongs to another "plane of reality" altogether and who, coming from a "strange, impossible world," sets the ideal of the pastoral and hence the hope of regeneration against the violence of the real world.[17] Certainly Fidelia is virtually pure symbol—the personified ideal of truth, who dares venture into the shore world only in disguise and who fears rejection even by the honest Manly until she has a chance to prove her fidelity. That she is very nearly overwhelmed by the darkness into which Manly sends her and that she emerges only after receiving a wound surely suggests her lack of immunity and the fate of truth in an imperfect world.

In terms of that world, indeed, it is finally only the comic realists—figures like Freeman and the minor Eliza—who offer any believable regenerative possibilities. Both see the world in no better a light than does Manly, but through their kind of "plain dealing" they seek not to quarrel with it but to make their peace and ultimately to find a transcendence through laughing acceptance. Recognizing that hatred actually stems from a frustrated love, Eliza declares to Olivia: "I must confess, I think we women as often discover where we love by railing, as men when they lie by their swearing; and the world is but a constant keeping gallant, whom we fail not to quarrel with when anything crosses us, yet cannot part with't for our hearts" (395). And when, at the end of the play, Manly offers to be reconciled to the "odious" world for Fidelia's sake and remarks, "my friend here would say, 'tis your estate that has made me friends with the world," Freeman's reply is almost an echo of Eliza: "I must confess I should; for I think most of our quarrels to the world are just such as we have to a handsome woman; only because we cannot enjoy her as we would do" (506, 507). Both statements, with their patent sexual overtones, surely represent one way of phrasing the perennial reaction that the comic spirit has to the moralist and the satirist.

The comedy-satire debate is, in fact, still going on as the play closes; but while the comic spirit is triumphant in believable terms (Freeman with his money and Jerry with his red breeches), the satirist and idealist can be rewarded only by a dream figure and hence on a stage where such a figure can exist. Fidelia has reconciled Manly to the shore world, but her very unreality is surely intended to make an audience ask how many idealists offstage ever find their Fidelias. Upon the stage the idealist's dream does survive, but given the real world, it must be the laughing realist, after all, who proves the better doctor. "Ridicule commonly decides great matters more forcibly and better than severity," and in the final analysis the "sea-lieutenant" would seem to have assumed command.

# [VIII]

# *Congreve's Apprenticeship*

---

DELUSION, n. The father of a most respectable family, comprising
Enthusiasm, Affection, Self-denial, Faith, Hope, Charity,
and many other goodly sons and daughters.
FLESH, n. The second person of the secular Trinity.

—AMBROSE BIERCE, *The Devil's Dictionary*

IF IT WERE NOT KNOWN FROM THE HISTORICAL RECORD THAT THE
plays of William Congreve belong to a generation twenty years
younger than that of Etherege and Wycherley, that conclusion
might well be drawn in any case from internal evidence, for along
with all the characteristics they share with the earlier comedies, they
reveal in addition a thoughtful quality which tends to mark the
end of a tradition rather than the beginning of one. Etherege and
Wycherley continually give the impression, each in his particular
way, of being very much involved with the heroes whose actions
they dramatize. They were themselves, in effect, participants in a
revolution in its progress, and their comic protagonists are centrally preoccupied with attaining the freedom to establish an identity and a way of life for themselves within a society that regards
them with suspicion.

In Congreve's comedies, however, the concern of the heroes and
heroines is not so much with achieving a life style as with maintaining, defending, and refining upon one which has already been

achieved and with wielding the power that belongs to them beautifully and well. As audience we bear witness to what they are able to do with what they are and how they are able to cope with the problems which confront them in their world. And the pungency and harmony and graceful control that Congreve achieves in his writing style are much the same qualities which his heroes and heroines are bent upon making dominant in the world they have created for themselves.

The fact remains, however, that the link with Etherege is a strong one—and if we must feel the connection with Wycherley as more remote, still Wycherley's plays did exert a certain thematic influence, and it is to his as well as Etherege's comic tradition that Congreve belongs, rather than to that of either sentimental or moral comedy.[1] It is true that after Bellmour his heroes are less libertine in their behavior and professions than their earlier counterparts, and that there is an increasingly less manifest concern with sexual matters, but the difference is actually more apparent than real; and they may be said to represent what amounts to a second step in the refining and civilizing process whose first step we have already noted in the development from the boisterous Sir Frederick Frollick to the more sophisticated Courtall and Dorimant. It is simply a matter of an increasingly subtle and self-conscious artistry.

Life, to the best of Congreve's heroes and heroines, remains a "plaything," and the denial of this attitude to Congreve himself which Dobrée implies in his fanciful Swift-Gay conversation seems largely to miss the point of the nature and significance of the play function: "Plaything?" Gay is made to question, "It was just as such, I thought, that he could not regard life, and far from asking too little of it, he always appeared to me to ask too greatly. His plays seem, in all their most wonderful scenes, to breathe a wish for an existence so exquisite, for beings so lovely in their persons, so delicate in their minds, that in despair he gave over creating them as patterns for mankind to imitate."[2] But the fact is, as has already been sufficiently emphasized, that to see life as a genuine plaything is by no means to see it simply frivolously or to ask "too little of it," but on the contrary to ask the maximum; and Gay's characterization actually defines the kind of "exquisite" existence which Congreve's heroes and heroines seek to achieve in the play sphere. On

Congreve's comic playground the challenges, if more elegantly delivered, have lost none of their difficulty.

## The Old Batchelor

REGARDLESS OF THE EVIDENCES in Congreve's first play of the influence of both Etherege and Wycherley, it is already marked by the intellectual seriousness and artistic awareness which were to characterize Congreve's comic vision throughout his career as a playwright. *The Old Batchelor* (1693) has been on one occasion described as "une farce avec toutes les qualités du genre";[3] but while certain farcical elements are undeniably present, they constitute something more than a young playwright's concession to an English audience's perennial delight in knock-about and horseplay, possessing as they do a decided thematic justification. As Dobrée suggests: "From the opening line of *The Old Batchelor* we are in the realm of ideas, and realize that we are in contact with a thinker."[4]

Of all Congreve's comic heroes Bellmour stands most clearly in the Dorimant-Horner tradition, but he possesses their high spirits without their astringency and reveals a philosophical streak which is new. Thus, in his opening debate with Vainlove, he defines explicitly what amounts to his modus vivendi in the world. "Wisdom's nothing but a pretending to know and believe more than we really do," he affirms. "You read of but one wise Man, and all that he knew was, that he knew nothing. Come, come, leave Business to Idlers, and Wisdom to Fools; they have need of 'em: Wit, be my Faculty, and Pleasure, my Occupation, and let Father Time shake his Glass. Let low and earthly souls grovel 'till they have work'd themselves six Foot deep into a Grave—Business is not my Element—I rowl in a higher Orb . . ." (25, 26).[5]

The business-pleasure opposition is, of course, already familiar to us from Wycherley, but Bellmour here makes clear at the outset that his dedication to pleasure amounts to a conscious philosophy. Sounding the note of both the skeptic and the Epicurean, he has earlier proclaimed: "And so must Time, my Friend, be close pursued, or lost. Business is the rub of Life, perverts our Aim, casts off the Bias, and leaves us wide and short of the intended Mark." And when Vainlove comments, "Pleasure, I guess you mean," Bellmour rejoins, "Ay, what else has meaning?" (25) In a world in which all we can know is that we know nothing, Bellmour finds his "meaning" in the immediate reality of being alive and of living life well. Hence when Vainlove asks him later: "Could you be content to go to Heav'n?" Bellmour replies, "Hum, not immediately, in my Conscience not heartily? I'd do a little more good in my Generation first, in order to deserve it" (55).

The word "Generation" with its implicit double meaning places Bellmour clearly on the side of life; and since "Heav'n" in this particular context refers to marriage, his remark further suggests that his attitude toward the married state is a good deal more realistic than that of Vainlove. Marriage, like Heaven, will perhaps come eventually, and he will accept it with his customary "tractability" ("there is a Fatality in Marriage") but meanwhile there are other pleasures to be tasted. He has a passion for living, and for him pleasure, far from signifying mere time-passing, means an unremitting activity in the interest of crowding as much life as possible into the immediate moment. Business he leaves to "Idlers."

His, then, is a life of "Wit" and "Pleasure," and the connection he makes between the "faculty" and the "occupation" is surely deliberate. He subscribes, in effect, to the Hobbesian way of thinking of which Thorpe has said significantly: "Of the factors that distinguish the active from the sluggish or dull intellect Hobbes regards none as of more importance than appetite. Thus he constantly and unequivocally emphasizes appetite as essential to a vigorous, lively, and orderly mind." And Thorpe then goes on to cite the passage from *Leviathan* in which Hobbes asserts:

> And therefore, a man who has no great passion for any of these things; but is, as men terme it indifferent; though he may be so farre a good man as to be free from giving Offence; yet he cannot possibly have either a great Fancy or much Judgement. For the Thoughts are to the Desires, as Scouts, and Spies, to range abroad, and find the way to the things Desired: All Stedinesse of the minds motion, and all quicknesse of the same, proceeding from thence. For as to have no Desire, is to be Dead: so to have weak Passions, is Dulnesse.[6]

The passage is an important one, for it is partly in such terms that the opposing characteristics of Bellmour and Vainlove are set before us. Bellmour, being made up of "Flesh and Blood," is "a Cormorant in Love" (29). He describes Laetitia as "a delicious Morsel" (27), and of his arrangement with Vainlove Sharper says: "you with Pleasure reap that Fruit, which he takes Pains to sow" (32). In short, he has appetites in abundance, and "Fruit" has much the same sexual implications as in Etherege's *Man of Mode*. Vainlove, on the other hand, is characterized by Sharper as "of very little Passion, very good Understanding, and very ill Nature" (31). And when Sharper urges him with respect to Araminta: "To her Man— a delicious Mellon pure and consenting ripe, and only waits thy cutting up," Vainlove demurs, " 'Tis an untimely Fruit," and Sharper exclaims in disgust, "Never leave this damn'd, illnatur'd whimsey, *Frank*? Thou hast a sickly peevish Appetite; only chew Love and cannot digest it" (72). Lacking Bellmour's "Passion" and "Appetite" for life as it is and his ready adaptability to whatever the circumstances require, Vainlove seems destined to regard every fruit as "untimely," and to find his satisfaction only in a continuing pursuit. "Truth on't is," says Bellmour of Araminta, "she fits his Temper best, is a kind of floating Island; sometimes seems in reach, then vanishes and keeps him busied in the search" (31).

The "ill nature" of which Sharper twice accuses Vainlove is, presumably, an aspect of that quarrel he makes with reality for not living up to his expectations. A "Contemplative Lover" who speaks of marriage to Araminta as going to "Heav'n," he is the romantic dreamer for whom real life can offer, he fears, no fulfillment equal to his dreams, and his is the dilemma which Congreve frequently touches on in his assessment of the human condition. Dobrée has described Congreve's central preoccupation as "the necessity to guard against disillusion,"[7] and the song which Araminta introduces in the second act sounds almost precisely this note:

I.

*Thus to a ripe, consenting Maid,*
*Poor, old, repenting* Delia *said,*
*Would you long preserve your Lover?*
*Would you still his Goddess reign?*

[182]

> *Never let him all discover,*
> *Never let him much obtain.*
>
> II.
> *Men will admire, adore and die,*
> *While wishing at your Feet they lye*
> *But admitting their Embraces,*
>    *Wakes 'em from the Golden Dream;*
> *Nothing's new besides our Faces,*
>    *Every Woman is the same.*    (50)

For Vainlove, who cherishes the "Golden Dream," and for Araminta, who would "still his Goddess reign," there is, indeed, as Araminta says, "too much Truth" in the words of the song, and the only way for them to guard against disillusion is to avoid ever bringing the heavenly expectation to the hard test of experience.

In fact the central theme of the play has to do in large part with precisely this juxtaposition of "heavenly" and "earthly" preoccupations—a juxtaposition to which Congreve has given repeated emphasis in his imagery. Norman Holland has commented, in his discussion of *The Old Batchelor,* on the great "metaphorical density of Congreve's prose"[8] and has gone on to supply us with a helpful and thoroughgoing examination of the various metaphorical patterns he discovers in the play. Perhaps most important among these are what he calls "images of weight" as opposed to "comparisons that tend to point the action up toward a supernatural level."[9] We may further note that the weight images are always in some way associated with animal or physical references and these in turn often with "fruit" and "appetite" references; and the heaven-earth opposition is also frequently expressed as a "Deity-Devil" contrast and an "illusion—clear-sightedness" one. In such terms Bellmour and Belinda belong, it would seem, to the Devil's party and thus to reality, while Vainlove keeps following a dream which in earthly terms is unattainable.

There is finally no answer to his dilemma, and the play supplies none. Bellmour sums up the hopelessly contradictory position when he exclaims: "But how the Devil dost thou expect to get her if she never yield? . . . Marry her without her Consent; thou'rt a Riddle beyond Woman—" (55). And in the closing scene of the play, when Vainlove actually proposes marriage to Araminta and she procrastinates by suggesting that they "take the Advantage of a little of our Friends Experience first," Bellmour comments aside: "O my Conscience she dares not consent, for fear he shou'd recant," and then says to them hopefully, "May be it may get you an Appetite to see us fall to before ye" (108). But as with everything in Vainlove's sphere, the "Appetite" remains a "may be"—a future possibility and not a present reality, and his difficulty remains unsolved.

Yet there is a way other than his of guarding against disillusion, and that is Bellmour's way (and Belinda's) of harboring no illusions in the first place. Belinda is persistently an antiromantic who jeers at "Darts, and Flames, and Altars" and tells Bellmour bluntly, "if you must talk impertinently, for Heavens sake let it be with Variety; don't come always, like the Devil, wrapt in Flames —I'll not hear a Sentence more, that begins with an, *I burn*—Or an, *I beseech you, Madam.*" To which Bellmour, undeterred, retorts: "But tell me how you would be ador'd—I am very tractable" (49, 50). Thus Belinda's "Altars" and her "for Heavens sake" are first undercut by her own "Devil" reference and then are picked up again in the "ador'd" of Bellmour's ironic reply. Theirs is the kind of witty antagonism already encountered in the exchanges between Courtall and Gatty, Dorimant and Harriet—an antagonism based on a clear-eyed recognition of the falsity of the romantic love tradition and a determination to eschew all illusion. Belinda possesses, in embryo, traces of that proud, independent spirit which is a part of Millamant's magnificence, and when Vainlove soulfully declares, "For as Love is a Deity, he must be serv'd by Prayer," she counters: "O Gad, would you would all pray to Love then, and let us alone" (49). To her "This Love," far from being "a Deity," "is the Devil, and sure to be in Love is to be possess'd" (45). And when she speaks disparagingly of "that filthy, awkward, two-leg'd Creature, Man" (44), it is not with the prudish hypocrisy of a Lady Fidget but as a part of her insistence on seeing things as they are. "Ha, ha, ha, love a Man!" she laughs; and to Araminta's affirmation, "yes, you would not love a Beast," she rejoins, "Of all Beasts not an Ass" (45).

Perhaps Belinda lacks the graceful detachment of a Harriet or a Millamant, but the language she uses accurately expresses her realistic nature as she opposes it to romantic dream. Even more important, however, it expresses her pitiless contempt for people who, through their awkward unimaginativeness, do not see the possibilities for making their heaviness light. More than one critic has pointed, for example, to Congreve's brilliant use of language in Belinda's devastating description of the "Country Girls": "Two such unlick'd Cubs! . . . Ay, O my Conscience, fat as Barn-Door Fowl: But so bedeck'd, you would have taken 'em for *Friezland* Hens, with their Feathers growing the wrong way—O such Outlandish Creatures!" (76) Not only the barnyard imagery, but the choppy, unfinished sentences and the repeated use of heavy and harsh consonants turn the passage into a sheer poetry of abuse. *Mere* earthiness is not enough, and out of reality she would make a new poetry.

Like Bellmour she would "rowl in a higher Orb." In short, both Belinda and Bellmour would first see man with clarity for the "awkward, two-leg'd Creature" he is and then they would, like Congreve himself, make of that "homely Fare . . . the Feast."[10] They would, as William Van Voris puts it in another context, build "a Corinthian crown on a Doric 'Base . . . Thus all below is Strength, and all above is Grace.' "[11] It is, however, as Congreve here suggests, by no means easy to see reality clearly, and his hero and heroine live in a world where nearly everyone is blind to both his own essential nature and everyone else's. Thus the animal metaphors so frequently to be found in the play are used as a means of continually undercutting human dreams and pretensions.

But not until well along in the play do we come upon a dialogue which indicates that there is more to the entire metaphorical pattern than at first meets the eye. It is at the point in Act V when the *miles gloriosus* Captain Bluffe, contemplating the possibilities of revenging himself on Sharper for the beating suffered at his hands, declares: "I am prepar'd for him now; and he shall find he might have safer rouz'd a sleeping Lion." For answer Sir Joseph cautions him: "Nay, don't speak so loud—I don't jest, as I did a little while ago—Look yonder—A-gad, if he should hear the Lion roar, he'd cudgel him into an Ass, and his primitive Braying. Don't you remember the Story in *Aesop's Fables,* Bully? A'gad, there are good

Morals to be pick'd out of *Aesop's Fables,* let me tell you that; and *Reynard the Fox* too" (95, 96).

Apparently it was Congreve's view also that there were "good Morals to be pick'd out of *Aesop's Fables* . . . and *Reynard the Fox,"* for much of the same emphasis on human pride and pomposity and human blindspots that runs through the beast fables is to be found also in the play; and further, the references to cormorants, asses, and lions already cited by no means exhaust the list. Sylvia is referred to at one point as being as "true as Turtle" (26); Vainlove's role in life is described as "continually starting of Hares for you to course" (27); Fondlewife is characterized as a "kind of Mongrel Zealot" (28); Captain Bluffe has occasion to remark, with reference to Sharper, that "every Cock will fight upon his own Dunghil" (41); Belinda declares in one instance to Bellmour: "O foh, your dumb Rhetorick is more ridiculous, than your talking Impertinence; as an Ape is a much more troublesome Animal than a Parrot" (51); Lucy's advice to Sylvia is: "Strike *Heartwell* home, before the Bait's worn off the Hook" (52); and once her conquest has been accomplished, Sylvia gloats, "Ha, ha, ha, an old Fox trapt—" (66); Lætitia describes the disguised Bellmour as "a Wolf in the cloathing of a Sheep" (86); and when Araminta asks Belinda what she has done to infuriate Heartwell, she replies, "Only touch'd a gall'd-Beast 'till he winchd" (104). And finally, the verses with which Heartwell closes the play sound very much as if Congreve is contributing a fable of his own:

> With gaudy Plumes and gingling Bells made proud,
> The youthful Beast sets forth, and neighs aloud.
> A Morning-Sun his Tinsell'd Harness gilds,
> And the first Stage a Down-Hill Green-sword yields.
> But, Oh—
> What rugged Ways attend the Noon of Life!
> (Our Sun declines,) and with what anxious Strife,
> What Pain we tug that galling Load, a Wife;
> All Coursers the first Heat with Vigour run;
> But 'tis with Whip and Spur the Race is won.

Aesop's beast fables offer, of course, paradigms (generally not very complimentary) of human behavior, and of their significance one recent commentator has observed: "The Greek looks into his

glass and sees a horrible picture of himself. It is always difficult to
be honest with oneself, and it is as though the fables were saying,
'It is not I but the animal in me that is like this.' Then comes the
moralist and says, 'No, you fool; this is yourself even more truly
than any ideal you may have.' "[12] To Congreve, who later penned
such lines as "Believe it, Men have ever been the same,/And all
the Golden Age, is but a Dream," the fables must have seemed to
offer unavoidable conclusions regarding the human condition; and
we have only to read Carlyle's tribute to the Reynard story to understand how deeply it too must have appealed to Congreve's own
temper and philosophy:

> Cunningly constructed, and not without a true poetic life, we must
> admit it to be . . . It is full of broad, rustic mirth; inexhaustible in
> comic devices; a World-Saturnalia . . . it is an Air-pageant from
> Fancy's Dream grotto, yet Wisdom lurks in it; as we gaze, the
> vision becomes poetic and prophetic. A true Irony must have dwelt
> in the poet's heart and head: here, under grotesque shadows, he
> gives us the saddest picture of Reality; yet for us without sadness;
> his figures mask themselves in uncouth, bestial vizards, and enact,
> gambolling; their Tragedy dissolves into sardonic grins. He has a
> deep artful Humour, sporting with the world and its evils in a kind
> mockery; this is the poetic soul, round which the outward material
> has fashioned itself into living coherence . . . for now, as then, "Pru-
> dence" is the only virtue sure of its reward, and Cunning triumphs
> where Honesty is worsted; and now, as then, it is the wise man's
> part to know this, and cheerfully look for it, and cheerfully defy it.[13]

Bellmour is, like Congreve himself, one of the cheerful defiers,
and so far as the *Fables* are concerned, that of "The Nightingale
and the Hawk" in some sense defines the philosophy of both:

> A nightingale perched on a high oak and was singing her usual
> song. A hungry hawk saw her and pounced upon her. When she
> was about to be killed, she appealed to the hawk to let her go, saying
> that there was not enough of her to fill a hawk's stomach. She beg-
> ged him, if he wanted food, to go after the larger birds. But the
> hawk replied "I would be a fool if I let go the food on hand and
> went off after some I had never seen."

The difference between Bellmour's philosophy of living and Vainlove's is surely suggested by the implications of the fable; and it

also touches on the familiar *carpe diem* theme which the fables as well as many of the comedies of the Restoration period include.

The prevailing tone of most of the fables and the *Reynard* stories is one of alternately mild and heavy irony—an irony compounded by the ever-present consciousness that the characters are, after all, beasts who are talking and acting like humans. And with his undercurrent of animal references Congreve subtly achieves a similar kind of irony in *The Old Batchelor,* albeit by a reverse method. Unlike Wycherley, he would seem here to view man's essential nature not in terms of a fundamental innocence corrupted by reason and conscience but as an ironic fact always undercutting human dreams of glory. Thus, for example, Vainlove, the "contemplative Lover" cherishing his "golden Dream," employs as his servant the redoubtable Setter, whose name supplies sufficient testimony as to his nature but who is, as Lucy remarks, "too true a *Valet de Chambre* not to affect his Master's Faults" (56). And when she goes on to deride him as a "Contemplative Pimp," he retorts in a tone of pompous self-importance: "Ha! what art, who thus maliciously hast awaken'd me, from my Dream of Glory? Speak thou vile Disturber—" But to Lucy he is, after all, only a "Beggars Curr" (56, 57); and hence, by implication, his dreams ("Why if I were known, I might come to be a great Man") are as irrevocably punctured by Lucy's irreverently realistic view as are Vainlove's by his valet's parody.

Setter, of course, belongs essentially to Bellmour's and Sharper's and Lucy's earthy reality. "I wonder," he says to himself, "to which of these two Gentlemen I do most properly appertain—the one uses me as his Attendant; the other (being the better acquainted with my Parts) employs me as a Pimp; why that's much the more honourable Employment—by all means—I follow one as my Master, t'other follows me as his Conductor" (56). Like Congreve's later Jeremy and Waitwell, he is an enthusiastic and inspired aider and abettor of his master's deceptions and intrigues, priding himself on his successful artistry and as efficient as a "Blood-Hound" (94) in sniffing out trickery and deceit.

All of the realists in the play know well enough that theirs is a world in which "Cunning triumphs where Honesty is worsted," and all of them in one way or another adhere to the *carpe diem* philosophy. In the perennial spirit of English comedy they act without illusions and often satisfy their appetite for living by shamelessly taking advantage of those less clear-sighted and more complacent than themselves. Thus Lucy addresses Sylvia: "in the Name of Opportunity mind your own Business. Strike *Heartwell* home, before the Bait's worn off the Hook. Age will come" (52). And she goes on: "dress up your Face in Innocence and Smiles; and dissemble the very want of Dissimulation. . . . Hang Art, Madam, and trust to Nature for dissembling. *Man, was by Nature Womans Cully made:/We, never are but by our selves betray'd*" (53). And Sylvia herself finally comes to acknowledge the truth of Lucy's observations: "Well, I find dissembling to our Sex is as natural as swimming to a *Negro;* we may depend upon our skill to save us at a plunge, tho' till then we never make the experiment—" (66).

Virtually every incident and every detail in the play serves to corroborate Lucy's basic insights—insights which sound much the same cynical note so frequently to be heard in the fables and the *Reynard* stories. In both cases, to be realistic about human nature is perhaps necessarily to be to some extent cynical, and yet in neither context is the prevailing mood by any means darkly pessimistic. In some sense the kind of comic spirit with which we are here concerned inevitably contains, by its very nature, a substratum of cynicism regarding human aspirations, and among the greatest of the Restoration comic playwrights there is always a touch of regret (which in Wycherley often becomes anger) at having to entertain the idea that "all the Golden Age, is but a Dream." (Indeed it may well be argued that it is the absence of this sense in Etherege that makes his plays seem finally, for all their undeniable sparkle, rather more brittle and less profound than those of his confrères.) Yet it is of the essence of the comic spirit which prevails in the plays of Congreve that, in a manner of speaking, it makes the best of the worst and molds life artfully and imaginatively and beautifully out of whatever raw materials are at hand. It is just this ability that is associated with Bellmour at the opening of the play when, in the midst of his lyrical flight ("I rowl in a higher Orb, and dwell—"), Vainlove interrupts him with, "In Castles i'th' Air of thy own building: That's thy Element, *Ned*—Well as high a Flyer as you are, I have a Lure may make you stoop." And after a single glance at the letter proffered him, Bellmour responds good-naturedly, "I marry Sir, I have a Hawks Eye at a Womans hand—" (26). The "Air" is always his natural "Element" but like the hawk of the fables he will always be ready to come to the "Lure."

In *The Old Batchelor* the characters may be said to divide themselves, much as in the beast narratives, into those who cling to illusions and those who reject them, into those who are blind to reality and those who see it for what it is (in Bellmour's case, with "a Hawks Eye"). The seeing and blindness opposition is used repeatedly, and the implication concerning the blind is, almost invariably, that they are self-deceived and that they do not, in fact, really want to see things clearly. Heartwell, Fondlewife, and Sir Joseph Wittol are all at some point in the play referred to as blind or unseeing, and they are, as a consequence, all too easily "betray'd" by those with an open eye for that very blindness.

Their blindnesses, however, are clearly not all of a piece. Sir Joseph's is simply that of a fool who is lacking wholly in wit and wisdom and who, in his vanity and cowardice, can be hoodwinked even by a blustering bully like Captain Bluffe. The latter has only to say to him threateningly: "Sir, I say you can't see; what d'ye say to that now?" for Sir Joseph to reply obediently, "I am blind" (44), and in the course of the play he is repeatedly used either as a "blind," as by Lætitia, or as a convenient dupe, as by Sharper and later by Bellmour and Setter. Never seeing beyond the surface of things, he is himself nothing but a surface. In its overblown pretentiousness the language he uses precisely reflects the inflated emptiness of his "knightly" affectations, and his so-called "wit" (that "faculty" so essential to living well) is dependent on a memory which is forever failing him: "I had a pretty thing to that purpose, if he han't frighted it out of my Memory" (38).

Fondlewife too is of course something of a fool, but at times he has, like Heartwell, "Reason" enough to recognize his own folly. His is for the most part, however, an "easie Faith" (90), and "Mongrel Zealot" that he is, he generally chooses to be a true believer in spite of the evidence of his senses. Proposing to give his wife "Instructions," to "reason" with her, he lectures her on "how heinous, and how crying a Sin, the Sin of Adultery is," even while knowing ("I will reason with myself") that his reasoning actually flies in the face of all reason ("to say truth, she's fonder of me, than she has reason to be"), and he entrusts her to the keeping of a man whose "Fanatick-Habit" inspires a faith obviously altogether false. And even when that faith has been shattered, he clings to his belief in his wife's innocence. "I do believe thee,—" he declares. "I won't believe my own Eyes" (90).

The assertion has an ironic echo a few lines later when the disguised Bellmour, whom Lucy has addressed as "Reverend Sir," unmasks himself. "Now, Goodness have Mercy upon me! Mr. *Bellmour!* is it you?" she exclaims. And when he rejoins, "Even I. What dost think?" she replies, "Think! That I shou'd not believe my Eyes, and that you are not what you seem to be" (91). In short, she recognizes at once the incongruity between the religious exterior and the natural man beneath it, between "Deity" and "Devil," and her refusal to believe her eyes is inspired, not like Fondlewife's by a false trust, but a well-justified distrust of outward innocence and piety. To "see with the eyes of faith" in the real world leads only to being misled and duped, and the implication would seem to be that it is not only Bellmour who makes use of "a swinging long spiritual Cloak, to cover carnal Knavery," for as Setter says, Tribulation Spintext wears a "black Patch . . . upon one Eye, as a penal Mourning for the ogling Offences of his Youth; and some say, with that Eye, he first discover'd the frailty of his Wife" (55).

Even Heartwell, for all his idealistic championing of honesty— "My Talent is chiefly that of speaking Truth" (34)[14]—and his confident assumptions that he is above the general human frailty, is finally proved as blind and self-deceived as the rest. "I am for having every body be what they pretend to be," he declares roundly, "a Whoremaster be a Whoremaster" (33). Yet Vainlove has already described him as a "pretended Woman-Hater," and he proves after all to possess no immunity from that "Infection" of love against which he rails. "I think I have baited too many of those Traps, to be caught in one my self" (34), he confidently affirms, but in his subsequent Reason-Appetite soliloquy, the thought of the "delicious, damn'd, dear, destructive Woman" is at last too much for all the arguments of his reason to withstand, and he very nearly becomes "an old Fox trapt—" Blinded by his own desires, he is caught by reality and proves an easy prey for a woman who can "dissemble the very want of Dissimulation," and the ironies multiply when he is ultimately saved by one artist in dissembling working against another. "*Heartwell* is my friend;" says Bellmour, "and tho' he be blind, I must not see him fall into the Snare, and unwittingly marry a Whore" (92). (Again, the insistent seeing-blindness opposition.)

In a world where even wisdom is "but a pretending to know and believe more than we really do," where values such as courage, honesty, innocence, and love are likely to prove mere pretenses, and where faces are all too easily masked, it is dangerous to take anything at face value or to make any commitment "unwittingly." As in the beast narratives, the world is full of traps for the gullible and the unwary, and only those possessed of Reynard's qualities of craft, eloquence, and open-eyed realism remain free to have their own way with life and, in effect, to "extract Gold" from the "dirt," as Bellmour describes the end of Sharper's designs on Sir Joseph (35), and to "stamp" their own "image on the Gold," as Sharper says of Bellmour's activities in affairs of love (32).

The obvious difference between Bellmour's or Sharper's, Belinda's or Lucy's kind of pretending and that of their less clear-sighted "victims" in the play is that the former involves no self-deception and no assumption of being other than one is. Belinda's "affectation" of indifference to Bellmour, for example, is an aspect of her wryly satirical temperament and of her self-appointed role as laughing commentator on the antics of that ridiculous creature the human animal. "*Araminta,*" she cries, "come I'll talk seriously to you now; could you but see with my Eyes, the buffoonry of one Scene of Address, a Lover, set out with all his Equipage and Appurtenances; O Gad! sure you would—But you play the Game, and consequently can't see the Miscarriages obvious to every stander by" (45).

As a "stander by" herself, she *sees* her own world and her part in it with an amused and detached objectivity which makes it highly entertaining. "Come, Mr. *Sharper,*" she exclaims, speaking as the essentially poetic soul that she is, "you and I will take a Turn, and laugh at the Vulgar—Both the great Vulgar and the small—Oh Gad! I have a great passion for *Cowley*—Don't you admire him?

... Ah so fine! So extreamly fine! So every thing in the World that I like—Oh Lord, walk this Way—I see a Couple, I'll give you their History" (80).

Clearly she is an actress who is fully aware of her role of witty sophisticate and who makes the most of it. Yet her performance here as well as the wittily aggressive counterattacks she launches against Bellmour amount to more than a superficial posing or affectation. Making fun of human absurdities is, in part, her way of having fun; and as Huizinga says, "it is precisely this fun-element that characterizes the essence of play."[15] Sentimentalities, stupidities, and gaucheries become in her hands fuel for her wit and ingenuity, and out of them she makes a spirited and artful game which she as the master player controls—a poem of her own writing. The "Variety" she demands of Bellmour she demands of life as well, and when she announces her decision to marry, she does so with her customary note of defiance: "O my Conscience, I cou'd find in my Heart to marry thee, purely to be rid of thee—At least, thou art so troublesome a Lover, there's Hopes thou'lt make a more than ordinary quiet Husband." And to Bellmour's rejoinder ("Courtship to Marriage, is but as the Musick in the Play-House, 'till the Curtain's drawn; but that once up, then opens the Scene of Pleasure"), she counters: "Oh, foh—no: Rather, Courtship to Marriage, as a very witty Prologue to a very dull Play" (101, 102). Plainly she is, like Harriet at the end of *The Man of Mode,* offering her lover a challenge—and one that she reasserts in her final words: "Prisoner, make much of your Fetters" (108).

And yet if each is sparring with the other and trading image for image in a tirelessly agile give-and-take of the kind we have witnessed in Etherege, each is also, in his own way, attacking and challenging verbally the dulling marital trap. And Bellmour can surely be counted on to rise to Belinda's dare. There may be a "Fatality in Marriage," but after all he knows himself for a "lucky Rogue" (91), and veteran actor that he is, his performance in the "Play" is not likely to be a dead one. With "Wit" as his chief "Faculty," he adjusts himself to the ways of his world with good-natured tolerance and then makes the most of them to create a pleasurable life for himself. Against the sharpness of Belinda's witty sallies, he opposes the light-heartedness of his own and acts whatever part comes his way with confidence and zest. He too is a player, and in him Belinda has found a poetic nature to counterpoint her own. From the moment when we hear him utter his opening sentiments on the subject of wit and wisdom, we cannot fail to know that we are confronted with a master of language and that seventeenth-century audiences had never before heard anything quite like this. What could have been in other hands than Congreve's a lifeless philosophical statement takes on, through its almost unanalyzable use of repetitions and balances, alliterations and antitheses, resolutions only established to be at once opened out again, and imagery which brings abstractions into the realm of concrete, dramatic immediacy, a rhythmic liveliness and comic grace which prove to be also characteristic of Bellmour himself. And the final statement recapitulates the sense of the entire passage with a sweeping verbal gesture that carries us from "groveling" depths to "rowling" heights in such a way as to impart the very feeling of flight.

Possessed of Dorimant's and Horner's insatiable appetite for life, Bellmour can soar psychologically as well as verbally and can manage almost invariably to get what he wants and to take full advantage of the fools around him. His talents for "Hypocrisie" and for improvisation ("Well, now, I know my Cue") are the familiar ones of his comic predecessors, and like them, he takes delight in the prospect of staging a good show ("Oh, what Sport will be here") and has the egotist's complete self-assurance ("I-gad let me tell you, my most prevailing Argument is express'd in dumb show").

With Setter as his trusted "Engineer" he sets about his designs with self-congratulatory effrontery. "Secure in my Disguise," he tells himself with satisfaction, "I have out-fac'd Suspicion and even dar'd Discovery—This Cloak my Sanctity, and trusty *Scarron's* Novels my Prayer-Book—Methinks I am the very Picture of *Montufar* in the *Hypocrites*—" (73). The prayer-book substitution proves a dangerous bit of bravado, and only Bellmour's quick invention and the "Impudence" of which, as Lætitia says thankfully, "he has a considerable Portion" (88), saves the day, for Fondle-wife eventually discovers the reputedly holy book to be entitled *The Innocent Adultery* and exclaims: "Ay, this is the Devil's *Pater-Noster*" (85). (Again, deity versus devil.)

The book is, of course, peculiarly appropriate to Bellmour who, true to his ancestral tradition, is of the Devil's party in the positive comic sense. "Very good!" he comments approvingly when first contemplating an assignation with Lætitia. "Then I must be disguised—With all my Heart—It adds a Gusto to an Amour; gives it the greater resemblance of Theft; and among us lewd Mortals, the deeper the Sin the sweeter" (27, 28). Later Setter affirms, in answer to Bellmour's question ("How goes the Project?"), "As all lewd Projects do, Sir, where the Devil prevents our Endeavours with Success" (55). And in the final act he exclaims in a similar vein as his new master enters: "Talk of the Devil—See where he comes." To which Sharper adds, "Hugging himself in his prosperous Mischief—No real Fanatick can look better pleas'd after a successful Sermon of Sedition" (94).

In the concluding scenes all the "prosperous" mischief-makers—Lucy, Sharper, Setter, and Bellmour—combine their impressive talents to lay a final trap for Sir Joseph and Captain Bluffe; and these two consummate fools, blinded to the end by their own vanities, walk docilely into the snare. For his part Heartwell, fresh from his narrow escape and equipped with a new clarity of vision, commends his friend by asserting: *"Bellmour,* I approve thy Mirth, and thank thee—And I cannot in gratitude (for I see which way thou art going) see thee fall into the same Snare, out of which thou hast deliver'd me" (107). But Bellmour too can "see" the trap, and we are left with little doubt that he, in committing himself "to lasting Durance," has done so with open eyes and will "make much of" his "Fetters." Traps and heavy loads are not for him, and we can be sure that he will continue to soar. Thus, as he prepares to "fall to" with "Appetite," it is he who commands the concluding dance, with Setter by his side to call the dancers in, while Vainlove continues his never-ending pursuit and Heartwell nurses his disillusion and sets out to "plod on alone."

## The Double-Dealer

CONGREVE'S SECOND COMEDY, in spite of the fact that it reveals many of the same thematic preoccupations as his first, strikes quite a different note, and what little pertinence it has to the present study lies, strangely enough, in its villain rather than in its hero, the latter being after all of very slight inherent interest. In some sense *The Double-Dealer* (1695) may be read thematically as a sequel to *The Old Batchelor,* constituting as it does a continuing examination of the dangers of credulity in a world where honesty is no match for cunning. The examination, however, takes place chiefly in the realm of melodrama rather than comedy, and the point of particular interest is the illustration it supplies of the close identity between comic knave and melodramatic villain.

The fact remains, however, that it is not finally a very satisfactory play, and it is hardly surprising to find Congreve acknowledging in his dedicatory letter: "I design'd the Moral first, and to that Moral I invented the Fable," in view of the fact that the characters, both in themselves and in their actions and relationships, seem often more allegorical than real—embodiments of an abstract idea who are never quite convincing as credible human beings in a credible world. In human terms they seem not to have captured the playwright's imagination, and their failure to come to life is paralleled by a similar failure in Congreve's language.

And further, the juxtaposition of light and serious elements, while understandable in view of Congreve's abstract concerns, has the effect of depriving both of their intended dramatic impact— with the farcical doings less entertaining than they ought to be and the serious affairs less emotionally compelling. The title of the play, its tragi-comic nature, and its central concern with deceptions as they relate to love and friendship indicate that Congreve may again have had Wycherley's *Plain Dealer* in the back of his mind as in his earlier creation of Heartwell, but whereas Wycherley's attitude is that of an involved and angry man, Congreve's seems, still more than in his earlier play, detached and speculative—as does that of the pair of young lovers on whom the action of the play focuses.

Like Wycherley, Congreve tended here to follow Ben Jonson in depicting a world made up of knaves on the one hand and fools on the other, but his attitude toward his fools is far lighter than either Jonson's or Wycherley's. And Mellefont and Cynthia represent a new dimension altogether, playing as they do the role of objective and often serious commentators, for whom commitment to each other means commitment to a world which may, after all, hold only disillusion. "'Tis an odd Game we're going to Play at:" says Cynthia; "What think you of drawing Stakes, and giving over in time?" But Mellefont protests: "No, hang't, that's not endeavouring to win, because it's possible we may lose; since we have shuffled and cut, let's e'en turn up Trump now." And the dialogue continues:

> Cynt. Then I find it's like Cards, if either of us have a good Hand it is an Accident of Fortune.
> Mel. No, Marriage is rather like a Game at Bowls, Fortune indeed makes the Match, and the two nearest, and sometimes the two farthest are together, but the Game depends intirely upon Judgement.

The song sung at this point sounds the familiar *carpe diem* note, and after a first stanza which warns: *"Thus, in doubting, she refuses;/And not winning, thus she loses,"* the second stanza concludes: *"Think, O think o'th' sad Condition,/To be past, yet wish Fruition"* (140, 141). In short, to refuse to play the game for fear of losing is to risk losing the possibilities for "fruition" altogether, and yet to commit oneself to it is, at least in Cynthia's view, to risk playing the fool, for as she puts it, "tho' Marriage makes Man and Wife one Flesh, it leaves 'em still two Fools; and they become more conspicuous by setting off one another" (140). The "gaming" and "luck" metaphors eventually prove to have a certain thematic significance in the play, but it may suffice for the moment simply to note that what the lovers seek finally to impose on the world is a pattern of their own in defiance of such rational considerations as "Fortune, Portion Settlement," and "Jointures." "Marriage is the Game that we hunt," remarks Mellefont, "and while we think that we only have it in View, I don't see but we have it in our Power," and he proposes to Cynthia that she "run most wilfully and unreasonably away with me this Moment, and be married." But Cynthia, who is more hard-headed and realistic than he, demands that he first provide a "very evident Demonstration of his Wit" in order to prove that he is indeed able to control his world as he "boasted" (170).

Behind the surface lightness of tone of both the earlier and later dialogues between Cynthia and Mellefont there is a sobriety that will to a greater or lesser degree prove to be an important aspect in the relationships of all of Congreve's pairs of lovers from this point on. All of them, in one way or another, face a serious dilemma as to how they are to maintain a life style on their own terms in a world that is either actively hostile and deceptive or frivolously indifferent. And in *The Double-Dealer,* which can probably more accurately be defined as a problem play than a comedy, the infrequent dialogues between the lovers represent isolated efforts at creative living in a society that is otherwise little more than a chaos of meaningless babblings and violent confusions.

In the abstract terms in which they would seem to have been first conceived, what Cynthia and Mellefont stand for, presumably, are the creative and joyous and free possibilities in human relationships as they are pitted against the destructive and divisive forces of the world in a struggle for dominance. Coleridge once took exception to Congreve's comedies by arguing that "Wickedness is no subject for comedy," and that making it his subject "was Congreve's greatest error and peculiar to him,"[16] and to some extent he was right. Although the kind of "wickedness" represented by Lady Touchwood—a destructiveness engendered by jealousy and frustrated love—is to be found, as we have seen, in the plays of Etherege and Wycherley as well (and indeed constitutes a crucial aspect of the challenge with which the *creatively* "wicked" comic spirit must deal), a figure like Maskwell *is* "peculiar" to Congreve; and in his possession of the cold, calculating quality and something of the "motiveless malignity" of an Iago, he does seem out of place in any comic scheme of things.

If, however, we regard *The Double-Dealer* as a further exploration of the dangers of gullibility in a world of deceptions, is it not possible to conclude that Congreve actually saw Maskwell as much the kind of villain of melodrama defined by Eric Bentley, as representing the opposite side of the coin from Bellmour? As already mentioned, the medieval Vice could reveal either destructive or creative potentials—could be either an Ambidexter or a Merygreeke. As master deceiver and manipulator, he could be, in his Machiavellianism, either positive or negative. And he could seek power, as does Bellmour, to the ends of achieving harmony, unity, and life, or as does Maskwell, in the cause of discord, confusion, and death. And nowhere do we have a better opportunity of seeing one potential compared with and distinguished from the other than in the two plays under discussion.

Both Bellmour and Maskwell are continually associated with the devil. Lady Touchwood calls Maskwell alternately "Insolent Devil" and "mollifying Devil," and Mellefont twice suggests, with ironic ignorance, that Lady Touchwood may well be in league with the devil. "O my precious Aunt, and the Devil in Conjunction," he declares on one occasion (145), and later he asserts: "This very next ensuing Hour of eight a Clock, is the last Minute of her Reign, unless the Devil assist her in *propria persona*" (170). But Maskwell's deviltry, unlike Bellmour's, is always directed at arousing and manipulating the angry and destructive passion of jealousy, whether he is dealing with Lady Touchwood herself by working on her "violent passion" for Mellefont—"Death, do you dally with my Passion?" she exclaims to him (132)—or striking through her at Lord Plyant—"Bless me, what makes my Father in such a Passion!—I never saw him thus before," says Cynthia, (142)— or at Lord Touchwood, who says of Mellefont, " 'Death, I'll have him stripp'd and turn'd naked out of my Doors this Moment, and let him rot and perish, incestuous Brute!" (153). Wherever Maskwell's machinations have been felt, there are references to death, incest, and unnaturalness within the family, and exclamations dealing with "Confusion and Hell," "Damnation," "Hell and Damnation," "Death and Furies," "Thou Serpent and first Tempter," "all the Host of Hell."

Like all the vice-figures, Maskwell is a defier of traditional moralities in the name of his own pleasure and profit, but in his hands the beauty and love he seeks become hideously perverted. "Cynthia," he declares, "let thy Beauty gild my Crimes; and whatsoever I commit of Treachery or Deceit, shall be imputed to me as a Merit—Treachery, what Treachery? Love cancels all the Bonds of Friendship, and sets Men right upon their first Foundations." And he goes on to conclude, "Duty to Kings, Piety to Parents, Gratitude to Benefactors, and Fidelity to Friends, are different and particular Ties: But the Name of Rival cuts 'em all asunder, and is a general Acquittance—Rival is equal, and Love like Death an universal Leveller of Mankind" (149). In thus equating love with death he reveals the fundamental negativeness of his outlook. And if we are expected to allow to Cynthia's name its traditional associations, as seems likely from Brisk's passing reference to Lady Plyant as "the very *Cynthia* of the Skies, and Queen of Stars" (209), then Maskwell's perverted view is perhaps still further reinforced by his later instructions to Saygrace: "When *Cynthia* comes, let there be no Light" (201).

Unlike his comic counterparts, Bellmour among them, he does not create marriages but destroys them, and the love he professes to feel for Cynthia would seem to have approximately the same validity as that which Iago expresses for Desdemona. In the Vice tradition, what he seeks is power ("to put *Cynthia* with all her Fortune into my Power") and the pleasure which the feeling of power gives—"oh, 'tis such a Pleasure, to angle for fair fac'd Fools!" (149). In fact the power struggle in the play anticipates the subtler, more complex one that Congreve was later to examine in *The Way of the World*.

Lord Touchwood describes Maskwell (not knowing, of course, to whom he is referring) as "some pitiful Contriver, envious of my Nephew's Merit" (150), and although the statement contains a characteristic underestimation of Maskwell's skills, it nonetheless accurately suggests one of the aspects of his desire for power which confirms his resemblance to Iago—notably the natural antipathy which vice or villainy feels toward virtue and hence the desire to prove that such virtue is, through gullibility or corruptibility, easily controllable.

The more closely we look at Maskwell the more struck we must be with the thinness of the line which separates him from his comic opposite numbers and with the similarity of the assumptions which lie behind his destructive plottings and the creative ones of a Bellmour. To read Bernard Spivack's description of Iago in the present context is surely to bring to mind one as insistently as the other:

> He is *homo emancipatus a Deo,* seeing the world and human life as self-sufficient on their own terms, obedient only to natural law, uninhibited and uninspired by any participation in divinity. In addition to his animal nature, man possesses the equipment of will and reason with which to fulfill or regulate his natural appetites. He is the king of beasts, crowned by his superior faculties. And society,

by the same token, is the arena of endless competition, more or less organized, between the appetites of one man and another, success attending him who knows "how to love himself" and how to manipulate the natures of other men. . . . As for love, it is simply physical appetite mediated by will and guided to fulfillment by libertine cunning. A sensible man of the world serves himself and does himself homage, takes his pleasure and profit wherever he finds them, plays to win by any trick, dissembles his intentions . . . he knows that the world belongs to the worldling, and that human beings, whatever else they may profess, are in reality moved only by egotism, appetite, and personal advantage.[17]

Both a Maskwell and a Bellmour are egotists and self-seekers. Both, on occasion, frankly acknowledge their own rascality. "I don't pretend to Honesty," Maskwell tells Lady Touchwood, "because you know I am a Rascal" (133). Both thrive on making mischief in the cause of pleasure. "What Mischief I do is to be paid with Pleasure," says Maskwell (156). And both gloat in smug self-congratulation over the success of their designs: "This is prosp'rous indeed" (195). Both are master showmen—"I encourag'd it for your Diversion: Tho' it made you a little uneasie for the present, yet the Reflection of it must needs be entertaining" (148)—and see themselves as notable performers—"This was a Master-Piece, and did not need my Help—tho' I stood ready for a Cue to come in and confirm all, had there been Occasion" (153, 154). And both evince infinite confidence in their own inventiveness—"If I gain a little Time, I shall not want Contrivance" (135)— and repeatedly demonstrate their talents for improvisation. With calm objectivity ("a sedate, a thinking Villain") they gather the strings of the world's puppets into their hands and proceed "by Stratagem" to maintain control: "No matter, Sir, don't trouble your Head, all's in my Power" (195).[18]

The difference between them, however, reveals to what diverse ends essentially similar naturalistic assumptions can lead and how fascinatingly double are the potentials of repressed human passions, for if in both instances "passions spin the plot," the passions involved are different ones in each case and are directed to wholly opposite ends. While one manipulator seeks to release bottled-up sensualities for life-giving purposes, the other seeks to release anger and envy to the end of bringing on chaos and destruction. While one takes advantage of self-deceived fools and self-righteous hypocrites, the other preys upon the credulity of innocence: "that hungry Gudgeon Credulity, will bite at any thing" (149). While one laughs in a mood of high spirits and tolerant acceptance, the other laughs with contempt. And while one "seizes the day" to the end of fitting as much life as possible into it, the other regards time as of the essence for keeping passions at their highest destructive and disruptive pitch: "Expedition" is Maskwell's watchword:

> One minute, gives Invention to destroy,
> What, to rebuild, will a whole Age employ.    (135)

Again, we are in a world where nothing can be taken at face value; "Why, let me see, I have the same Face, the same Words and Accents, when I speak what I do think; and when I speak what I do not think—the very same—and dear Dissimulation is the only Art, not to be known from Nature" (149, 150). Maskwell's lines are a sinister echo of Lucy's comic contention in *The Old Batchelor*. In such a world, as Cynthia knows, anyone who seeks to shape life to his own ends must be able to offer a "Demonstration of Wit," and she will allow to Mellefont only one excuse should his "Plot miscarry." "Why if you give me very clear Demonstration that it was the Devil, I'll allow for irresistible Odds. But if I find it to be only Chance, or Destiny, or unlucky Stars, or any thing but the very Devil, I'm inexorable" (171). As it proves, of course, the odds *are* very nearly irresistible, for the lovers are confronted with an opponent who can lay his destructive traps with such devilish cunning that he can make virtually everyone around him see white as black and black as white. Repeatedly, through the whisperings in ears that he contrives behind the scenes, Mellefont is arraigned as an "Unnatural Villain" and a man of "unparallel'd Wickedness," while Maskwell himself acts his own preplanned role in the foreground with such convincing effect that, like Iago, he is continually praised for being "scrupulously honest" and for his "Unequall'd Virtue!" And while he makes treachery appear friendship and friendship treachery, he audaciously tells the truth about his plot to Mellefont in such a way that truth itself is perverted to false ends: *"No Mask like open Truth to cover Lies"* (195). So far as he is concerned, "Why, *qui vult decipi decipiatur*—'Tis no Fault of mine, I have told 'em in plain Terms, how easie 'tis for me to cheat 'em; and if they will not hear the Serpent's Hiss, they must be stung into Experience, and future Caution" (200).

At the opposite extreme to Maskwell, in this world of deceptions and pretenses, stand self-deceived fools like the Plyants, the Froths, and Mr. Brisk; and through them Congreve dramatizes another kind of extreme perversion of human responses with which Mellefont and Cynthia are confronted. The point being made about all these fools would seem to be that they live in a social world so silly and superficial (so "frothy") as to represent a wholesale travesty of the possibilities of love, of laughter, and of wit (whether the term is applied to poetry or invention or simple understanding). In their hands all such possibilities have been completely emptied of meaning. Thus Sir Paul Plyant, whose daughter describes him as "so very silly," complacently takes everyone for what he pretends to be—including Mr. Brisk, whom he regards as "such a merry facetious Person, he, he, he" (177). And while he is laughing in all the wrong contexts, Lord Froth refuses to laugh at all. "There is nothing more unbecoming a Man of Quality, than to Laugh" (129). "But does your Lordship never see Comedies?" asks Mellefont; and Lord Froth replies: "O yes, sometimes,—But I never laugh." And Careless subsequently demands: "Where the Devil's the Wit, in not laughing when a Man has a Mind to't" (130). Brisk's idea of wit, expressed in the same scene, is equally fatuous ("I'Gad, I love to be malicious"); and later he convicts himself of such fatuity even more irrevocably: "Pox on't, why should I disparage my Parts by thinking what to say? None but dull Rogues *think;* witty Men, like rich Fellows, are always ready for all Expences; while your Blockheads, like poor needy Scoundrels, are forced to examine their Stock, and forecast the Changes of the Day. Here she comes, I'll seem not to see her, and try to win her with a new airy Invention of my own, hem!" (178) And meanwhile Lady Froth's ostensibly serious efforts at writing an "Heroick Poem" actually have proved her capable of nothing but a witless and altogether ridiculous invention.

Everything in the world of these five fools, including love, is effectively reduced to mere silliness. "My Lord," exclaims Lady

Froth, "I have been telling *Cynthia,* how much I have been in love with you; I swear I have; I'm not asham'd to own it now; Ah! it makes my Heart leap, I vow I sigh when I think on't: My dear Lord! Ha, ha, ha, do you remember, my Lord? [*Squeezes him by the Hand, looks kindly on him, sighs and then laughs out*" (137). Indeed almost every scene in which these fools appear rings with empty "ha, ha, ha's," and "he, he, he's," which are set against Maskwell's wholly sinister "ha, ha, ha" and which rise to a climax in the affecting love scene between Brisk and Lady Froth:

> L. Froth. . . . But did you talk of Love? O*Parnassus!* Who would have thought Mr. *Brisk* could have been in Love, ha, ha, ha. O Heav'ns I thought you cou'd have no Mistress but the Nine Muses.
> Brisk. No more I have I'gad, for I adore 'em all in your Ladyship —Let me perish, I don't know whether to be splenatick, or airy upon't; the Deuce take me, if I can tell whether I am glad or sorry that your Ladyship has made the Discovery.
> L. Froth. O be merry by all means—Prince *Volscius* in Love! Ha, ha, ha.
> Brisk. O barbarous, to turn me into Ridicule! Yet, ha, ha, ha. The Deuce take me, I can't help laughing my self, ha, ha, ha; yet by Heav'ns I have a violent passion for your Ladyship, seriously.
> L. Froth. Seriously? Ha, ha, ha.
> Brisk. Seriously, ha, ha, ha. Gad I have, for all I laugh.
> L. Froth. Ha, ha, ha! What d'ye think I laugh at? Ha, ha, ha.
> Brisk. Me I'gad, ha, ha.
> L. Froth. No the Deuce take me if I don't laugh at my self; for hang me if I have not a violent Passion for Mr. *Brisk,* ha, ha, ha.
> Brisk. Seriously?
> L. Froth. Seriously, ha, ha, ha.
> Brisk. That's well enough; let me perish, ha, ha, ha. O miraculous, what a happy Discovery. Ah my dear charming Lady *Froth!*
> L. Foth. Oh my adored Mr. *Brisk!*    (179, 180)

In effect, Mellefont and Cynthia are caught between such perversions of poetry and wit and laughter and such foolish masquerades of "seriousness" and "violent Passion" on the one hand and Maskwell's cynical perversions on the other; and their relationship is set against the kind which exists between Brisk and Lady Froth and that which obtains between Maskwell and Lady Touchwood. Faced with such alternatives, Cynthia toys with a grimly ironic conclusion in her speculations: "'Tis not so hard to counter-feit Joy in the Depth of Affliction, as to dissemble Mirth in Company of Fools—Why should I call 'em Fools? The World thinks better of 'em; for these have Quality and Education, Wit and fine Conversation, are receiv'd and admir'd by the World—If not, they like and admire themselves—And why is not that true Wisdom, for 'tis Happiness: And for ought I know, we have misapply'd the Name all this while, and mistaken the Thing: Since

> *If Happiness in Self-content is plac'd,*
> *The Wise are Wretched, and Fools only Bless'd."*      (168, 169)

And much the same sentiment is later echoed by Lord Touchwood when he remarks to Sir Paul Plyant with reference to his being cuckolded: "Don't you know that you're a Fool, Brother?" And then, when Sir Paul answers, "A Fool; he, he, he, you're merry—No, no, not I, I know no such Matter," he goes on to conclude: "Why then you don't know half your Happiness" (197). In short, it is just possible that in a world of passions and deceptions igno-rance is bliss—and also that one perhaps does just as well to sit back complacently and trust to providence to assure a happy outcome.

Sir Paul, in fact, is forever appealing to "Providence" and at-tributing to it whatever he takes to be a welcome turn in his fortunes. But it is, ironically, not providence which brings him "happiness" but his own insistent self-delusion; and the conclusion indicated by the play as a whole is clearly that human fortunes rest to a great extent in human hands and that he who would not be easily duped in a deceitful, naturalistic world must have the wit to seek the causes for his good or bad fortunes in human agencies and at the same time to seize upon whatever possibilities luck or chance may bring his way and put them to service in his own be-half. Presumably it is this recognition which prompts Mellefont's view of marriage ("Marriage is rather like a Game of Bowls, For-tune indeed makes the Match . . . but the Game depends intirely upon Judgement"). And it would seem to be on a similar assump-tion that Cynthia denies to Mellefont any excuse for failure attrib-uted to "Chance, or Destiny, or unlucky Stars" and that Mellefont himself later cries: "O I could curse my Stars, Fate, and Chance; all Causes and Accidents of Fortune in this Life! But to what

Purpose?" (191) To what purpose, indeed, when it is Maskwell who is the real cause. And subsequently it is by taking advantage of her luck in discovering Lady Touchwood and Maskwell in conference that Cynthia is finally able to confirm her suspicions: "this may be lucky—My Lord, let me intreat you to stand behind this Skreen, and listen; perhaps this Chance may give you Proof of what you ne'er could have believ'd from my Suspicions" (204).

Maskwell himself trusts as little as possible to chance and as much as possible to invention ("Thanks, my Invention") and to management ("here comes the Man that I must manage") to bring him the power he seeks, and as for determining the source of his inspirations, about that question he cares very little: "By Heav'n I have it . . . Was it my Brain or Providence? No matter which—I will deceive 'em all, and yet secure my self, 'twas a lucky Thought!" (155) And it is only when Lord Touchwood at last resorts to a counter-invention ("For once, I'll add my Plot too") that he succeeds in trapping his adversary.

Congreve has taken pains to show that Mellefont himself is no simpleminded, gullible fool who will blindly walk into any trap a deceptive world lays for him. He knows from the outset the dangers Lady Touchwood's passion for him poses, and he is on his guard against her. "O, I would have no room for serious Design; for I am jealous of a Plot," he tells Careless. "I would have Noise and Impertinence keep my Lady *Touchwood's* Head from working: for Hell is not more busie than her Brain, nor contains more Devils, than that Imaginations" (125). Yet for all his cynical pronouncements about the deceptiveness and the *"destroying Pow'r"* of women (192), he is unprepared for Maskwell's kind of ingenious, cold-blooded cunning, which defies all "different and particular Ties," and it is finally Careless—a man "a little superstitious in Physiognomy" (127)—who recognizes the treachery.

Perhaps the implication is that it takes a devil to know a devil, for Careless represents the closest approximation that *The Double-Dealer* affords to a genuinely comic protagonist, and in some sense his actions recall those of Bellmour and supply, within the context of this play, a comic parallel and contrast to those of Maskwell, throwing the latter's destructiveness into sharper relief. He too, under cover of friendship, is engaged in treachery. "O Friendship!"

exclaims Lord Plyant, upon discovering Careless's love letter, "What art thou but a Name!" (182) And he is called an "Ungrateful Monster" when discovered. And possessed of the usual cleverness and inventiveness of his kind, he allays Lord Plyant's suspicions by quickly devising an ingenious explanation with which to carry off his plot. In a series of scenes in which his actions are reminiscent of Horner's, he easily takes advantage of Lord Plyant's stupid complacency and, by acting to perfection the role of whining lover, insinuates himself behind Lady Plyant's "honourable" defenses. His victim, however, is "an old fond Husband," and his ends are not, like Maskwell's, the negative ones of dividing and destroying but the positive ones of goodnaturedly helping out a friend and promoting the Mellefont-Cynthia union, while at the same time catering to his own pleasure and to the sexual satisfaction Lady Plyant's virginal pose has kept her from achieving. The scenes devoted to his machinations are not then, as one critic would have it, simply "irrelevant comic interludes of gay social satire."[19] They point up the creative possibilities of such machinations as opposed to the destructive potential of Maskwell.

As the final unmaskings of the play take place, it becomes the predictable role of the fools to look on with uncomprehending astonishment; and we hear Sir Paul exclaiming: "here's the strangest Revolution, all turn'd topsie turvy; as I hope for Providence" (208). Both he and Lord Froth remain blissfully deceived to the end; and Brisk and Lady Froth, complacent in the success of their own little deception, supply, as might be anticipated, a jarringly inappropriate commentary upon the serious proceedings—a commentary which serves once more to underline their own fatuousness and their complete detachment from reality. "This is all very surprising, let me perish," declares Brisk; and Lady Froth adds: "You know I told you *Saturn* look'd a little more angry than usual" (210).

But the proceedings to which they are witnesses do not, after all, emanate from providence or from the stars, and if justice is at last done, it is because one group of plotters has finally outwitted the other. Both Lord Touchwood and Mellefont have adopted disguises and have thereby at last managed to catch the would-be deceivers in their own trap; and only thus have the creative and unifying forces managed to triumph. Lady Touchwood and Maskwell stand finally in appropriate isolation, Maskwell's kinship with Iago being once again pointed up as he meets his fate with an unrepentent taciturnity ("are you silent, Monster?"). And Lord Touchwood's concluding speech lends fitting emphasis to the unity and creative potential of Mellefont and Cynthia as they emerge to assume dominance over the sterility and destructiveness of the villians:

> Let me join your Hands:—Unwearied Nights, and wishing Days attend you both; mutual Love, lasting Health, and circling Joys, tread round each happy Year of your long Lives.
>
> > *Let secret Villany from hence be warn'd;*
> > *Howe'er in private Mischiefs are conceiv'd,*
> > *Torture and Shame attend their open Birth;*
> > *Like Vipers in the Womb, base Treachery lies,*
> > *Still gnawing that, whence first it did arise;*
> > *No sooner born, but the Vile Parent dies.*

The language here, however, is unworthy of Congreve, and in its general flatness it indicates essentially what is wrong with the play as a whole. In dramatic terms the opposition between the positive and negative forces is finally as lacking in genuine tensions as this cliché-ridden poetic sentiment which resolves it, and one is left with the uncomfortable feeling that in reality the destructive forces have been defeated not through Careless's and Mellefont's and Cynthia's controlling hands but through Congreve's. Dramatically speaking, if anyone can be said to carry the day, it is the villains and the fools, for it is apparently they who really interested Congreve in this instance, while the forces for life and love caught in between evidently remained for him as they do for us rather lifeless allegorical representations and hence seem finally undeserving of the triumph given them.

# [ IX ]

## *Love for Love*

---

IMPUNITY, n. Wealth.
VIRTUES, n. pl. Certain abstentions.

AMBROSE BIERCE, *The Devil's Dictionary*

IN SPITE OF ITS RATHER SIMPLE PLOT LINE, CONGREVE'S THIRD PLAY IS
perhaps his most complex, weaving as it does into an elaborate and
at times confusing pattern the themes of dishonesty and truth, freedom and restriction, sanity and madness. As a part of this pattern,
both the hero and the heroine, while they retain many of the essential and familiar characteristics of the comic protagonist, also reveal
in certain passages a rather disconcerting philosophical seriousness.
In this connection, in fact, William Van Voris, following up a suggestion made by Norman Holland as to the Lockean overtones to
be found, regards the play as Congreve's rather sardonic putting
to the test of Locke's conclusions.[1] Yet the comic element has not
on this account faded wholly into the background. The comic challenge is, it is true, being given in rather different terms, but the artfulness and egotism, the impudence and earthiness, the balance
between detachment and involvement characteristic of the comic
spirit still belong to Valentine and Angelica, and it is upon the
machinations of one or the other of them that much of the dramatic
situation hinges. Nor is their world, in the last analysis, any less
naturalistic than that of their predecessors.

The situation that confronts us at the outset is the familiar one of an unnatural confinement—a situation which is of course often basic to a comic scheme. In this instance the result of the restriction has been the denial to Valentine of the Lockean "Life, Liberty, and Property." The "forc'd Confinement" to which he is subjected by the "unnatural Usage" of his father has to do with cutting him off from his inheritance and hence with depriving him of his right to live and love freely (having obliged him to shut himself away from his clamorous creditors and hence also from Angelica). Like Wycherley's Hippolita, he has been put under "Restraint" just in his "rambling age," and has been, as his servant Jeremy puts it, reduced to "Starving and Poverty" (220). And when he ventures to tax his father with the "Barbarity" of such a course, Sir Sampson exclaims: "Impudence! Why, Sirrah, mayn't I do what I please? Are not you my Slave? . . . How came you here, Sir? Here, to stand here, upon those two Legs, and look erect with that audacious Face, hah? Answer me that? Did you come a Volunteer into the World? Or did I, with the lawful Authority of a Parent, press you to the Service?" (250, 251) In short, Sir Sampson represents, in Locke's terms, an unnatural force denying basic human rights and in comic terms, that law and authority against which the audacious spirit of youth is to assert its defiance and its right to freedom and pleasure.

Much the same fundamental opposition obtains also between Angelica and her uncle Foresight, and the words she utters upon her first entrance at once establish her view of things, coming as they do hard on the heels of Foresight's observation that "tis now three a Clock, a very good Hour for Business." "Is it not," she demands, "a good Hour for Pleasure too, Uncle?" (241, 242) To Foresight she is a "Jill-flirt," a "malapert Slut," a "provoking Minx," and he objects: "What, wou'd you be gadding too? Sure all Females are mad today—It is of evil Portent, and bodes Mischief to the Master of a Family—" But Angelica makes merciless fun of his faith in "Prophecy" and retorts: "But my Inclinations are in force; I have a mind to go abroad" (242, 243).

Like Valentine, she represents "la jeunesse même,"[2] and it is characteristic of "l'éternal jeune homme" that his faults, as defined by a conservative and repressive society, have to do with "Love and Pleasurable Expense." In Sir Sampson's view Valentine is an "Ungracious Prodigal" and in Foresight's he is a "Prodigal Spendthrift

Gallant," but it is Valentine's Lockean contention (and also the contention made in the name of youth and of comedy) that his Passions, Inclinations, Affections, Appetites, Senses" are as inborn and natural a part of him as his "Reason." "I am of my self," he argues, "a plain easie simple Creature; and to be kept at small Expence; but the Retinue that you gave me are craving and invincible; they are so many Devils that you have rais'd, and will have Employment" (251). And he goes on to point out that "Fortune was provident enough to supply all the Necessities of my Nature; if I had my right of Inheritance" (252). Angelica represents to him "Riches, Health and Liberty at once, to a despairing, starving, and abandon'd Wretch" (303), and it is his father's severity, his failure in "civil government," which has at once condemned his son's appetites to starvation and cut him off from his life-giving love.

And in fact Sir Sampson proposes to cut his son off still more irrevocably by vengefully marrying Angelica himself. Full of a wholly "unreasonable" confidence in his own physical prowess, he would, ironically, deny to his son the very liberty of "going abroad" and taking his pleasure which he prides himself on having enjoyed. "I tell you," he proclaims boastfully to Foresight, "I have travell'd old *Fircu,* and know the Globe. I have seen the *Antipodes,* where the Sun rises at Midnight, and sets at Noon-Day. . . . I know the length of the Emperor of *China's* foot; have kiss'd the *Great Mogul's* Slipper, and rid a Hunting upon an Elephant with the Cham of *Tartary,*—Body o'me, I have made a Cuckold of a King, and the present Majesty of *Bantam* is the Issue of these Loins" (247). And to Angelica he talks confidently of his "warm Blood" and his "Vigour" and declares: "Odd, *Sampson's* a very good Name for an able Fellow: Your *Sampsons* were strong Dogs from the Beginning." To which Angelica rejoins: "Have a care, and don't over-act your Part—If you remember, *Sampson,* the strongest of the Name, pull'd an old House over his Head at last" (316).

The words amount to both a threat and a warning, were not Sir Sampson too self-deceived by his own vanity to heed them, for the fact obvious to everyone but himself is that he is one of those who, like Foresight, has "a Stomach to a Wedding Supper, when the Pidgeons ought rather to be laid to his Feet" (303). As Ben says of his father, "I fear his Fire's little better than Tinder; may-hap it will only serve to light up a Match for some Body else" (324). And Angelica's warning has a clear parallel with that "Prophecie" which so terrifies Foresight:

> *When Housewifes all the House forsake*
> *And leave good Man to Brew and Bake,*
> *Withouten Guile, then be it said,*
> *That House doth stond upon its Head;*
> *And when the Head is set in Grond,*
> *No marl, if it be fruitful fond.*    (242)

Clearly, both Sir Sampson's and Foresight's "houses" are destined to fall, their "governments" to topple. Both men have lost touch with what Van Voris, pursuing the Lockean overtones, has called "natural association"; and hence they possess "distorted ideas" leading to "wild imaginings."[3] Like Foresight, Sir Sampson would usurp the province that belongs by natural right to youth and would hence supply one more example of the kind of relationship of which Valentine speaks when he prophesies that in the future as in the present "Wives and Husbands will drive distinct Trades, and Care and Pleasure separately occupy the Family" (302).

The entire play is, in fact, concerned with the relationships not only between fathers and children but between wives and husbands, so far as "civil government" is concerned; and nearly all such relationships in the play fail deplorably, in one way or another, to achieve a balanced unity based on mutual respect for individual right. The title of the play suggests what both kinds of relationship ought to involve and what Valentine and Angelica at last give promise of achieving. And for all his "Fustian," Tattle accurately expresses the suitability of their match when he remarks: "you will pardon me, if from a just weight of his Merit, with your Ladiship's good Judgment, I form'd the Ballance of a reciprocal Affection" (263).

It is just this "Ballance of a reciprocal Affection" which is missing in virtually all the other family relationships in the play and which leads to disunity and strife. Poor foolish Foresight, for all his concern with being "the Master of a Family," seldom finds himself with any family of which to be master. "What," he exclaims typically, "are all the Women of my Family abroad? Is not my Wife come home? Nor my Sister, nor my Daughter?" And that daughter to whom he refers finds that the woman she should reasonably call her mother is eager to disclaim any such relationship:

> MISS. Mother, Mother, Mother, look you here.
> MRS. FORE. Fie, fie, Miss, how you bawl—Besides, I have told you, you must not call me Mother.
> MISS. What must I call you then, are you not my Father's Wife?
> MRS. FORE. Madam; you must say Madam—By my Soul, I shall fancy my self old indeed, to have this great Girl call me Mother—
> (256)

In the matter of denying parenthood, however, it is Sir Sampson who is, of course, the chief offender. "Why, who are you, Sir?" he asks Valentine at one point. And when the reply comes, "Your Son, Sir," he continues: "That's more than I know, Sir, and I believe not" (250). The only balances which obtain between Valentine and his father are of a wholly negative kind and serve only to set them against each other. Thus Valentine in his "madness" finds occasion to match his father's rejection with a denial of his own. "Who is that?" he inquires. To which Sir Sampson cries, "Gads bobs, does he not know me? . . . I am thy own Father," and Valentine rejoins: "It may be so—I did not know you" (291). In an earlier scene, when Valentine has had ample reason to speak sardonically of Sir Sampson's "Fatherly Fondness," Sir Sampson himself suggests that "your filial Piety, and my fatherly Fondness wou'd fit like two Tallies" (249). And toward the end of the play, upon Valentine's admitting his "Counterfeit" madness and Sir Sampson's subsequent exclamation, "what to cheat me? to cheat your Father?" it is again Valentine's turn to point out the logical *quid pro quo*: "Indeed, I thought, Sir, when the Father endeavour'd to undo the Son, it was a reasonable return of Nature" (327, 328). Nor is Sir Sampson's relationship with his other son a great deal different. So far as Ben is concerned, if his father addresses him "in a surly sort of manner," he has every right to return the compliment ("and Gad I answer'd 'en as surlily"); and when Mrs. Frail self-righteously reproaches him, "And were you this undutiful and graceless Wretch to your Father?" he retorts, "Then why was he graceless first" (299).

Sir Sampson, by consistently practicing an absolute and overbearing authoritarianism, misuses his strength and seeks to impose his will in opposition to the natural inclinations of both his sons. "What, I warrant my Son thought nothing belong'd to a Father, but Forgiveness and Affection; no Authority, no Correction, no Arbitrary Power" (246). "Arbitrary Power" is, of course, precisely what he exercises, and rebellion is the natural result. "What tho'f he be my Father," Ben protests, "I an't bound Prentice to 'en:—so faith I told'n in plain Terms, if I were minded to marry, I'd marry to please my self, not him" (298). It is not the son but the father who is lacking in "natural affection" and who "has not a Drachm of generous Love about him" (268), and the concern that Sir Sampson manifests over Valentine's madness—"Miracle! the Monster grows loving," says Scandal (293)—turns out, as might have been expected, to have its basis in self-interest, in his own desire to manage his disinheritance proceedings expeditiously.

Valentine, in point of fact, reveals more genuine concern and affection for his bastard son than does Sir Sampson for his own legally begotten offspring, and it is presumably with an eye to pointing up the contrast that Congreve introduces that strange little scene in Act I in which a wet nurse seeks admittance to Valentine with "one of your Children from *Twitnam*." For all his reduced circumstances and hence his understandable anger at so untimely a visitor ("cou'd she find no other time to fling my Sins in my Face"),[4] he nonetheless *"Gives Mony,"* and Scandal, as Godfather, follows suit ("My blessing to the Boy, with this Token . . . of my Love"). And when Scandal suggests that the nurse "not work so hard, that she may not smell so vigorously," Valentine cautions, "Scandal, don't spoil my Boy's Milk" (225, 226). *His* son's appetites are to have their satisfaction.

Thematically such a scene reveals what Congreve evidently assumes to be a natural human reaction where the father-son relationship is concerned, with Valentine taking for granted his responsibility as Sir Sampson (who is "inhuman" and a "Monster") does not. Both Scandal and Valentine are putting money to the uses of life and love rather than subordinating life and love to monetary considerations, and Valentine's behavior here anticipates his profession toward the end of the play that "I never valu'd Fortune, but as it was surservient to my Pleasure" (328), with this earlier instance of his loving and "generous" nature paralleling the later one.

The central question which the play asks, however, is whether either naturalness or any kind of honesty is often possible in human relationships given a world where people almost invariably behave inhumanly, unnaturally, dishonestly, and where interest is the dominant motive. And in this connection the deliberate contrast drawn in the subplot between Ben and Prue is instructive. Ben is childlike, and Prue actually is a child. But while Ben is determined to retain his innocence and to remain at liberty to follow his own inclinations and to speak his mind, Prue gives promise of being willing to adapt readily to civilized duplicities and ultimately of becoming yet another hypocrite on the pattern of Mrs. Foresight and Mrs. Frail.

Ben's mode of life is closely akin to Manly's in that he chooses to rebel against social dishonesties in a "plain and honest" way and to abandon the civilized world altogether in favor of the open seas and an essentially solitary existence. "I'll tell you why I don't much stand toward Matrimony," he says. "I love to roam about from Port to Port, and from Land to Land: I could never abide to be Portbound, as we call it: Now a man that is marry'd, has as it were, d'ye see, his Feet in the Bilboes, and may-hap mayn't get 'em out again when he wou'd. . . . A Man that is marry'd, d'ye see, is no more like another Man, than a Gally-Slave is like one of us free Sailors, he is chain'd to an Oar all his Life; and may-hap forc'd to tug a leaky Vessel into the Bargain" (270). All of Ben's language is filled not only with the predictable sea and sailing imagery, but with frequent references to free and unfettered motion as opposed to restraint, and with constant "look you's" and "d'ye see's" that suggest the clearsightedness and honesty of his nature.

More than one critic has commented that, for all his dramatic liveliness, he is actually out of place in the play, and certainly he hardly seems to belong to a drawing-room setting. As Sir Sampson says, "he wants a little polishing" (270). But in terms of the play's central themes, his being out of place is exactly the point, and Congreve has deliberately drawn him in such a way as to make him stand apart from a world in which his kind of freedom and candor is far to seek. He is innocent, completely devoid of artfulness. Possessed of a kind of natural wit and given to a wholly truthful assessment of the follies he encounters, he is basically childlike in his reactions and is quick to anger when his own good-natured honesty of response fails to inspire a like one.

But he is also, by the same token, hopelessly gullible and hence ill-equipped to deal with the ways of a deceitful and self-seeking, indeed a "monstrous," world. What he expects from others is the same balance of give and take by which he himself naturally and instinctively lives. When, for example, Sir Sampson asserts, "I would not marry for thy sake," he replies with characteristic straightforwardness: "Nay, what does that signifie?—an you marry again—Why then, I'll go to Sea again, so there's one for t'other" (270). And later he declares: "I mean all in good part: For if I give a Jest, I'll take a Jest: And so Forsooth you may be as free with me" (271). He thus proposes to live always by the honest tit-for-tat morality of the sea. "The short of the thing is," he informs Miss Prue, "that if you like me, and I like you, we may chance to swing in a Hammock together" (272). And when her response is to call him an "ugly thing," he declares: "if you shou'd give such Language at Sea, you'd have a Cat o' Nine Tails laid cross your Shoulders" (273). But such are not the ways of civilization, and having narrowly escaped from being ensnared by the devious, money-minded Mrs. Frail, whose flatteries he has accepted at face value, honest Ben has little recourse but to reject that civilization and return to the sea where he has been bred and where there is some truth to his conviction that "it's but a Folly to lie" (272).

On her first appearance Prue is also an innocent, having until the present moment "never been out of the Country" (237), but unlike Ben she shows an immediate aptitude for the kind of education in deceit that Tattle has to offer. At first, she seems to resemble Margery Pinchwife. She has the same frankly physical nature and the same naive assumption that what she wants she will get. And her journey from country to town represents, as in Wycherley, what may be regarded as a journey from innocence to experience. But in Prue's case the journey carries with it a turning from open-hearted honesty to calculating deceitfulness.

Thus Tattle becomes her initiator into the ways of maturity, as she begins to explore the possibilities of adult experience: "I warrant she's fond o' seeing the Town," remarks her nurse (241)—possibilities which, once recognized, are not to be easily set aside. "What, must I go to Bed to Nurse again," she protests, when her hopes in Tattle have failed to materialize, "and be a Child as long as she's an old Woman? Indeed but I won't. For now my mind is set upon a Man, I will have a Man some way or other" (321). It is, appropriately, her nurse who "saves" her from succumbing to the first seductive threat that she encounters, and the confined position at which she finally arrives reaffirms the dilemma that confronts all youthful and free inclinations in a repressive, authoritarian adult social world. "Here take your young Mistress, and lock her up presently," Foresight bids her nurse, "'till farther Orders from me—" (322). In Miss Prue's case, however, the chances are that she will not stay locked up for long, not because like Ben she will abandon the social world but because she has taken to the dishonesties of civilization and adulthood with instant enthusiasm. "I like it better than our old fashion'd Country way of speaking one's Mind . . ." she tells Tattle, "I always had a great Mind to tell Lies—but they frighted me, and said it was a Sin" (260).

Ben, for his part, really escapes the dilemma by choosing to remain a child—to avoid a commitment to civilization and to retreat to the world of innocence whence he has come. He is for the undisciplined, instinctive life of "us free sailors" ("the happiest, merriest Men alive"), with lusty ballads and rollicking dances and appetites readily satisfied. "We're merry Folks, we Sailors, we han't much to care for. Thus we live at Sea; eat Bisket, and drink Flip; put on a clean Shirt once a Quarter—Come home, and lye with our Land-ladies once a Year, get rid of a little Mony; and then put off with the next fair Wind" (285).

The main plot offers, however, an alternative other than Ben's for remaining true to oneself and retaining the freedom to speak one's mind—an alternative which does not involve abandoning the civilized world—and that is accepting the challenge which Sir Sampson unconsciously voices when he bids Valentine to "live by your Wits" (253). It is this challenge which is taken up in various ways by Valentine and Angelica, Jeremy and Scandal, all of whom live by design in a designing world while never succumbing to self-deception or hypocrisy. All of them are at one time or another called "rogues," and all are bent on remaining free to pursue their own life and pleasure—their own honest inclinations—amid the prevailing atmosphere of deceit and of the arbitrary exercise of authority. And all are, finally, completely realistic in recognizing the pitfalls all around them and the need for artfulness and cunning in a world where it will always be true, as Valentine puts it, that "Knaves will thrive thro' Craft, and Fools thro' Fortune; and Honesty will go as it did, Frost-nipt in a Summer Suit" (302).

It is true that Scandal's frankness at first appears to be a kind of misanthropic plain dealing in the Manly vein. The "Pictures" he draws are all "Satires, Descriptions, Characters, and Lampoons," and he is as outspoken in his pronouncements as is Ben. "I love to speak my Mind," he tells Mrs. Foresight at the end of Act III, scene xiv. And as the ensuing scene between Ben and Mrs. Frail commences, we hear Ben echoing the same sentiment, almost word for word: "Mess, I love to speak my Mind." In neither case is the practice likely to lead to prosperity, and at one point the piqued Valentine cautions Scandal as to the danger: "*Scandal,* learn to spare your Friends, and do not provoke your Enemies; this Liberty of your Tongue, will one Day bring a Confinement on your Body, my Friend" (225).

As it proves, however, Scandal is considerably more worldly wise and calculating in his plain dealing than at first appears, and when Mrs. Foresight says accusingly, "you have a villainous Character; you are a Libertine in Speech, as well as Practice," he sounds, in his response, a good deal more like a Horner than a Manly: "you mistake, the Liberty I take in talking, is purely affected, for the Service of your Sex. He that first cries out stop Thief, is often he that has stol'n the Treasure. I am a Jugler, that act by Confederacy; and if you please, we'll put a Trick upon the World" (282). Like Horner he thoroughly enjoys his reputation for being "impudent" and a "devil" and delights in playing tricks on fools like Foresight "in the Name of Love and Pleasure" (279). And he has equally few illusions as to the meaningfulness of words such as "Conscience and Honour" with which Mrs. Foresight momentarily holds him off: "Why, Honour is a publick Enemy; and Conscience a Domestick Thief; and he that wou'd secure his Pleasure, must pay a Tribute to one, and go halves with t'other" (281). Indeed he is a considerably purer comic character than is the often rather serious Valentine, and the remark that Holland unaccountably attributes to Valentine actually belongs to him ("I know of no effectual difference between continued Affection and Reality" [262])[5] and is a part of that insistently realistic outlook which recognizes human identities for the elusive and inconstant things they are.

The kind of world with which Scandal is equipped to deal, then, is that of a Mrs. Foresight and a Mrs. Frail—both women who are constantly contriving to "put a Trick upon the World" and both representatives of a selfish, mercenary, hypocritical society. Mrs. Foresight at one point exclaims to her friend: "I'll swear you can keep your Countenance purely, you'd make an admirable Player," and Mrs. Frail retorts: "I'll swear you have a great deal of Confidence, and in my Mind too much for the Stage" (254). Both, in fact, are well versed in the ways of the deceptive adult world. But although they can manage to trap a gullible "Booby" like Ben easily enough, they are not so successful when they fix their sights on Valentine as a still more lucrative prospect, for then they encounter plotters too clever for them, and the deceivers are handily outdeceived.

Indeed they all become unwittingly the subject for a comedy of Scandal's and Jeremy's devising. With all the bold effrontery of their comic kind, the two rogues contrive a means of using the vanity and the mercenary motives of both Tattle and Mrs. Frail to create an entertaining little diversion for themselves. "It may make us sport," says Scandal (301), falling back on the time-honored expression of the self-satisfied mischief-maker, and in Jeremy he has a collaborator who is no mean wit in his own right.

In many respects Jeremy is simply a later version of Bellmour's Setter in *The Old Batchelor,* but with Setter's earthy, appetitive nature and impudent self-confidence, he combines an educated intelligence—"I have the Seeds of Rhetorick and Oratory in my Head —I have been at *Cambridge*" (317)—and a seemingly inexhaustible capacity for turning out witty similes. And the point seems to be that he is, ironically, a good deal wittier and a good deal wiser in the ways of the world than men like Sir Sampson and Foresight, each of whom prides himself on his superior wisdom. For all that he "was born in a Cellar" of a father who was a "Chairman" and a mother who "sold Oisters in Winter, and Cucumbers in Summer" (252), he is made up of the same basic ingredients—carries the same "huge Train of Attendants"—as Valentine himself, and the implication is that he is fully justified in maintaining with equal outspokenness his objection to their being starved and impoverished.

It is the eminently sensible, practical-minded Jeremy who protests against the first role in which Valentine chooses to cast himself to the end of avoiding starvation. As the play opens, Valentine is playing the philosopher. A book in his hand, he is heard bidding Jeremy go "to Breakfast," while he himself continues to pore over Epictetus, which he calls "a Feast for an Emperor": "refine your Appetite," he advises, "learn to live upon Instruction; feast your Mind, and mortifie your Flesh; Read, and take your Nourishment in at your Eyes; shut up your Mouth, and chew the Cud of Understanding." But Jeremy remains unconvinced. "You'll grow devilish fat upon this Paper Diet," he sneers. "Will *Plato* be Bail for you? Or *Diogenes,* because he understands Confinement, and liv'd in a Tub, go to Prison for you? 'Slife, Sir, what do you mean, to mew your self up here with three or four musty Books, in Commendation of Starving and Poverty?" And when Valentine next proposes to "write a Play," Scandal joins with Jeremy in proclaiming the impracticality of such a line of action: "Impotent and vain! Who would die a Martyr to Sense in a Country where the Religion is Folly? . . . No, turn Pimp, Flatterer, Quack, Lawyer, Parson, be Chaplain to an Atheist, or Stallion to an old Woman, any thing but Poet; a Modern Poet is worse, more servile, timorous, and fawning, than any I have nam'd: Without you could retrieve the Ancient Honours of the Name, recall the Stage of *Athens,* and be allow'd the Force of open honest Satire" (223, 224).

Yet to "write a Play" is, in a manner of speaking, just what Valentine does; and he contrives his own role in such a way as to satisfy Scandal's conditions—to "be allow'd the Force of open honest Satire." By "playing the Madman" (286) and proclaiming "I am Truth" (291), he achieves much the same sort of freedom to arraign his society directly and aggressively that was enjoyed by Horner in his assumed impotence and hence innocence. Ben, as a genuine innocent, can "speak his mind" on social and sexual matters with the kind of childlike openness which belonged to Margery Pinchwife and which is indulged (he "wants a little polishing") without calling down on itself the repressive wrath of a civilized world—a world in which "All well-bred Persons Lie" (259). But in a case like Valentine's, where his prosperity depends on social acceptance and where there has been a clear commitment to the adult world, free speaking is only possible by indirection (his own awareness of this fact being plainly indicated by his earlier warning to Scandal), and thus his pretended madness becomes a device to win him the indulgence he requires. Ben's "Sea-Wit" may be heard unprotestingly, but Valentine can only find an audience for his kind of wit and sense by pretending to be "out of his wits." "He is indeed here, Sir, and not here, Sir . . . he has lost himself," Jeremy informs Sir Sampson (290). Hence he can no longer be held accountable for his words and actions. Strictly speaking, they are no longer his. And safe in his lie, he gives voice unsparingly to the truth; secure in his "Masque of Madness" (308), he becomes a "Poet" who "frankly speaks his Mind," and undertakes the "bold Essay" ("to lash this Crying Age"), as Congreve himself has declared in the Prologue that he was setting out to do in his own play.

But Valentine's "Project" has also, of course, more practical ends in view, and it is to the attainment of these ends that Scandal and Jeremy lend their ingenuity. As expert actors, they assume principal roles. "You are witty, you Rogue, I shall want your Help," Valentine has earlier told Jeremy in connection with his intentions of becoming a playwright (221). The design he has contrived is one whereby he may at once be able to hold Sir Sampson and his lawyer at bay and trick Angelica into declaring her love—and thus retain his fortune and gain his love at a single stroke. By pretending to be out of his senses, he plans to create a world governed by wit rather than by folly and one in which fortune will be "subservient to Pleasure," in short, one in which his appetites will find their satisfaction. "You know your Cue" (289), Scandal tells Jeremy, as they take up their parts under Valentine's direction, and so far as their designs on Sir Sampson are concerned, all goes well.

But in thinking himself capable of so easily outwitting Angelica, Valentine has reckoned without the strength of an adversary who is as determined as he to remain her own master. "He has a Mind to try, whether his playing the Madman, won't make her play the Fool, and fall in Love with him," Jeremy explains to Scandal. But instead of achieving "Love for Love" by means of his comedy of deceptions, he finds himself played "Trick for Trick" (288). "I am not the Fool you take me for;" Angelica assures him, "and you are mad, and don't know it" (311). And she thereupon neatly turns his play inside out. Proving as expert as he in acting a role and having discovered his trick, she at once sets about contriving a design of her own. She is, indeed, as Sir Sampson pronounces her, "cunning, a wary Baggage" (315), with an inventiveness which is more than a match for Valentine's own. And even while her design is only beginning to take shape, she manages to prove as elusive in her sanity as Valentine in his "madness." The balances are virtually perfect. She too can seem to be "both here . . . and not here." "What is she gone, Sir?" Jeremy asks Scandal, and he rejoins, "Gone; why she was never here, nor any where else; nor I don't know her if I see her; nor you neither." Whereupon Jeremy exclaims: "Good lack! What's the matter now? Are any more of us to be mad?" (289).

In short, this is a world in which not only do sons not know their fathers or fathers their sons, but hardly anyone really knows either himself or anyone else. As Van Voris points out, Congreve is here playing Locke's treatises against one another. In a world where each individual has created out of "the ideas that filter through his imperfect senses . . . a private reality," the resulting "government looks anything but civil; the human capacity for misunderstanding seems infinite; and the age of reason dawns on madness."[6]

Thus, in the final acts we are bearing witness to the madness of an entire society, virtually every one of the members of which seems to be "mad for want of his Wits," and hence operating at cross-purposes to everyone else. "All mad, I think—" says Ben to Mrs. Frail; "Flesh, I believe all the *Calentures* of the Sea are come ashore, for my part" (297, 298). And not long afterward, he has occasion to think Mrs. Frail mad as well: "O Lord, O Lord, she's mad, poor young Woman, Love has turn'd her Senses" (299). The fever seems to spread alarmingly. "Heav'n keep us all in our Senses —" cries Foresight, "I fear there is a contagious Frenzy abroad. . . . Well, I shall run mad next" (322). And he asks of Ben regarding Sir Sampson's and Angelica's rumored match: "Well, but they are not mad, that is, not Lunatick?" To which Ben replies: "I don't know what you call Madness—But she's mad for a Husband, and

he's horn mad, I think, or they'd ne'er make a Match together"
(323).

What Angelica does, in these terms, is to take over and extend
Valentine's "comedy," casting him for her own purposes as the real
madman of the piece. "Nay Faith, now let us understand one another, Hypocrisie apart—" he protests. "The Comedy draws toward
an end, and let us think of leaving acting, and be our selves . . . I tell
you the Farce is done" (308, 309). But her tricks are still to be
played, and if Valentine's comedy is over, hers has just begun.
"Wou'd any thing, but a Madman, complain of Uncertainty?" she
asks; "Uncertainty and Expectation are the Joys of Life. Security
is an insipid thing, and the overtaking and possessing of a Wish,
discovers the Folly of the Chase. Never let us know one another
better; for the Pleasure of a Masquerade is done, when we come to
shew our Faces" (310, 311).

The dilemma here is the same as that which confronted Vainlove
and Araminta in *The Old Batchelor*. Angelica too harbors a "fear
of disillusion," and her praise of "Uncertainty" finds an echo in
Scandal's "Opinion" a few lines further on

> *That Women are like Tricks by slight of Hand,*
> *Which, to admire, we should not understand.*    (311)

And earlier, in reply to her question "Do you know me, *Valentine?*" her "mad" lover has replied: "You're a Woman,—One to
whom Heav'n gave Beauty, when it grafted Roses on a Briar. You
are the Reflection of Heav'n in a Pond, and he that leaps at you is
sunk" (306). Nor does the song that he thereupon asks to have sung
("the Song that I like") offer much reassurance:

I.

> *I tell thee, Charmion, could I Time retrieve,*
> *And could again begin to Love and Live,*
> *To you I should my earliest Off-ring give;*
> *I know, my Eyes would lead my Heart to you,*
> *And I should all my Vows and Oaths renew,*
> *But to be plain, I never would be true.*

II.

> *For by our weak and weary Truth, I find,*
> *Love hates to center in a Point assign'd;*

*But runs with Joy the Circle of the Mind.*
*Then never let us chain what shou'd be free,*
*But for Relief of either Sex agree:*
*Since Women love to change, and so do we.*

Truth in this play apparently carries, as in Wycherley, the double sense of honesty and fidelity, and in both senses, experience has shown it to be "weak and weary." Thus Angelica is justifiably on her guard and is determined to know the truth of Valentine's professions before she will allow him to "know her" for what she really feels—and she is equally determined not to be denied her own right to independence and freedom: "you must pardon me, if I think my own Inclinations have a better Right to dispose of my Person, than yours" (328). Revelling in a consciousness of her own cleverness and in her power to know the real world and to make it her plaything (as witness her impudent and rather coarsely suggestive taunting of Foresight early in the play), she unscrupulously sets out to demonstrate that she can outwit her witty lover and beat him at his own game.

As in *The Old Batchelor* there are two requirements for guarding against disillusion in a civilized and deceptive world—and in this case a rather ironically Lockean world made up of multiple "private realities" and in which self-interest is the primary human motive. One is "cunning"; the other is "wariness" (a wariness which, with whatever reluctance, banishes all illusions at the outset and accepts no professions without testing their truth). The obvious foils to the hero and heroine in this regard are Tattle and Mrs. Frail, who having dreamed of (and indeed intrigued toward) marriage with Angelica and Valentine respectively, end finally by being "trickt . . . into one another." Hence it becomes quite literally the case with them that "the Pleasure of a Masquerade is done, when we come to shew our Faces." Having flung off their disguises, they can confront each other only with dismay. The balance to which the machinations of Scandal and Jeremy have led is, in this instance, the ironic one of "interest for interest," and Tattle's "Constancy" bids fair to be short-lived. "If the Gentleman is in Disorder for want of a Wife," he remarks of Sir Sampson, "I can spare him mine" (330). And meanwhile both Sir Sampson and Foresight have also suffered from a severe disillusion. In Sir Sampson's case the gap between what he is and what he thinks himself to be and in Foresight's that between what he knows and what he thinks he knows proves a grotesquely wide one. Both have "over-acted their parts," and in the end Sir Sampson states the truth for both of them: "You're an illiterate old Fool, and I'm another" (330).

Given a world of unstable identities, of men and women who "love to change," and of passions which are "unreasonable and involuntary" (289), constancy is seldom found and commitment to marriage can only be regarded as dangerous. If it is possible to find a "Heav'n" at all, it is only possible by first knowing all pitfalls and then by picking one's way warily among them. "I . . . know you both," says Angelica finally to Sir Sampson and his son, and it is only on the basis of that knowledge that she at last resolves to "have done dissembling" and to make known her own true feelings. Only when Valentine shows himself capable of the ultimate madness of placing love before "Interest" (" 'Sdeath," exclaims Scandal, "you are not mad indeed, to ruin your self?" [328]) does he make a gesture extreme enough to convince the skeptical Angelica. Only then does the harmonious "Love for Love" balance and unity become possible; and only then does Scandal, as master of the revels, call up the dancers: "methinks 'tis pity they shou'd not be employ'd when the Match is so much mended. *Valentine,* tho' it be Morning, we may have a Dance" (330). And even at this point Angelica, like Etherege's Harriet, remains cautious: "Have a Care of Promises;" she tells Valentine, "you know you are apt to run more in Debt than you are able to pay."

And after all, is such a balance really possible beyond the confines of a stage? Van Voris has pointed out that Valentine's constancy is referred to by Angelica as a " '*Miracle*' that works only for '*to Day*,' "[7] and is not Congreve finally telling us by means of the extravagant and romanticizing closing professions of his comic protagonists that we are being supplied with a kind of storybook ending? He has given us fair warning in the Prologue as to the satiric intent of his play:

> *Since the* Plain-Dealer's *Scenes of Manly Rage,*
> *Not one has dar'd to lash this Crying Age.*
> *This time, the Poet owns the bold Essay,*
> *Yet hopes there's no Ill-manners in his Play.*

In short, *The Plain Dealer* was in Congreve's mind as he wrote, and again there is the implication that it is "only on Stages that we see/ Truth pleasing or rewarded Honesty." Like Fidelia's, Valentine's and Angelica's very names mark them as the characters of romance; and if their fate is exemplary, it is also rare. Only the isolated example of Angelica has converted Scandal (leading him to confess that "all Women are not like Fortune, blind in bestowing Favours"), and in Angelica's words "How few, like *Valentine,* would persevere even to Martyrdom and sacrifice their Interest to their Constancy!" He is, that is to say, as much a "Miracle" as Angelica herself—and also, by implication, that ideal balance of "Love for Love" that they at last achieve.

# [ X ]

# The Way of the World

MARRIAGE, n. The state or condition of a community consisting
of a master, a mistress and two slaves, making in all, two.
REPARTEE, n. Prudent insult in retort. Practiced by gentlemen
with a constitutional aversion to violence, but a strong
disposition to offend.

—AMBROSE BIERCE, *The Devil's Dictionary*

THE FORMIDABLY SOPHISTICATED HERO AND HEROINE OF CONGREVE'S
last comedy (1700) would seem to have come a long way indeed
from the audacious, ebullient, down-to-earth world of Sir Frederick
Frollick and a longer way still from the primitive high spirits of the
earlier English comic rogues. And in fact John Palmer has gone so
far as to assert of Congreve's plays that they have virtually nothing
English about them. "The root of his comic appeal," he writes, "is in
the pretense that man has no feeling deeper than an epigram may
carry; no aspiration higher than a fine coat may express; no impulse
sharper than a smile may cover; no joy more thrilling than a nod
may contain; no sorrow bitterer than a pretty oath may convey....
Certainly it cannot be said that the plays of Congreve struck an
English vein."[1]

If *The Way of the World* included none but characters like Witwoud and Petulant, Palmer's assertions about Congreve would, presumably, have to be accepted without demur. But to argue such a

lack of depth² in the play as a whole is to allow almost all the true "root of his comic appeal" to go unheeded. Indeed the play loses virtually all its genuine dramatic impact as soon as one fails to sense that if Mirabell is the complete gentleman and Millamant the complete lady, each retains, nonetheless, that core of irrepressible naturalness and aggressive independence and individuality by now sufficiently recognizable, and further that the play which they dominate is fairly bursting with sexual and emotional implications. The human passions constitute the very center of both impact and meaning (nowhere in Restoration comedy do passions more clearly "spin the plot"); and we will do well at the outset to recall Bernard Harris's characterization of Congreve's language rhythm as "the articulation . . . of an inexhaustible human energy, a 'refinement' fuelled upon gross matter."

What Mirabell and Millamant represent, in effect, is the ultimate step in a refining process that we have seen to have been going on in Restoration comedy. Mirabell is characterized by a beautifully finished worldliness and self-possession from which all the blatant crudity of a Sir Frederick Frollick or a Horner and the self-conscious flamboyance and devilishness of a Dorimant have disappeared. Fully aware of the follies and knaveries of his world, he always treads cautiously, while good-naturedly making the best of them, and meanwhile he moves from chocolate house to park, from park to drawing room, with complete savoir-faire and the grace fostered by flexibility and control. The spirit and charm of youth and freedom and life are undeniably his, and no woman in the play can help falling in love with him. As Foible says, "Mr. *Mirabell* is such a sweet winning Gentleman" (383). For all that his libertinism is already behind him as the play opens, it is a part of his nature, and he is not above making use of his seductive powers when the occasion demands.

It is Millamant, however, who is the real master (or rather, mistress) of the revels, and perhaps Mirabell's own summation is the only wholly adequate one: "Think of you! To think of a Whirlwind, tho' 'twere in a Whirlwind, were a Case of more steady Contemplation" (375). From the moment when she "sails" onto the stage, she is in perpetual motion, shamelessly indulgent in her own capriciousness and quite outrageously egotistical and overbearing.

"I please my self," she announces; and that, so far as she is concerned, is that. She will have the world on her own terms or not at all—a place beautiful and exciting and free, a poem of her own making. And she is forever acting the part of herself and at the same time standing back to admire the result. The prosaic world is altogether too dull an atmosphere in which to be able to draw breath. Love letters will do for pinning up one's hair, but only "those in Verse . . . I never pin up my Hair with Prose" (371).

As the play begins, however, neither Millamant nor Mirabell has succeeded in making prevail within their chaotically passionate world the kind of artistry each has achieved on the individual level. As in *Love for Love,* the family of which they are a part is a kind of representation in little of a society, and the play examines the manner in which authority is asserted and the human emotions expressed within its bounds. The power structure is continually being altered and forced into varying realignments depending on which of the family members is able to exert the greatest control, and the question finally being posed (much the same one as in *The Double-Dealer*) has to do with whether a creative or a destructive rule will triumph.

In these terms the key male opposition is that between Mirabell and Fainall, and it is they whom we see maneuvering for position as the play opens, with fortune for the moment favoring the latter. "You are a fortunate Man, Mr. *Fainall*," Mirabell remarks in the opening line with immediate reference to a game of cards, and as it proves in the ensuing dialogue, Mirabell has at this point lost also in the larger social game being played—a loss due significantly not to fortune but to the treachery of Fainall's "friend" Mrs. Marwood. Hence Mirabell has been at this juncture assigned to a position outside that central circle in which the power of the family resides and inside which Millamant stands as the sought-after prize. "Seeing me," Mirabell says to Fainall, "they all put on their grave Faces, whisper'd one another; then complain'd aloud of the Vapours, and after fell into a profound Silence" (344).

The game in which Mirabell and Fainall are involved is the familiar one of intrigues and deceptions, and Mirabell's latest deceptive maneuver (one reminiscent of Courtall's in *She wou'd if she cou'd,* of which Congreve's play awakens a good many echoes) has only served to separate him further from Millamant. "The Discovery of your sham Addresses to her, to conceal your Love to her Niece, has provok'd this Separation!" Fainall informs him gratuitously. "Had you dissembl'd better, Things might have continu'd in the State of Nature" (345). The aspect of the situation which does not now accord with the "State of Nature" has to do with the exclusion of "all the Male Sex" from the inner circle, and since this unnatural state of affairs has been engineered by Mrs. Marwood, she becomes, with the very first mention made of her, identified as an agent of divisiveness and negativism (a role which her name of course confirms). And thus it is she, along with Fainall, who holds the controlling position at the beginning.

Mirabell's machinations, by contrast, are undertaken altogether in the cause of love, and it is through lovemaking that he seeks to win to his side the imposing Lady Wishfort, who must always be taken into account as the ultimate source of power within the family. Having been exposed in his first pretense, in which he himself has played the whining lover, he is setting out, as the action begins, to contrive a fresh and quite similar deception, the plan being now to disguise his own servant Waitwell as Sir Rowland and to cast him in the role of lover, and thus to approach Lady Wishfort again through her appetitive nature and thereby to turn her vengefulness to positive account. Thus, in effect, Mirabell becomes the author of an entire play.

His plot is intended quite clearly to be a case of bare-faced blackmail, undertaken with that same ruthlessness and optimistic confidence of success which are the familiar attributes of the comic hero. "I have been engag'd in a Matter of some sort of Mirth," Mirabell informs Fainall, "which is not yet Ripe for Discovery" (347). It has been objected on occasion that Mirabell's lovemaking to a pathetic and "superannuated" woman smacks of a deplorable lack of principle. But the objection has been made by critics who have also felt sympathy for Mrs. Loveit and who must mistakenly be regarding Mirabell as a romantic hero and not as the comic one that he is—the kind of hero from whom unprincipled behavior is to be expected in such a life-and-death matter as Mirabell has in hand. Certainly he possesses the comic hero's never-say-die resiliency, for having been in this second attempt again thwarted by Mrs. Marwood, he returns to the attack undaunted, this time playing the repentent sinner; and so persuasive is his "false insinuating tongue," that Lady Wishfort's love is reawakened in spite of herself: "Oh, he has Witchcraft in his Eyes and Tongue;—When I did not see him I cou'd have brib'd a Villain to his Assassination; but his Appearance rakes the Embers which have so long lain smother'd in my Breast" (434).

The imagery sets life against death, and throughout the play Mirabell is, in the tradition of his kind, a promoter of marriages. His final words have to do with a promise to "contribute all that in me lyes to a Reunion" (440). Such marriages are, of course, as might be expected, those which in one way or another serve his own interest, and that between Waitwell and Foible has been designed with a shrewd eye to the advantages that may accrue to himself from winning Foible to his side in the game of deceptions in which he is involved. Nor is that his only motive. As he explains to Mrs. Fainall, "I wou'd not tempt my Servant to betray me by trusting him too far. If your Mother, in hopes to ruin me, shou'd consent to marry my pretended Uncle, he might, like *Mosca* in the *Fox,* stand upon Terms; so I made him sure before-hand" (368, 369). He knows well enough the treacherous, deceptive nature of his world, and it has been with the caution born of such knowledge that he has previously taken care to safeguard the interests of Mrs. Fainall at the time of promoting her marriage and thus has been able to save her (and himself) from ruin: "Thank Mr. *Mirabell,* a cautious Friend, to whose Advice all is owing" (439).

The central workers of treachery are, it is obvious, Fainall and Mrs. Marwood, and the relationship which obtains between them as allies in the game of deception has a clear parallel with that earlier unholy alliance between Maskwell and Lady Touchwood in *The Double-Dealer.* In the present case, however, the positions are almost exactly reversed. It is now Mrs. Marwood who is the Iago-like villain of the piece. It is she who is a "mischievous Devil" and proves capable of thinking up "Ingenious Mischief," and it is she who manages things so as to have her opponent regarded as a "wheadling Villain" while she herself maintains with Lady Wishfort her credit for being "a dear Friend" who "is all Goodness." Working on Fainall's passions of greed and jealousy, she turns him with cold calculation into an instrument for carrying out the destructive designs born of her own hatred. "You Married her to keep you;" she says to him with callous cynicism regarding the wife of whose premarital affair he has just become cognizant; "and if you can contrive to have her keep you better than you expected; why should you not keep her longer than you intended?" And when he demands, "The Means, the Means," she has them ready at hand, as well as her own ways of keeping the deception going by working on passions other than his: "Discover to my Lady your Wife's Conduct; threaten to part with her—My Lady loves her, and will come to any Composition to save her Reputation. Take the Opportunity of breaking it, just upon the Discovery of this Imposture. My Lady will be enrag'd beyond Bounds, and sacrifice Niece, and Fortune, and all at that Conjuncture. And let me alone to keep her warm; if she shou'd flag in her part, I will not fail to prompt her" (398). Lady Wishfort herself knows the ways of the world well enough to have exclaimed to her earlier: "Ah dear *Marwood,* what's Integrity to an Opportunity?" But of course she is deluded as to just who it is in her world who "carries Poison in his Tongue that wou'd corrupt Integrity it self" (379).

The word "Integrity" has, it may be noted, a special importance in this particular context, carrying as it does implications of unity as well as honesty, for it is clearly to the end of wreaking havoc and disunity that a wholly destructive opportunist like Mrs. Marwood directs her endeavors. The kind of marriage into which Fainall has entered—motivated by greed and characterized by "mutual falsehood"—is exceeded in its essentially negative quality only by that which Mrs. Marwood describes to Mrs. Fainall as the one kind into which she herself could be persuaded to enter: "if I cou'd but find one that lov'd me very well, and would be throughly sensible of ill Usage, I think I should do my self the Violence of undergoing the Ceremony." And when Mrs. Fainall inquires, "You wou'd not make him a Cuckold?" she replies grimly, "No; but I'd make him believe I did, and that's as bad." And she goes on to explain with vindictive satisfaction her reason for only pretending the offense: "O if he shou'd ever discover it, he wou'd then know the worst, and be out of his Pain; but I wou'd have him ever to continue upon the Rack of Fear and Jealousie" (361).

The obvious foil to the death-oriented Mrs. Marwood is the life-

oriented Millamant, and yet just as Mirabell and Fainall bear a
superficial resemblance to each other in their libertinism and propensity to intrigue, so do the two ladies in their willfulness and
their desire for power. The more closely we consider the dialogue
of the play, the more apparent it becomes that Congreve has contrived it in terms of a number of basic oppositions having to do
with the direction given to the fundamental human emotions; and
one of these oppositions reveals itself in the Millamant-Marwood
contrast. It begins to come into clearer focus a few scenes after the
Fainall-Marwood exchange when Millamant also talks of the pleasure of inflicting pain ("I love to give Pain"), and upon Mirabell's
objecting, "You wou'd affect a Cruelty which is not in your Nature;
your true Vanity is in the Power of pleasing," she promptly rejoins: "Ones Cruelty is ones Power, and when one parts with ones
Cruelty, one parts with ones Power, and when one has parted with
that, I fancy one's old and ugly" (371, 372). Millamant, in short,
is quite as capable of sounding vindictive as Mrs. Marwood, and
she too professes to "detest" and "hate" Mirabell (389). Both are
gloriers, rejoicing in their own superiority.

Yet there is unquestionably a vital difference between these two
power-conscious ladies—a difference of a kind already encountered
in *The Double-Dealer* but now defined far more subtly and persuasively and pursued in its complexities a good deal more exten-
sively. What Congreve illustrates here once again is the hair-thin
line that separates the comic from the tragic, the creative from the
destructive, where the human passions in general and sexual antagonism and aggressiveness in particular are concerned. The desire to give pain is, as ought perhaps to go without saying, one
element in the struggle for power characterizing an intense sexual
relationship in which a complexity of passions is involved; and the
violence of these passions is not to be ignored or sentimentalized
away. The heat they generate has as much possibility of exploding
destructively as of being expressed creatively and artistically. And
in these terms, Mrs. Marwood on the one hand and Millamant on
the other suggest, in their sharply emphasized juxtaposition, the
alternate potentialities.

That Millamant is a woman who lives with special intensity
seems to be a fact which has escaped more than one of her senti-

mental admirers and a good many of those detractors who have
glibly dismissed her as a mere coquette. Kathleen Lynch has suggested that Congreve intended to portray her as a comic heroine who
is to be laughed at as well as with, since while she herself is laughing
at the patent fools in the play, we as audience find her laughable
(in a "genial and sympathetic" way) in her inability to express
her genuine nature, restricted as she is by the rigid forms imposed
by her society.[3] But does not the whole point of her character and
of her position in the play rest on the fact that she evolves her own
forms and her own rules by which to express her own vital nature?
So natural and artless does she manage to appear that even Mirabell
himself is not able to decide whether she owes her charm to art or
nature: "Her Follies are so natural, or so artful, that they become
her" (348). Her style of life achieves, in fact, much the same quality
that Sprat once attributed to Cowley's style of writing: "a natural
easiness and unaffected grace where nothing seems to be studied
yet everything is extraordinary."[4]

Virtually every one of her appearances on the stage confirms that
she possesses a nature as potentially violent as Mrs. Marwood's. And
her name itself suggests her innate aggressiveness. It is surely no
ladylike refinement that explains the instant domination of the
scene which she seizes at every entrance and in every dialogue and
which almost invariably gives a quality of breathlessness to her
repartees. "You have a Colour, what's the matter?" asks Mrs. Marwood on one of these occasions, and Millamant exclaims: "That
horrid Fellow *Petulant* has provok'd me into a Flame—I have
broke my fan—*Mincing,* lend me yours;—Is not all the Powder out
of my Hair?" (386) And when, in the following scene, Mrs. Marwood confronts her with the fact that her love for Mirabell has
become public knowledge, she goes on to observe concerning Millamant's reactions, "You are nettl'd. . . . Indeed, my Dear, you'll
tear another Fan, if you don't mitigate those violent Airs" (388).
The intensity of her responses is continually apparent but never
escapes the bounds of graceful control (she remains always the
conscious player), and her final open declaration to Mrs. Fainall
of her love for Mirabell proves completely characteristic: "Well,
If *Mirabell* should not make a good husband, I am a lost thing;—
for I find I love him violently" (410).

[234]

What Millamant does, however, in contrast to Mrs. Marwood, is to give expression to her nature in a wholly creative way. She is an artist of life who contrives for herself a style completely expressive of her own vital depths; and indeed Huizinga might almost have had her specifically in mind in his discussion of "the elegant convolutions and luxuriance of the Rococo," for he points out that "beneath all this finery the spirit of the age was seeking a way back to Nature, but a way with style. . . . Few periods of art have managed to balance play and seriousness as gracefully as the Rococo."[5]

The note of seriousness is always to be heard as a part of Millamant's gaiety, and informing her style is that streak of deliberate cruelty which she equates with the power of her youth and beauty. Whether she is mercilessly taunting her lover ("Ha, ha, ha, What wou'd you give, that you cou'd help loving me?" [374]), or gloating in triumph over her rejected rival ("I am a Sybil if I am not amaz'd to think what he can see in me. I'll take my Death, I think you are handsomer—and within a Year or two as young.—If you cou'd but stay for me, I shou'd overtake you—" [389]), or mocking at the gaucheries of her would-be wooer, Sir Wilfull ("Ah Rustick, ruder than *Gothick*." [404]), she asserts her power in a way that would seem almost primitive were it not for the playful spirit and for the style with which she carries it off, and she herself remarks at one point, in the midst of her gloating superiority: "I must laugh, ha, ha, ha; tho' I grant you 'tis a little barbarous, ha, ha, ha" (388). And doubtless there is more than a little barbarity, not to mention hunger for power, in the nature of the sentiments conveyed in the song which she commands to be sung at this juncture:

I.
*Love's but the Frailty of the Mind,*
*When 'tis not with Ambition join'd;*
*A sickly Flame, which if not fed expires;*
*And feeding, wastes in Self-consuming Fires.*

II.
*'Tis not to wound a wanton Boy*
*Or am'rous Youth, that gives the Joy;*
*But 'tis the Glory to have pierc'd a Swain,*
*For whom inferior Beauties sigh'd in vain.*

III.

*Then I alone the Conquest prize,*
*When I insult a Rival's Eyes:*
*If there's Delight in Love, 'tis when I see*
*That Heart which others bleed for, bleed for me.*

Throughout the play love is spoken of, as here, in terms of what at first sight may seem the merely hackneyed metaphor of fire and flame. (We may recall also Lady Wishfort's reference to Mirabell: "his Appearance rakes the Embers.") Such references, however, take on a decided significance when it is noted that the same metaphor also recurs in connection with the passions of anger and jealousy and hence serves to reinforce the central creation-destruction antithesis. The fire metaphor, as used by Fainall and Mrs. Marwood, has always a negative implication. "Your mutual Jealousies of one another," Fainall tells Mrs. Marwood, alluding to her conversation with Mrs. Fainall, "have made you clash 'till you have both struck Fire. I have seen the warm Confession red'ning on your Cheeks, and sparkling from your Eyes" (364). And not only does Mrs. Marwood propose, with regard to Lady Wishfort, "to keep her warm" but she herself intends to "play the Incendiary" (399). In both cases the references have to do with sowing discord, and it is, of course, the intent of Mrs. Marwood, motivated by her own jealousy-inspired hatred, to work upon the passion of jealousy wherever she finds it, and most notably in Fainall and Lady Wishfort, until she succeeds in arousing its full destructive potential and in directing it to the end of preventing Mirabell's marriage to Millamant. In her case it is a matter of hatred's generating hatred, of heat's generating more heat until a destructive explosion is produced.

Thus it is while under her sway that Lady Wishfort sees Mirabell as a "Spend-thrift Prodigal." When Mrs. Marwood manages to change her love for him into an intense hatred (to smother the embers of love), she begins to think of avenging measures even to the extreme of wholesale annihilation ("I'll have him murder'd. I'll have him poison'd. Where does he eat? I'll marry a Drawer to have him poison'd in his Wine" [380, 381]) or a disinheritance which will, as in the case of Sir Sampson's punishment of Valentine, deprive him of the means of life ("No, don't kill him at once, Sir *Rowland,* starve him gradually Inch by Inch" [417]).

In some sense the source of all the heat generated in the world of the play, whether in the service of life or death, is Lady Wishfort, who holds, for all her superficial "humours" overtones, a highly complex position at its symbolic center. It is presumably of significance that she does not appear on the stage until the opening of Act III—a means used by Congreve to point up her focal position and to suggest, at the same time, how heavily she makes her presence and her power felt even when physically absent. As head of the family, she represents the source of ultimate authority—and just how irrationally, not to say chaotically, that authority is exercised becomes at once apparent upon her initial appearance, as she sends a bewildered and terrified waiting woman scurrying frantically about in a vain effort to satisfy her passionate and imperious demands.

The possessor of a confused and frustrated emotional nature, she bends in any direction the strongest wind blows her, since her rebellious passions are always, in effect, straining against and breaking from the "Decorums" and "Forms" by which she has chosen to bind them, much as her real face, that "old peel'd Wall," is forever breaking through in spite of all her efforts to spread over it a smooth false surface (382). As Sir Wilfull points out reassuringly to Mirabell later: "she dare not frown desperately, because her Face is none of her own; 'Sheart, and she shou'd her Forehead wou'd wrinkle like the Coat of a Cream-cheese" (432). In short, the kind of "Art" she employs—as Foible tells her, "a little Art once made your Picture like you; and now a little of the same Art must make you like your Picture" (382)—does not express the truth of what she is, either in the matter of cosmetics or as regards the "Forms" of her social personality, and her name suggests something of her frustrations and vain longings. The overcivilized "Order" she prepares for the reception of Sir Rowland corresponds with her careful preplanning of the "first Impression" she seeks to make—"I won't lye neither, but loll and lean upon one Elbow" (401)—both of them wholly belying her own aggressively passionate nature. And similarly, her language often has an over-elegance and pretentious formality quite at odds with the raging intensities which it covers, as when she says to Witwoud about Sir Wilfull: "Dear Cousin *Witwoud* get him away, and you will bind me to you inviolably. I have an Affair of moment that invades me with some Precipitation—You will oblige me to all Futurity"—a line immediately preceded by her raging arraignment of Sir Wilfull: "Good lack! what shall I do with this beastly Tumbril?— Go lie down and sleep, you Sot—Or as I'm a Person, I'll have you bastinado'd with Broom-sticks. Call up the Wenches with Broomsticks" (415).

She exercises a tyranny over her own natural inclinations which has its counterpart in a like tyrannical behavior where the members of her family are concerned, and one of the most significant aspects of that tyranny has to do with her Puritanism. "Shrine of Virtue" that she is, she vehemently denies that there is, in her "yielding" to Sir Rowland, "the least Scruple of Carnality" (417), and the books that are prominent in her library and which she recommends to Mrs. Marwood (one wonders if there is not some irony in her description of them as "Books over the Chimney") are *"Quarles* and *Pryn,* and the *Short View of the Stage,* with *Bunyan's* Works" (379).

In point of fact, Congreve has, in his characterization of Lady Wishfort, devised a devastating reply to Jeremy Collier, which far surpasses in its effectiveness his feeble attempts at expostulation and self-defense in his earlier essay. Mirabell identifies her in the opening scene of the play as "the Foundress of this Sect" (the "Sect" being the cabal which excludes men and hence goes against the "State of Nature"). Is not Congreve actually saying in effect: *here* is what comes of maintaining over any society (as well as over any individual personality) this kind of moralistic control, with its total failure to give scope to the fundamental human passions? Is he not saying: here are the confusions and perversions and destructive violences which are likely to result when such passions at last break through? It is, it may be noted, Collier's brand of "Education" to which Lady Wishfort's daughter has been subjected:

> LADY. . . . I promise you, her Education has been unexceptionable
> —I may say it; for I chiefly made it my own Care to initiate her very

Infancy in the Rudiments of Virtue, and to impress upon her tender Years a young Odium and Aversion to the very sight of Men,— ay Friend, she would have shriek'd if she had but seen a Man, 'till she was in her Teens. As I'm a Person 'tis true—She was never suffer'd to play with a Male-Child, tho' but in Coats; Nay her very Babies were of the *Feminine Gender,*—O, she never look'd a Man in the Face but her own Father, or the Chaplain, and him we made a shift to put upon her for a Woman, by the help of his long Garments, and his sleek Face; 'till she was going in her Fifteen.

MRS. MAR. 'Twas much she should be deceiv'd so long.

LADY. I warrant you, or she would never have born to have been catechiz'd by him; and have heard his long Lectures against Singing and Dancing, and such Debaucheries; and going to filthy Plays; and prophane Musick-meetings, where the lewd Trebles squeek nothing but Bawdy, and the Bases roar Blasphemy. O, she would have swoon'd at the Sight or Name of an obscene Play-Book—and can I think after all this, that my Daughter can be Naught? What, a Whore? And thought it Excommunication to set her Foot within the Door of a Play-House.   (427)

And to that daughter herself Lady Wishfort exclaims: "O Daughter, Daughter, is it possible thou should'st be my Child, Bone of my Bone, and Flesh of my Flesh, and as I may say, another Me, and yet transgress the most minute Particle of severe Virtue? Is it possible you should lean aside to Iniquity, who have been cast in the direct Mold of Virtue? I have not only been a Mold but a Pattern for you, and a Model for you, after you were brought into the World" (425, 426).

The wording of Lady Wishfort's outburst at this point is of particular interest, because it calls at once to mind one of the items included by Mirabell shortly before in his matrimonial proviso. "I denounce," he has declared, "against all strait Lacing, squeezing for a Shape, 'till you mould my Boy's Head like a Sugar-loaf; and instead of a Man-Child, make me Father to a Crooked-billet" (408). In other words, Mirabell proposes that his child be left free to develop naturally and humanly, without any straight-laced inhibitions imposed from without, and he also demands of Millamant her natural face. "MIRA. *Item,* I Article that you continue to like your own Face, as long as I shall: And while it passes currant with me, that you endeavour not to new Coin it" (408). The contrast between his convictions in this regard and Lady Wishfort's (both having to do with molding) brings out as explicitly as anything in the play the terms of the central opposition.

Together Mirabell and Millamant represent the comic and creative and artistic forces of life and youth in their family and society, seeking to influence Lady Wishfort to their advantage as Fainall and Mrs. Marwood seek to influence her to theirs. One couple stands for the establishment of a new pattern of freedom, the other for the prolonging of an old pattern of tyranny and negativism where the human emotions are concerned. Indeed, what Millamant and Mrs. Marwood represent, in some sense, are the alternate possibilities for love and hatred, freedom and tyranny, available to Lady Wishfort herself as the central focus of power, and upon the triumph of one or the other hangs the whole question of how power is to be wielded in the new generation. What Millamant alone of the three women has achieved is a style within which her own nature may find creative expression. For all that Mirabell taxes her with "the variety of your Disposition" (374) and for all her seeming contradictions of whim, she is never for a moment at the mercy of her own emotions or of any externally imposed social stricture. Not only does she not allow passion, much less sentiment, to exert any tyranny over her, as is the case at times with Lady Wishfort, but as a rational being she does not tyrannize over her own natural inclinations as does that lady in her Puritanical moments.

Instead, she persistently challenges such tyrannies with all the gaiety and arrogance of which the comic spirit is capable, reveling in her own barbarity as well as in the beautifully harmonious and lively world of her own creation. As Ashley Thorndike has put it: "Her merriment has the insouciance of Puck's and the airiness of Ariel's. Happy in her own quickness of wit she exults less at the inferiority of others than at her own celerity which outdistances all competitors."[6] Her laughter rings out through the play, and indeed we can almost hear her proclaiming at times with Puck, "What fools these mortals be!" The wry comic detachment she consistently maintains from both herself and her world is one of the sources of her power—a power which she has no intention of losing even in deference to love. "I'll fly and be follow'd to the last

Moment," she declares, "tho' I am upon the very Verge of Matrimony, I expect you should sollicit me as much as if I were wavering at the Grate of a Monastery, with one Foot over the Threshold. I'll be sollicited to the very last, nay and afterwards" (405).

Thus Mirabell is actually involved in two games at once, each as demanding of ingenuity as the other. He has not only to outwit the destructive intriguers who threaten him and to win to his side the indecisive Lady Wishfort, but he has also to rise to the new challenge that Millamant audaciously flings at him. And the challenge is even more formidable than that ironic dare which Harriet has issued to Dorimant on the subject of "that great rambling lone house" in Hampshire, for Millamant is an even more witty and accomplished woman and she insists upon having a vital and excitingly unpredictable relationship—and wants nothing to do with a docile submissiveness on either side. No sooner has she chided Mirabell for his "offensive Freedom" in scolding her for the company she keeps ("I shan't endure to be reprimanded, nor instructed; 'tis so dull to act always by Advice, and so tedious to be told of ones Faults" [374]) than she turns about and makes outrageous fun of him for playing the heavy lover. In effect, she is challenging him to regard himself and their relationship with the same amused objectivity as she herself does. "Sententious *Mirabell!*" she cries. "Prithee don't look with that violent and inflexible wise Face, like *Solomon* at the dividing of the Child in an old Tapestry Hanging. . . . Well, after all there is something very moving in a Lovesick Face. Ha, ha, ha—Well I won't laugh, don't be peevish—Heigho! Now I'll be melancholy, as melancholy as a Watchlight." Was there ever a more shameless glorier? Yet she knows, with Santayana, that in its "intrinsic aspect existence is nothing tragic or sad, but rather something joyful, hearty, and merry," and she possesses what he describes as a "buoyant and full-blooded soul" which "has quick senses and miscellaneous sympathies; it changes with the changing world; and when not too much starved or thwarted by circumstances, it finds all things vivid and comic."[7]

Always the actress, Millamant plays every role with deliberate and delighted exaggeration, thus giving to it an artistic heightening. What she fears most in her relationship with Mirabell is that "we shall be sick of one another" (374), and the very fact that she dramatizes and mocks at both her own fears and her love indicates their genuineness. "I'll take my Death I'm in a horrid Fright," she exclaims to Mrs. Fainall, and when her friend says impatiently: "Fy, fy, have him, have him, and tell him so in plain Terms: For I am sure you have a Mind to him," Millamant replies: "Are you? I think I have—and the horrid Man looks as if he thought so too— Well, you ridiculous thing you, I'll have you—I won't be kiss'd, nor I won't be thank'd—Here kiss by Hand tho'" (409).

Even her moments of seriousness have in them an element of self-dramatization and self-mockery which adds to their depth and leads us to feel their truth as no sentimentalizing tone ever could. From her withdrawn position in the early scenes of Act IV, for example, she views herself and her world with absolute clarity: "I am thoughtful, and wou'd amuse my self . . . I would confer with my own Thoughts" (402). And Congreve conveys the sense of her restless intensity through stage directions that describe her as continually *"walking about"* as she repeats snatches from Suck-ling's poetry. Perpetually in graceful motion, she lives in a self-contained poetic world, from which she peremptorily dismisses the awkward, bumbling Sir Wilfull; and his total incapacity to respond to her on her own poetic level is underlined by his il-literately mistaking her praise of Suckling for an animal reference (which, incidentally, serves also as an apt commentary on his own nature). But if Sir Wilfull is no match for her, Mirabell at once demonstrates that he can more than hold his own, for as Millamant returns to her recitations after Sir Wilfull's ignominious exit— *"Like* Phoebus *sung the no less am'rous Boy"*—Mirabell enters with the succeeding line glibly at command: *"Like* Daphne *she, as Lovely and as Coy"*—and smoothly turns it into a means for pur-suing his own amorous cause.

Theirs is a game of wit played with more skill and artistry than any other in Restoration comedy. From the first, it is a power strug-gle in which each is forever seizing the offensive from the other and in which the sexual implications are never far below the surface. As with previously considered wit combats, the tension of the game is the result of the mutual attraction existing between the antag-onists as each attempts to retain his sense of freedom and control.

And it is a tension that is immediately apparent upon their first encounter when, in response to Mirabell's comments on her vanity and his subsequent contention that "Beauty is the Lover's Gift," Millamant counters by adroitly turning both sallies back upon his own head. "O the Vanity of these Men! . . . Beauty the Lover's Gift—Lord, what is a Lover, that it can give? Why one makes Lovers as fast as one pleases, and they live as long as one pleases, and they die as soon as one pleases: And then if one pleases one makes more" (372). In short, she returns arrogance for arrogance, and with good measure, by making the lover merely an object (an "it") whose very existence depends on a woman's indulgence. The world, including the lovers in it, is one's own to create. And further, her characteristic use of the impersonal pronoun when referring to herself has the effect of giving her not only an unassailable objectivity but a superior position of aloofness and detachment which makes her, from the attacker's vantage point, a peculiarly elusive opponent.

There is no doubt that Millamant knows her own powers of wit and charm nor that she makes use of them quite brazenly in assuring that she will have her own way with her world, but the important point to keep in mind is that she never uses that power as a tyrannical and repressive force. Mirabell may, on occasion, accuse her of tyranny, and it can hardly be denied that she more than once treats him with deliberate high-handedness, but there is always the saving comic detachment. She *plays* at tyranny as she plays at cruelty, and what her love of power ultimately comes to is a love of freedom—a freedom without which there can be no genuinely creative artistry. Her jealous guarding of that power is tantamount to the protection of her right to an artistic selfhood, and it is a right which she acknowledges to belong to Mirabell as well (although she can always slyly manage to convey the impression that her decision to "let him follow his own Way" involves a generous concession on her own part).

The demands she makes in the duly celebrated proviso scene all have to do with safeguarding her own power to remain free and mistress of herself ("I'll never marry, unless I am first made sure of my Will and Pleasure" [406]) and with making sure that there will be no sinking into the dullness of being taken for granted.

But by freedom she also means, clearly enough, that she will not be tyrannized over by her own passions or relax into any banal sentimentality; and through her tone of elegant boredom (as in her reference to "the agreeable Fatigues of Sollicitation") she establishes herself safely at a distance from any such degradation. Not for her the uncontrolled violences and intensities of a Lady Wishfort. And even as she is concluding the outline of her "Conditions," she impudently leaves the impression that her agreeing to marry by no means constitutes a surrender but rather is a queenly condescension: "These Articles subscrib'd, if I continue to endure you a little longer, I may by degrees dwindle into a Wife" (407).

The language of the proviso scene is beyond doubt as masterful as anything in Congreve, or for that matter in seventeenth-century comedy, conveying as it does a sense of profound tensions and intensities under magnificent control. Here, more effectively than anywhere else in Congreve's work, his dialogue captures that precariously achieved union of earth and air (or as one critic has put it, of truth and beauty)[8] which we have seen to have been a central thematic preoccupation of his even in his first play. Indeed, it may well be suggested that the proposed marriage between Mirabell and Millamant represents just this union, for virtually all of Mirabell's dialogue is made up of thinly disguised sex suggestions and is filled with senuous and animal references ("Oil'd-skins . . . Hog's Bones, Hare's Gall, Pig Water, and the Marrow of a roasted Cat"; "*Orange-Brandy . . . Anniseed, Cinamon, Citron* and *Barbado's-Waters*"). And as Holland points out, these earthy demands are presented in methodically reasoned statements ("*Imprimis* then, I covenant . . ."; "*Item,* I Article . . ."), while Millamant meets his conditions with cries of "Odious" and "Detestable" (which recall her earlier, "loathing" of the "Country and every thing that relates to it") and makes her whimsical demands without regard to any sort of logic whatever and in a tone of airy offhandedness.

But if we feel the unmistakable tension which exists between them as they make their bargain, we cannot fail to see also that they are essentially in agreement on the question of liberty and that the wit on both sides constitutes a verbal attack on the degrading, freedom-denying conventions in their own society. When, for example, Millamant assumes the role of tyrant, she does so obviously in mockery (one of her demands is to "be sole Empress of my Tea-Table") and with her customary air of amused objectivity; and in response to Mirabell's request for a like "Liberty to offer Conditions," she pronounces from her throne: "You have free leave, propose your utmost, speak and spare not." And when the Contract has at last been concluded and Mirabell has established his right to take exception to her freedoms wherever they threaten to infringe upon his own convictions in the matter of what he wants in a wife, Millamant dismisses him from her presence with an imperial admission that he has perhaps deserved her queenly favors: "Ay, go, go. In the mean time I suppose you have said something to please me." And we can imagine Mirabell making an exaggerated bow as he replies: "I am all Obedience" (410). In the final analysis there has been no sacrifice of integrity on either side.

Millamant's and Mirabell's consummately acted little drama clearly makes a commentary by way of parody on Lady Wishfort's world—a world in which the tyrannies are altogether too genuine and threaten to become the dominant mode.[9] In the succeeding act it is Fainall who is laying down the "Conditions" in deadly earnest: "I . . . am content you shall enjoy your own proper Estate during Life," he informs Lady Wishfort, "on Condition you oblige your self never to marry." The word "condition" occurs again a few lines later, as Mrs. Marwood remarks: "That Condition, I dare answer, my Lady will consent to, without Difficulty." And should Lady Wishfort, as she protests, require marriage "in case of Necessity; as of Health," Fainall goes on to say that he will "reserve to my self the Power to chuse for you" (429)—an ironic reversal of Lady Wishfort's own earlier action in having chosen her daughter's first husband. It is now her turn to wish "to be deliver'd from this Tyranny" (435), and it is, of course, the realistic Mirabell who delivers her, at a time when she herself can conceive of no recourse but an escape to a dream world about whose actual existence Congreve himself had no illusions: "Dear *Marwood,* let us leave the World, and retire by our selves and be Shepherdesses" (425).

Throughout the play similar contrasts have been piling up—Fainall's relationships of mutual distrust, hatred, and jealousy with both his own wife and Mrs. Marwood set against Mirabell's relationship with Millamant based on mutual love and forbearance.

There have been, all along, oppositions set up between destructive and creative conflict, destructive and creative design and pretense, and what might be termed destructive cynicism and creative realism, and by the beginning of Act V the result of the negative dominance has been to throw the whole family into a state of violent confusion, while the result of the positive one has been the emergence in embryo of a new family group characterized by an artistically and wittily achieved balance and control of conflicting elements.

The only characters who have remained almost wholly uninvolved from beginning to end are Witwoud and Petulant, and the reason for their lack of involvement is not far to seek. In their preoccupation with social affectations and surface polish they have been dissociated altogether from any vital energies whatsoever, whether positive or negative, which would identify them with the human community and have become little more than empty caricatures of human beings. The manner of their initial appearance, emerging from a card game at the chocolate house with Witwoud the loser, suggests that Congreve intended us to regard them as in some sense parallel to the earlier pair of card-players, with Witwoud representing a would-be Mirabell and Petulant a would-be Fainall. Witwoud has taken on the surface attributes of Mirabell's wit, but as the latter points out, his verbal sallies are wholly dependent on a none-too-reliable memory ("Gad I have forgot what I was going to say to you . . . my Memory is such a Memory") and "some few Scraps of other Folks Wit," and hence the "great Fire" of his so-called wit ("I confess I do blaze to Day, I am too bright") is totally without heat.[10] In fact, he does not know a real fire from a fake one ("he will . . . call downright Rudeness and ill Language, Satire and Fire"). And Petulant's self-styled malice ("pox I'm malicious, Man") and his refined libertinism ("they must wait or rub off, if I want Appetite") bear a superficial resemblance to Fainall's while amounting in reality to mere exhibitionism.

Indeed there is every indication that neither Witwoud nor Petulant is quite a bona fide representative of the male sex, for as Fainall explains to Mirabell in regard to the ladies' "Cabal-Nights": "it was once propos'd that all the Male Sex shou'd be excepted; but some body mov'd that to avoid Scandal there might be one Man

of the Community; upon which *Witwoud* and *Petulant* were en-
roll'd Members" (345). They have, in fact, much in common with
the "de-natured" Sir Fopling Flutter; and Witwoud bears a further
resemblance to him in his having been, in Sir Wilfull's words,
"bound to a Maker of Fops" and having, as a result of his education, denied his own origins ("'tis not modish to know Relations
in Town"). In the final analysis, therefore, neither Witwoud nor
Petulant has any meaningful contact with the vital realities of
family or society, and Sir Wilfull is quite right in concluding, "I
think they may be spar'd," for the responses of both to the dis-
ruptions and ultimate realignments of the fifth act are, like Brisk's
in *The Double-Dealer,* completely fatuous and uncomprehending:

PET. For my part, I say little—I think things are best off or on.
WIT. I gad I understand nothing of the matter,—I'm in a Maze
yet, like a Dog in a Dancing-School.     (440)

And Sir Wilfull himself can also "be spar'd," as he himself
knows. For all his hearty honesty and good nature and his sturdy,
straightforward masculinity, he is a discordant element— a "Booby"
like Ben Legend, who "stinks" of the stables and the barnyard
(the pig is the animal twice associated with him) as does Ben of
the salt seas. Norman Holland suggests that whereas Witwoud and
Petulant are all form and no content, Sir Wilfull is all content and
no form,[11] and there is a good deal of justification for the assessment. Yet surely Sir Wilfull makes, nonetheless, a more positive
contribution to the overall comic spirit of the play than such a
characterization would indicate, for he represents honest human
vitality at its pre-social best, neither Puritanically denied (Lady
Wishfort, looking down from her Puritanical heights, calls him a
"beastly Pagan") nor perverted to destructive ends.

Sir Wilfull is the Sir Joslin Jolly of the piece, the buffoon who
supplies the farcical note. His language is full of references to hard
drinking, maidenheads, and wenching, and the rollicking, high-
spirited drinking scene toward the end of Act IV, of which he is
the guiding spirit, abounds in exuberant life and stands in marked
contrast to the coldly sober, dark and destructive confusions which
have become rife at the opening of Act V—confusions which reach
their climax in the closing scenes as Fainall runs at his wife with

drawn sword and Mrs. Marwood, in reply to a warning not "to stifle your Resentment," mutters: "Yes, it shall have Vent—and to your Confusion, or I'll perish in the Attempt" (439).

Thus there is surely importance in the fact that it is to Sir Wilfull that Mirabell and Millamant turn for help in bringing about their final *coup de grace*. Millamant of course rejects him as a suitor, thus rejecting nature uncivilized by art and choosing instead an art which, like her own, has refined upon nature. But symbolically Sir Wilfull stands for the raw natural energies she and Mirabell have converted into a radiant, harmonious beam of light and the raucous high spirits they have formed into the controlled gaiety of the dance of life. And if we have any remaining doubts as to the elemental naturalness which informs their art, we should have none after hearing the final words they speak to each other:

> MILLA. Why does not the Man take me? Wou'd you have me give my self to you over again?
> MIRA. Ay, and over and over again;
> 
> *Kisses her Hand.*
> I wou'd have you as often as possibly I can. Well, Heav'n grant I love you not too well, that's all my Fear.
> SIR WIL. 'Sheart you'll have time enough to toy after you're married; or if you will toy now, let us have a Dance in the mean time; that we who are not Lovers may have some other Employment, besides looking on.

It is Millamant's and Mirabell's ultimate achievement to have "socialized" the passions and to have contrived the kind of dance which, as Havelock Ellis insists, "is imperatively needed to give poise to the nerves, schooling to the emotions, strength to the will, and to harmonise the feelings and the intellect with the body which supports them."[12] After them, the comic spirit of Restoration drama could scarcely have aspired to any higher development.

# [ XI ]

## *Epilogue*

---

PANTING and perspiring, they run and never arrive. They would
all like to stop but dare not as long as the others are running.
What makes them run so frantically, as though they were driven
by the threatening swish of an invisible whip wielded by an
invisible slave driver? The driver and the whip they carry in
their own minds. If one of them finally stops and begins
leisurely to whistle a tune or watch a passing cloud or picks up
a stone and with childish curiosity turns it around in his
hand, they all look upon him first with astonishment and then
with contempt and disgust. They call him names, a dreamer
or a parasite, a theoretician or a schizophrenic . . . They not only
do not understand him—they not only despise him but "they
hate him as their own sin."

—FRANZ ALEXANDER, *Our Age of Unreason*

IF IT WAS THE CASE, AS GAYLEY SUGGESTS, THAT THE VICE OF THE
English morality plays "found a house of correction" and "left a
stage," the comic heroes of Vanbrugh and Farquhar may be said
to have done almost precisely the reverse: having found a stage,
they left a house of correction. "Humor at present seems to be de-
parting from the stage," Oliver Goldsmith was complaining by
1772, "and it will soon happen that our comic players will have
nothing left for it but a fine coat and a song. It depends upon the

audience whether they will actually drive those poor merry creatures from the stage, or sit at a play as gloomy as at the Taber-
nacle."[1] To attempt to determine just why such a development
had occurred would take us, of course, far beyond the scope of the
present study, but perhaps a few speculations may at least be haz-
arded.

Certainly it is clear that by 1700, when *The Way of the World*
was produced and met with at best a lukewarm reception, the
stage was coming increasingly under attack—an attack launched
mainly on Puritanical and moralistic grounds. And it was from
the charge of immorality that Restoration comedy was to suffer
for the next two hundred years—through the Victorian period and
beyond. Yet Puritanism was hardly a new phenomenon in the
late seventeenth century. As Cazamian has pointed out, the merry
Englishman had from the beginning possessed also his somber
side: "The inward turn and the preoccupation with a moral world,
severely checking and limiting the appetites of the natural man,
developed from within, as did the love of pleasure and of fun; the
Puritans were neither more nor less native and national than the
merry-Englanders; only they appear to have received more en-
couragement, after all, from the conditions and circumstances in
which English civilization had to grow; and their relative victory
was a case of a manifold personality organizing itself, when the
time came for it to be stabilized, around what was in fact its most
powerful tendency."[2]

It was this tendency which was reasserting its dominance as the
seventeenth century drew to a close, but the point to be accorded
special emphasis is that it now had a new and not inconsiderable
ally in the cause of repressive sobriety—namely, an increasingly
influential middle-class mentality almost invariably hostile to the
comic or play spirit. In his extensive consideration of the arguments
and counterarguments that succeeded Collier's much-heralded condemnation of the contemporary stage, Joseph Wood Krutch notes
that "there is much stress on the ill effects of plays upon the middle
class, and the theater is attacked not only on strictly moral grounds
but also on the charge that it tends to undermine the industry and
application necessary for success in trade."[3] Krutch earlier points
out that it was not the contemporary theater alone which was being

censured, but all theater and indeed all art, since art by its very nature is rooted in delight and in a love of life and hence is at odds with the Christian ascetic doctrine; and surely he might have gone on to add that it is equally at odds with the cause of bourgeois prosperity, for he cites that pillar of the middle class Daniel Defoe as having regarded the wits "as the devil's particular modern privy consellors."[4]

Defoe could, of course, well have said the same thing of the wits' fictional counterparts among the heroes and heroines of Restoration comedy, all of whom are, like their more obviously primitive comic predecessors, intimately associated in their individual ways not only with the devil but with the world and the flesh as well. And the fact would seem to be that the roguish, laughing challenge they kept flinging at moral complacency and at anyone given to regarding himself with unrelieved seriousness was not one which a newly established bourgeois society felt able to accept or even to tolerate. To insist upon and to revel in the possibilities in life for love and freedom and pleasure and harmony and beauty, to oppose to the rigid dictates of humorless good sense the delights of behaving a little passionately or a little madly, to suggest that play has perhaps a value in and for itself and that time is more than money—how could a bourgeois society whose emphasis lay on hard, productive work and firm self-discipline not see all such premises as dangerously subversive?

It was a society which was nothing if not serious, an adult world which would have been quite happy to forget or deny its own childhood; and reason and common sense (and virtue that paid off) were becoming its watchwords. The new heroes of the new "comedies"—if such they could be called—were sentimentalized figures who were shown in the course of the dramatic development the patent error of their undisciplined and antisocial ways and in the end came docilely and gratefully to heel. And so it was that by 1772 Goldsmith had ample reason to caution: "it will be but a just punishment, that when, by our being too fastidious, we have banished humor from the stage, we should ourselves be deprived of the art of laughing."

It was not, however, simply the art of laughing at stake but the very art of living and the spirit of play and ultimately a genuinely meaningful morality. George Santayana wrote in his essay "The Comic Mask":

> Reason cannot stand alone; brute habit and blind play are at the bottom of art and morals, and unless irrational impulses and fancies are kept alive, the life of reason collapses for sheer emptiness. . . . Moralists have habitually aimed at suppression, wisely perhaps at first, when they were preaching to men of spirit; but why continue to harp on propriety and unselfishness and labour, when we are little but labour-machines already, and have hardly any self or any passions left to indulge? Perhaps the time has come to suspend those exhortations, and to encourage us to be sometimes a little lively, and see if we can invent something worth saying or doing. We should then be living in the spirit of comedy, and the world would grow young. . . . We should be constantly original without effort and without shame, somewhat as we are in dreams, and consistent only in sincerity.[5]

It was just in this spirit that the comic heroes and heroines of the Restoration stage contrived to live. In their artistry, their inventiveness, their aggressive insistence on freedom and joyous expansiveness, even in their ruthlessness, they imparted to their lives, within the boundaries of time, an intensity and vitality and *integrity* which went far beyond mere immorality or frivolity or rebelion for its own sake. And when we, in our stuffy self-righteousness, reject them, we do so to our loss, and the rejection constitutes an admission of our own inadequacy of response to their honesty and to the spirit of lively youth which they embody.

# N O T E S

Chapter I. *Prologue*

1. L. C. Knights, "Restoration Comedy: The Reality and the Myth," *Explorations* (New York: New York Univ. Press, 1964), p. 168.

2. John Wain, "Restoration Comedy and its Modern Critics," *Essays in Criticism,* VI (October, 1956), 377. "One of the main checks on one's natural wish to take Restoration comedy seriously," says Wain, "is, of course, the frightful confusion it exhibits whenever a moral attitude is to be taken up. Critics who enthusiastically recommend its fearless questioning of fundamental social questions, or indignantly deny that it is 'immoral', seldom argue their case with any plausibility. . . . We do expect an artist to have *artistic* morality; to take up a consistent attitude toward problems of conduct, and not merely to trifle with them. Trifling is exactly what these dramatists are doing."

3. Perhaps we cannot do better, in seeking support for this point, than to cite a succinct textbook summary of the differences between French and English comedy: "the French thought of comedy more as a socializing force than the English did. Elizabethan comedy often dealt sympathetically with the opposition of an individual to recognized social authority. . . . Society in general says that the authority of parents and guardians and political rulers is a safeguard for social institutions and should be respected. Shakespeare would be one of the last to deny this; yet he writes a play in which recognized social authority is made tyrannical and ridiculous and the rebelling individual is given the complete sympathy of the audience. This tendency to sympathize with the individual and to defy social authority is typical of English and American comedy, whether in the sixteenth century or the twentieth. It does not mean that the English stage has made a persistent campaign of nearly four hundred years to tear down authority, or that the English think society is generally wrong. It does mean, and this is the important point, that the English audience has always been more interested in the individual than in the social group. . . . The social implications of

this justification of the rebelling individual and the condemnation of social authority and social conventions are seldom considered. . . . While English comedy usually justified the individual in his revolt against social conventions and social authority, Molière justifies society and ridicules the non-conforming individual." Fred B. Millett and Gerald Eades Bentley, *The Art of the Drama* (New York: D. Appleton-Century, 1935), pp. 99, 100.

4. Eric Bentley, *The Life of the Drama* (New York: Atheneum, 1964), p. 226.

5. Charles Baudelaire, "On the Essence of Laughter," *The Mirror of Art,* trans. and ed. Jonathan Mayne (New York: Phaidon, 1955), pp. 147–49.

6. Louis Cazamian, *The Development of English Humor, Parts I and II* (Durham, N.C.: Duke Univ. Press, 1952), p. 15.

7. "While the virtues talked, the vices acted," says Bernard Spivack, "and by their physical exuberance and verbal pungency transmuted the pious monotony of the homily into the profane excitement of the play." *Shakespeare and the Allegory of Evil* (New York: Columbia Univ. Press, 1958), p. 123.

8. It may be noted that Northrop Frye, in identifying various *eiron* types in comedy, discusses the "tricky slave" ("the *architectus* of the comic action") and the English Vice in the same general terms and talks of Shakespeare's Puck as combining aspects of both: "such a character carries out the will of the author to reach a happy ending. He is in fact the spirit of comedy." He might well, however, also have established an identity between the Vice and the parasite, since he defines the parasite as the "oldest buffoon" and describes the buffoon type as functioning "to increase the mood of festivity rather than to contribute to the plot." The Vice in fact does both, being both "entertainer" and *"architectus." Anatomy of Criticism; Four Essays* (Princeton, N.J.: Princeton Univ. Press, 1957), pp. 173–75.

9. Thomas Babington Macaulay, "Comic Dramatists of the Restoration," *Critical and Historical Essays* (Leipzig: Bernhard Tauchnitz, 1850), p. 148.

10. Quoted in Norman Holland, *The First Modern Comedies: the Significance of Etherege, Wycherley, and Congreve* (Cambridge, Mass.: Harvard Univ. Press, 1959), p. 201.

11. Cazamian, *Development of English Humor,* p. 160.

12. Wylie Sypher, "The Meanings of Comedy," *Comedy,* ed. Wylie Sypher (Garden City, N.Y.: Doubleday Anchor Books, 1956), p. 200.

13. It may well be that the explanation for the appearance of such a comedy at this particular time has to do also with the aristocratic monopoly of the theater between 1660 and 1700. As G. Wilson Knight has observed, in a passage which has special pertinence to this study: "The proper function of comedy is to assist the assimilation of instinct, especially sexual instinct. . . . Whatever might be true of southern Europe, or even of France, Protestant

Britain had too firm a sense of sin to engage in any wholesale comic and communal relaxation. The medieval 'Feast of Fools' was not popular in England. And yet morality and convention alone are impotent; the stuff of life is there whatever we think of it, and it is comedy's business to face it. The next step is accordingly a facing not of the instinct alone as a simple force of nature, but of instinct recognized simultaneously as sin, as inevitable, and as honourable. For such subtleties the middle classes had neither the inclination nor the language. Clarification could only come through an aristocratic daring and a sophisticated expression." *The Golden Labyrinth: A Study of British Drama* (New York: Norton, 1962), p. 130.

## CHAPTER II. *Dramatis Personæ*

1. Johan Huizinga, *Homo Ludens, A Study of the Play Element in Culture* (Boston: Beacon Press, 1955), p. 1.

2. Ibid., p. 4.

3. Hence we find, even as early as the embryonic comic sequences in the morality plays, vice-figures with names like New-Gyse and Now-a-Days (*Mankind*), Nicol Newfangle (*Like Will to Like*), and Imagination (*Hyckscorner*).

4. Huizinga, *Homo Ludens*, p. 132.

5. James Sully, *An Essay on Laughter: Its Forms, Its Causes, Its Development, and Its Value* (New York: Longmans, Green, 1907), p. 146.

6. Huizinga, *Homo Ludens*, p. 8.

7. Eric Bentley, *The Life of the Drama* (New York: Atheneum, 1964), pp. 239, 240.

8. Huizinga, *Homo Ludens*, p. 10. And Huizinga continues in this same passage: "Into an imperfect world and into the confusion of life it brings a temporary, a limited perfection. Play demands order absolute and supreme. The least deviation from it 'spoils the game', robs it of its character and makes it worthless. The profound affinity between play and order is perhaps the reason why play . . . seems to lie to such a large extent in the field of aesthetics. Play has a tendency to be beautiful. It may be that this aesthetic factor is identical with the impulse to create orderly form, which animates play in all its aspects. The words we use to denote the elements of play belong for the most part to aesthetics, terms with which we try to describe the effects of beauty: tension, poise, balance, contrast, variation, solution, resolution, etc."

9. In this connection Huizinga writes (*Homo Ludens*, p. 119): "Poiesis . . . is a play-function. It proceeds within the play-ground of the mind, in a world of its own which the mind creates for it. There things have a very differ-

ent physiognomy from the one they wear in 'ordinary life', and are bound by ties other than those of logic and causality. If a serious statement be defined as one that may be made in terms of waking life, poetry will never rise to the level of seriousness. It lies beyond seriousness, on that more primitive and original level where the child, the animal, the savage and the seer belong, in the region of dream, enchantment, ecstacy, laughter. To understand poetry we must be capable of donning the child's soul like a magic cloak and of forsaking man's wisdom for the child's."

10. Havelock Ellis, *The Dance of Life* (Boston and New York: Houghton Mifflin, 1923), p. 182.

11. Huizinga, *Homo Ludens*, p. 51.

12. Lane Cooper, *An Aristotelian Theory of Comedy* (New York: Harcourt, Brace, 1922), p. 25.

13. Huizinga, *Homo Ludens*, p. 164.

14. Ellis, *The Dance of Life*, p. 38. And Huizinga reveals much the same conviction in citing Plato's explanation of Play (*Homo Ludens*, pp. 159, 160): "how all young creatures cannot keep either their bodies or their voices still, how they must continually be moving and making a noise for joy, leaping and skipping and dancing and uttering all manner of cries. But whereas all other creatures know not the distinction between order and disorder which is called rhythm and harmony, to us men the same gods who were given us as companions in the dance have granted the perception of rhythm and harmony, which is invariably accompanied by pleasure."

15. Ellis, *The Dance of Life*, p. 48.

16. *Representative English Comedies: From the Beginnings to Shakespeare*, ed. Charles Mills Gayley, 3 vols. (New York: Macmillan, 1907), I, liv.

17. Bernard Spivack, *Shakespeare and the Allegory of Evil* (New York: Columbia Univ. Press, 1958), p. 192.

18. Ibid. The passage in Spivack continues: " 'Farewel my masters our partes we haue playd' is the valedictory of the Vice to the audience attending *Enough Is as Good as a Feast*. Ah, my masters, how like you this play?' asks Nichol Newfangle toward the end of *Like Will to Like*. And the first words of the Vice in *A Marriage between Wit and Wisdom* are equally thespian:

> Al sirra, my master,
>> How fare you at this blessed day?
> What, I wen, all this company
>> Are come to se a play!"

19. Ola Elizabeth Winslow, *Low Comedy as a Structural Element in English Drama: from the beginnings to 1642* (Menasha, Wis.: Collegiate Press, 1926), p. 63.

20. Spivack, *Shakespeare and the Allegory of Evil,* p. 192.

21. "Only after the gradual disappearance of the 'apron' in the eighteenth century," observes Allardyce Nicoll, "did the actors retire behind the foot-lights into the interior of the stage itself, abandoning their sense of kinship with the audience and becoming far-off figures set in a distant world." *A History of Restoration Drama 1660–1700* (Cambridge: Cambridge Press, 1923), p. 32.

22. Spivack, *Shakespeare and the Allegory of Evil,* p. 162.

23. Robert Withington, "The Development of the 'Vice,'" *Essays in Memory of Barrett Wendell* eds W. R. Castle and Paul Kaufman (Cambridge, Mass.: Harvard Univ. Press, 1926), p. 155.

24. Spivack, *Shakespeare and the Allegory of Evil,* p. 189.

25. It is especially difficult in this connection to understand how Norman Holland has reached his conclusions about language in the seventeenth century being "regarded as an outside . . . within which the real substance, thought, lay hidden." (*The First Modern Comedies: the Significance of Etherege, Wycherley, and Congreve* [Cambridge, Mass.: Harvard Univ. Press, 1959], p. 51) The fact that Dryden frequently uses clothing images for language does not by any means necessarily confirm the point. Bernard Harris has pointed out that Dryden himself put "his language in the service of basic human instincts"—and thereby "was making more possible in the drama the fullest presentation of experience." "The Dialect of those Fanatic Times," *Restoration Theatre,* Stratford-upon-Avon Studies 6 (London: Edward Arnold, 1965), 26.

26. Oscar Wilde, "The Critic as Artist, Part I," *Intentions* (New York: Modern Library, n.d.), p. 119.

27. Susanne K. Langer, *Feeling and Form* (New York: Scribner, 1953), p. 349.

28. As Henry Ten Eyck Perry points out: "the phallus, as the symbol of procreation, became an object of divine worship in ancient Greece, as it still is in some parts of the world. Its worship expressed man's gratitude for the gift of life itself; here we come close to the mystery of the true nature of comedy. We are glad to be alive, and we show by laughter our sense of exuberant well-being. Throughout its history, comedy has leaned heavily upon vulgarity and coarseness, because, like the Greek phallus, they have a logical relation to vitality and animal high spirits." *Masters of Dramatic Comedy and their Social Themes* (Cambridge, Mass.: Harvard Univ. Press, 1939), pp. 3, 4.

29. John Wilson has summarized the case for the prosecution: "Wit for its own sake, obscenity merely for the pleasure of being obscene, the insinuation which is more indecent than the broadest vulgarity, the rewarding of the wicked and the neglect, if not chastising, of the good—these are the things

prized in the upside-down world of Restoration comedy." *The Influence of Beaumont and Fletcher on Restoration Drama* (Columbus, Ohio: Ohio State Univ. Press, 1928), p. 30.

30. Ellis, *The Dance of Life,* p. 283.

31. L. C. Knights, "Restoration Comedy: The Reality and the Myth," *Explorations* (New York: New York Univ. Press, 1964), p. 161.

32. John Palmer, *Comedy* (New York: George H. Doran, 1919), pp. 51, 52.

33. Ibid., p. 52.

34. Nicoll, *A History of Restoration Drama,* p. 185. Nicoll's definition of the comedy of manners, which has gone virtually unchallenged for a good many years, reads as follows: "In the main, we may say, the invariable elements of the comedy of manners are the presence of at least one pair of witty lovers, the woman as emancipated as the man, their dialogue free and graceful, an air of refined cynicism over the whole production, the plot of less consequence than the wit, an absence of crude realism, a total lack of any emotion whatsoever."

35. Sigmund Freud, *Wit and Its Relation to the Unconscious,* Authorized English Edition, A. A. Brill (New York: Moffatt, Yard, 1916), pp. 145, 146.

36. Langer, *Feeling and Form,* pp. 335, 336.

37. Henry Ten Eyck Perry, *The Comic Spirit in Restoration Drama: Studies in the Comedy of Etherege, Wycherley, Congreve, Vanbrugh and Farquhar* (New York: Russell & Russell, 1962), p. 140.

38. Sully, *An Essay on Laughter,* p. 112.

39. Perry, *The Comic Spirit in Restoration Drama,* p. 26.

40. "The Dialect of those Fanatic Times," *Restoration Theatre,* p. 36.

41. As George Williamson says of seventeenth-century wit, it "may take the form of fanciful exaggeration, resemblance, dissimilitude, incongruity, contradiction, or covert intimation, but its associations must always involve the surprising or unexpected." *The Proper Wit of Poetry* (Chicago: Univ. of Chicago Press, 1961), p. 15.

42. Thomas Hobbes, *Leviathan* (London: J. M. Dent & Sons, 1947), p. 33.

43. Withington, "The Development of the 'Vice;' " *Essays in Memory of Barrett Wendell,* p. 163.

44. Henri Bergson, "Laughter," *Comedy,* ed. Wylie Sypher (Garden City, N.Y.: Doubleday Anchor Books, 1956), p. 129.

45. Charles Baudelaire, "On the Essence of Laughter," *The Mirror of Art,* trans. and ed. Jonathan Mayne (New York: Phaidon, 1955), pp. 138, 139.

46. Clarence deWitt Thorpe, *The Aesthetic Theory of Thomas Hobbes:*

*With Special Reference to His Contribution to the Psychological Approach in English Literary Criticism* (Ann Arbor: Univ. of Michigan Press, 1940), p. 147.

47. Ellis, *The Dance of Life,* pp. 306, 307.

48. In the course of defining the comic plot, Eric Bentley remarks: "The desire to live is not merely love of living. It is also greed. Comedy deals with the itch to own the material world. Hence its interest in gluttons who imbibe part of this world, and misers who hoard another part. And from *devouring* and *clutching,* human nature makes a swift leap to *stealing.* In how many comic plots there is theft or the intention of theft! If men did not wish to break the tenth commandment, comic plotting, as we know it, could never have come into being." *Life of the Drama,* p. 304.

49. Ibid., pp. 248, 249. It is interesting to note that Bentley states further: "Puck could be the knave of a farce. He is not deep or purposive enough to be a villain. He is a trouble-maker by accident and even by nature but not always by design and never with intent to do serious damage. He is a prank-ster—like Harlequin."

50. Spivack, *Shakespeare and the Allegory of Evil,* pp. 46, 47.

51. Northrop Frye, *Anatomy of Criticism; Four Essays* (Princeton, N.J.: Princeton Univ. Press, 1957), p. 173.

52. Langer, *Feeling and Form,* p. 343.

53. Wilde, "The Critic as Artist, Part I," *Intentions,* pp. 126,127.

54. Sypher, "The Meanings of Comedy," *Comedy,* ed. Wylie Sypher, p. 223.

55. Elizabeth Mignon, *Crabbed Age and Youth: The Old Men and Women in the Restoration Comedy of Manners* (Durham, N.C.: Duke Univ. Press, 1947), pp. 29, 37.

56. David S. Berkeley, "*Préciosité* and the Restoration Comedy of Manners," *Huntington Library Quarterly,* XVIII (February, 1955), 109.

57. John Harold Wilson, *The Court Wits of the Restoration: An Introduction* (Princeton, N.J.: Princeton Univ. Press, 1948), p. 94.

58. Gellert Spencer Alleman, *Matrimonial Law and the Materials of Restoration Comedy* (Philadelphia: Univ. of Pennsylvania, 1942).

59. Wilson, *Court Wits of the Restoration,* p. 176.

60. Quoted in Bonamy Dobrée, *Restoration Comedy 1660–1720* (Oxford: Clarendon Press, 1924), p. 32.

61. Frye, *Anatomy of Criticism,* p. 182.

62. Langer, *Feeling and Form,* p. 333.

63. As Anne Righter writes: "The truewits and their ladies are painfully aware that the institutionalization of love may be its death, that time and habit are terrible enemies. They must marry if they are to possess one another

at all, yet they confront this solution at the end of the play with a dubiety which, in Elizabethan comedy, had been reserved only for clowns and fools; for Launce and his slovenly milkmaid; Touchstone and Audrey. Dorimant and Harriet, Millamant and Mirabell, describe marriage as the risk they take, not as the end of the story." "Heroic Tragedy," *Restoration Theatre*, Stratford-upon-Avon Studies 6 (London: Edward Arnold Ltd., 1965), 153, 154.

64. Lionel Trilling, *Freud and the Crisis of Our Culture* (Boston: Beacon Press, 1955), pp. 37, 43.

65. Thorpe, *The Aesthetic Theory of Thomas Hobbes,* p. 123.

66. Ibid., p. 22.

67. Quoted in Ellis, *The Dance of Life,* p. 24.

68. C. D. Cecil, "Libertine and *Précieux* Elements in Restoration Comedy," *Essays in Criticism,* IX (July, 1959), 243.

69. Quoted in K. M. P. Burton, *Restoration Literature* (London: Hutchinson Univ. Library, 1958), p. 35.

70. Huizinga, *Homo Ludens,* p. 211.

71. Basil Willey, *The Seventeenth Century Background* (Garden City, N.Y.: Doubleday Anchor Books, 1953), p. 112.

72. Ellis, *The Dance of Life,* p. xi. It may be true in this connection that Restoration comedy demands a kind of "mannered" acting, but the thematic content of the plays plainly requires that a distinction be made between the "manners" of the fop and those of the rake-hero. The danger of ignoring such a distinction is critical, for it may allow us to forget the sexuality, the aggressiveness, the passion for power that lie behind the manners of the heroes to give them their vitality, and to keep the plays from being nothing more than tea-party chatter and mincing little dances of a heel and a toe and a step, step, step. Much of the theme of Etherege's *Man of Mode* rests on precisely the fop-rake distinction. It is always of the essence of the fop's absurdities that he parades all the surface manners of the rake while possessing none of the vital sexuality which gives the rakish manners their content and meaning.

73. Margaret L. Wiley, *The Subtle Knot: Creative Scepticism in Seventeenth-Century England* (Cambridge, Mass.: Harvard Univ. Press, 1952), p. 18. "The sceptic picks up and lays down the dogmatisms of men according to what their tendency is and to whether they forward or obstruct his progress toward the highest truth he can conceive. . . . Here is another point at which mysticism and scepticism lie very close to each other. Both require a flexibility which veers to receive the truth from whatever direction it blows" (p. 24).

74. C. Maurice Bowra, *The Greek Experience* (New York and Toronto: New American Library, 1957), p. 85.

CHAPTER III. *The Beginnings in Etherege*

1. *The Lettterbook of Sir George Etherege,* ed. Sybil Rosenfeld (London: Oxford Univ. Press, 1928), p. 189. (Ratisbon 18/28 April, 87. To Mr. Corbet)

2. Ibid., p. 142. (Ratisbon 2/12 Feb. 86/7)

3. Lane Cooper, *An Aristotelian Theory of Comedy* (New York: Harcourt, Brace, 1922), pp. 205, 206.

4. John Palmer, *The Comedy of Manners* (London: G. Bell & Sons, 1913), p. 91. Palmer maintains that Etherege "intercepted without effort for his immediate purpose the things that came to him, and gracefully encountered the one problem which his generation acutely recognized. Whether it were fighting the Dutch, defeating the policy of Achitophel, tying a riband, or writing a play—style was the man. There was form and there was bad form. The whole duty of man was to find the one, and to eschew the other."

5. There is clearly a danger in representing Etherege's thinking as more complex than it actually was, and it is hardly accurate to describe his purpose "as the desire to weigh many perceptions of reality, the crux of thought lying in the belief that there are many realities of relative worth and that the state of man is one upon which many conflicting realities operate." According to this view, Etherege's method is "to pit different perceptions of reality against one another in an effort to recreate that complexity of vision that life affords." The words are Rose Zimbardo's (*Wycherley's Drama: A Link in the Development of English Satire* [New Haven: Yale Univ. Press, 1965], p. 4), in which she expresses her agreement with Dale Underwood's basic thesis—that from the "point of multiple vision, the comic ritual of the plays is primarily one in which man in the pride and assertiveness of his wit progressively reveals its and his own general insufficiency and confusion." *Etherege and the Seventeenth-Century Comedy of Manners* (New Haven: Yale Univ. Press, 1957), p. 110.

6. Alfred Harbage, *Cavalier Drama: An Historical and Critical Supplement to the Study of the Elizabethan and Restoration Stage* (New York: Modern Language Association of America, 1936), p. 87.

7. John Harold Wilson, *The Court Wits of the Restoration: An Introduction* (Princeton, N.J.: Princeton Univ. Press, 1948), p. 150.

8. Jocelyn Powell, "George Etherege and the Form of Comedy," *Restora-*

*tion Theatre,* Stratford-upon-Avon Studies 6 (London: Edward Arnold, 1965), 46, 48.

9. Alfred Harbage points out, in this connection: "The admirable rakes of Elizabethan drama, from Prince Hal in *Henry IV* to Wellborn in *A New Way to Pay Old Debts* had been at bottom sound and substantial citizens; Sir Frederick is *not* at bottom a sound and substantial citizen, and for this reason is not besmirched by his indiscretions and is in no need of rehabilitation." (*Cavalier Drama,* p. 87).

10. Wylie Sypher, "The Meanings of Comedy," *Comedy,* ed. Wylie Sypher (Garden City, N.Y.: Doubleday Anchor Books, 1956), p. 225.

11. *The Dramatic Works of Sir George Etherege,* ed. H. F. B. Brett-Smith, 2 vols. (Oxford: Basil Blackwell, 1927), I, 1–88. References to this volume will appear in parentheses within the text.

12. James Sully, *An Essay on Laughter: Its Form, Its Causes, Its Development, and Its Value* (New York: Longmans, Green, 1907), pp. 281, 282.

13. What Mrs. Langer says of the action of comedy may be seen to be especially applicable here: "Destiny in the guise of Fortune is the fabric of comedy; it is developed by comic action, which is the upset and recovery of the protagonist's equilibrium, his contest with the world and his triumph by wit, luck, personal power, or even humorous, or ironical, or philosophical acceptance of mischance. Whatever the theme . . . the immediate sense of life is the underlying feeling of comedy, and dictates its rhythmically structured unity, that is to say its organic form. . . . The feeling of comedy is a feeling of heightened vitality, challenged wit and will, engaged in the great game with Chance. The real antagonist is the World." *Feeling and Form* (New York: Scribner, 1953), pp. 331, 348, 349.

14. J. Y. T. Greig, *The Psychology of Laughter and Comedy* (London: George Allen & Unwin, 1923), p. 98.

15. Langer, *Feeling and Form,* p. 342.

16. Sigmund Freud, *Wit and Its Relation to the Unconscious,* Authorized English Edition, A. A. Brill (New York: Moffatt, Yard, 1916), pp. 145–53.

17. Quoted in Greig, *Psychology of Laughter and Comedy,* pp. 97, 98.

18. Powell, "George Etherege and the Form of Comedy," *Restoration Theatre,* p. 46.

19. Ibid., 48.

20. "Farah," *Shadows on the Grass* (London: Michael Joseph, 1961), p. 10.

21. *The Dramatic Works of Sir George Etherege,* ed. H. F. B. Brett-Smith, 2 vols. (Oxford: Basil Blackwell, 1927), II, 89–180. Again page references to this volume will appear in parentheses within the text.

22. Underwood, *Etherege,* p. 101.

23. Sydney Smith, cited in J. C. Gregory, *The Nature of Laughter* (London: Kegan Paul, Trench, Trubner, 1924), p. 91.

24. Powell, "George Etherege and the Form of Comedy," *Restoration Theatre*, p. 54.

25. Francis MacDonald Cornford, *The Origin of Attic Comedy* (London: Edward Arnold, 1914), p. 139.

26. W. Wycherley, *Miscellany Poems: as Satyrs, Epistles, Love-Verses, Songs, Sonnets* (London, 1704), p. 246.

CHAPTER IV. *The Man of Mode, or Sir Fopling Flutter*

1. Bergson speaks of the source of the comic as "*some rigidity or other* applied to the mobility of life, in an awkward attempt to follow its lines and counterfeit its suppleness," and he goes on to say: "It might almost be said that every fashion is laughable in some respect. Only, when we are dealing with the fashion of the day, we are so accustomed to it that the garment seems, in our mind, to form one with the individual wearing it. We do not separate them in imagination. The idea no longer occurs to us to contrast the inert rigidity of the covering with the living suppleness of the object covered: consequently, the comic here remains in a latent condition. It will only succeed in emerging when the natural incompatibility is so deep-seated between the covering and the covered that even an immemorial association fails to cement this union: a case in point is our head and top hat." "Laughter," *Comedy,* ed. Wylie Sypher (Garden City, N.Y.: Doubleday Anchor Books, 1956), p. 85.

2. In view of Etherege's patent insistence on these differences between Sir Fopling and Dorimant, it is astonishing that so many recent critics have largely denied the existence of any such distinction. Jocelyn Powell has actually reversed the differences, making an observation about Dorimant and his world which can in reality only be justified with specific reference to Sir Fopling: "in the society Etherege portrays manners have become not a means to an end, but an end in themselves . . . that which was intended to express feeling, now dictates to it, and manners prevent the intercourse they were designed to aid." She then goes on to suggest quite rightly that the "energy of love and of living is expressed in the communication between human beings," but denies, in effect, that Dorimant and Harriet manage to express any such "energy," hamstrung as they are by "the lightness and elegance of fashion." And the issue becomes further confused when Sir Fopling is seen as the heir to the "lyrical and musical life and energy" of Sir Frederick Frollick and Sir Joslin Jolly—"picking up the realism of the play and turning it

into a dance," and when the example of Dorimant is held up as one in which "form has become a substitute for feeling." "George Etherege and the Form of Comedy," *Restoration Theatre*, Stratford-upon-Avon Studies 6 (London: Edward Arnold, 1965), 66–68.

3. Bergson, "Laughter," *Comedy*, p. 89.

4. Oscar Wilde, "The Truth of Masks," *Intentions* (New York: Modern Library, n.d.), p. 241.

5. Harris, "The Dialect of those Fanatic Times," *Restoration Theatre*, Stratford-upon-Avon Studies 6 (London: Edward Arnold, 1965), 29, 30.

6. Dale Underwood, *Etherege and the Seventeenth-Century Comedy of Manners* (New Haven: Yale Univ. Press, 1957), p. 88. The song, of which Underwood says that there is a " 'satanic' posture embedded in the verses' synthetic pastoralisms," includes the lines:

> *The threatning danger to remove*
> *She whisper'd in her Ear,*
> *Ah Phillis, if you would not love,*
> *This Shepheard do not hear.*
>
> *None ever had so strange an Art*
> *His passion to convey*
> *Into a listning Virgins heart*
> *And steal her Soul away.*

7. James Sully, *An Essay on Laughter: Its Forms, Its Causes, Its Development, and Its Value* (New York: Longmans, Green, 1907), p. 97.

8. Quoted in Havelock Ellis, *The Dance of Life* (Boston and New York: Houghton Mifflin, 1923), pp. 11, 12.

CHAPTER V. *Wycherley's Early Plays*

1. John Palmer, *Comedy* (New York: George H. Doran, 1919), p. 52.

2. J. Auffret, "Wycherley et ses Maîtres les Moralistes," *Études Anglaises*, XV (Octobre-Décembre, 1962), p. 387.

3. Rose Zimbardo, for example, who is also bent on establishing a connection with the classical satirists, writes: "The satirist's battleground is indeed here and now, but his very point is that reality, because it is vice-ridden is not 'uncomplicated.' In the satirist's eyes virtue is uncomplicated, truth is simple, honesty is obvious. On the other hand, vice is complex. It resorts to duplicity, complication, and distortion in its efforts to cloud the distinction between good and evil, true and false. Wycherley, then, must be as concerned as Etherege with the world of illusion and delusion, but false appearance

interests him not in itself but as it shows how far human life deviates from what it should be." In her view Wycherley's plays "are not comedies at all"; they are satires. *Wycherley's Drama: A Link in the Development of English Satire* (New Haven: Yale Univ. Press, 1965), pp. 3, 14, 15.

4. Julian Symons, "Restoration Comedy (Reconsiderations II)," *Kenyon Review,* VII (Spring, 1945), 188.

5. W. Wycherley, *Miscellany Poems: as Satyrs, Epistles, Love-Verses, Songs, Sonnets* (London, 1704), p. 182.

6. Bonamy Dobrée, *Restoration Comedy 1660–1720* (Oxford: Clarendon Press, 1924), p. 85. Dobrée states flatly at this point that "Wycherley's joy was spoiled by his puritanism."

7. W. H. Auden, "Bryon: The Making of a Comic Poet," *The New York Review of Books,* VII (August 18, 1966), 14.

8. Malcolm Elwin, *The Playgoer's Handbook to Restoration Drama* (London: Jonathan Cape, 1928), p. 74.

9. Norman Holland has tried to establish the importance of these plays, but ultimately he arrives at the conclusion, not particularly complimentary to Wycherley's profundity, that "Wycherley's unique contribution to Restoration comedy was a sense that folly, evil, and limitations to happiness were all related, that there is a right way and a wrong way." *The First Modern Comedies: the Significance of Etherege, Wycherley, and Congreve* (Cambridge, Mass.: Harvard Univ. Press, 1959), p. 70.

10. *William Wycherley,* ed. W. C. Ward (London: T. Fisher Unwin, n.d.). This single volume contains all four plays, and the page numbers in parentheses in this chapter and in chapters VI and VII will all refer to it.

11. Zimbardo, *Wycherley's Drama,* p. 33.

12. Ibid., pp. 33, 34, 40.

13. Ibid., p. 45.

14. Ibid., p. 39.

15. Ibid., pp. 39, 40.

16. Ibid., p. 40.

17. It is impossible to see, however, how Hippolita can at any point in the play be regarded as "a representation of ideal love"—especially if by that phrase Mrs. Zimbardo means, as in her earlier discussion of Christina, "supersensuous love." *Wycherley's Drama,* p. 52.

CHAPTER VI. *The Country Wife*

1. Charles Perromat, *William Wycherley. Sa Vie—Son Oeuvre* (Paris, Librairies Felix Alcan, 1921), p. 224.

2. Anne Righter, "William Wycherley," *Restoration Theatre,* Stratford-upon-Avon Studies 6 (London: Edward Arnold, 1965), 79.

3. Rose Zimbardo, *Wycherley's Drama: A Link in the Development of English Satire* (New Haven: Yale Univ. Press, 1965), p. 95.

4. Ibid., pp. 154, 155, 159.

5. Norman Holland, *The First Modern Comedies: the Significance of Etherege, Wycherley, and Congreve* (Cambridge, Mass.: Harvard Univ. Press, 1959), p. 73.

6. Quoted in Perromat, *William Wycherley,* p. 225.

7. Wylie Sypher, "The Meanings of Comedy," *Comedy,* ed. Wylie Sypher (Garden City, N.Y.: Doubleday Anchor Books, 1956), p. 247.

8. Ibid., p. 241.

9. Sigmund Freud, *Wit and Its Relation to the Unconscious,* Authorized English Edition, A. A. Brill (New York: Moffatt, Yard, 1916), pp. 290, 291.

10. W. Wycherley, *Miscellany Poems: as Satyrs, Epistles, Love-Verses, Songs, Sonnets* (London, 1704), pp. 117–19.

11. Ibid., p. 122.

12. Perromat, *William Wycherley,* p. 345.

### CHAPTER VII. *The Plain Dealer*

1. Rose Zimbardo, *Wycherley's Drama: A Link in the Development of English Satire* (New Haven: Yale Univ. Press, 1965), pp. 73–75.

2. Thomas Fujimura, *The Restoration Comedy of Wit* (Princeton, N.J.: Princeton Univ. Press, 1952), p. 148; and Norman Holland, *The First Modern Comedies; the Significance of Etherege, Wycherley, and Congreve* (Cambridge, Mass.: Harvard Univ. Press, 1959), pp. 98, 99. According to Holland, "Manly is a dupe, not a hero. His railing only blinds himself. Neither is he a moralist. What he objects to in society is not wrongdoing, but the unwillingness to admit it—pretense and affectation. He carries his demands for sincerity to absurd lengths . . . Manly's virtue is his failing: he cannot—or is unwilling to—tell the copy from the real. . . . The attitude of the other people in the play proves conclusively that Manly is not to be taken seriously."

3. Fujimura, *The Restoration Comedy of Wit,* p. 147. Fujimura, however, does not pursue the matter beyond remarking that "the severity of Manly, in his extreme misanthropy, is contrasted unfavorably with the ridicule that Eliza and Freeman resort to, which is more effective in exposing coxcombs."

4. Holland, in his summary statement, argues as follows: "*The Plain-Dealer,* then, does not simply make a statement about the baseness of the Restoration. In a uniquely comic way it asks a question: Can an idealist find his ideal in this imperfect world in which appearances can never really be consistent with nature? . . . The wise man like Freeman accepts the contradiction between appearance and nature and deals with the inner, important attributes. . . . But finally, there is a special kind of folly, the idealist's, touched with godliness, that tries to escape the paradox, to run away to sea or the West Indies: this is Manly's folly and Fidelia's. In this sense, *The Plain-Dealer* is, like all great comic art, *encomium moriae,* the praise of Manly's folly in fighting the contradictions of society and Freeman's in accepting them. The play becomes an almost cosmic right-way—wrong-way simile: by showing us two wrong ways of this world, the ending implies a right way—improbable, unreal, in short, supernatural." *First Modern Comedies,* pp. 108, 109. The principal point of disagreement, as set forth here, will have to do with Holland's "*encomium moriae*" conclusions (as well as with his suggestion that "Manly is not to be taken seriously"). Manly states in the Prologue that his audience will regard his as "a fool's part," and since the audience is clearly under attack throughout the Prologue, their reaction can certainly not be taken to be Wycherley's.

5. Mrs. Zimbardo writes: "When we recognize the play as formal satire, Freeman's role at once becomes clear; he is the adversarius. His function is to take a position opposite that of the satirist, Manly, and to provoke the satirist's attack. As we have seen, the adversarius may assume any of a number of shapes. Freeman's is a type quite common in Roman satire. He is one of the very number whom the satirist scorns. But he detaches himself from the crowd and draws near the satirist where he plays the role of devil's advocate. Freeman is not on the side of virtue. He does not want to convince Manly that the world is not really full of hypocrites, but rather he champions the position that hypocrisy is the way of the world, the means to success. He hopes, in effect, to reason the satirist to the side of unreason, to win him to the very vice he stands most firmly against." *Wycherley's Drama,* pp. 127, 128.

6. W. H. Auden, "Byron: the Making of a Comic Poet," *The New York Review of Books,* VII August 18, 1966), 14.

7. Zimbardo, *Wycherley's Drama,* p. 80.

8. Jerome Bruner, *Toward a Theory of Instruction* (New York: Norton, 1968), pp. 129, 130.

9. Johan Huizinga, *Homo Ludens, A Study of the Play Element in Culture* (Boston: Beacon Press, 1956), p. 11. "The spoil-sport," says Huizinga, "is not the same as the false player, the cheat; for the latter pretends to be

playing the game and, on the face of it, still acknowledges the magic circle. It is curious to note how much more lenient society is to the cheat than to the spoil-sport. This is because the spoil-sport shatters the play-world itself. By withdrawing from the game he reveals the relativity and fragility of the play-world in which he had temporarily shut himself with others. He robs play of its *illusion*—a pregnant word that means literally 'in-play' . . . Therefore he must be cast out, for he threatens the existence of the play-community."

10. Northrop Frye, *Anatomy of Criticism; Four Essays* (Princeton, N.J.: Princeton Univ. Press, 1952), p. 176.

11. Holland, *First Modern Comedies,* p. 98.

12. Wylie Sypher, "The Meanings of Comedy," *Comedy,* ed. Wylie Sypher (Garden City, N.Y.: Doubleday Anchor Books, 1956), p. 246.

13. J. Y. T. Greig, *The Psychology of Laughter and Comedy* (London: George Allen & Unwin, 1923), pp. 174, 175.

14. George Meredith, "Essay on Comedy, " *Comedy,* ed. Wylie Sypher, p. 16.

15. One of the most convincing parts of Mrs. Zimbardo's analysis of Manly suggests that we view him in "Everyman" terms. *Wycherley's Drama,* pp. 143–45.

16. Zimbardo, *Wycherley's Drama,* p. 127.

17. E. M. W. Tillyard, *Shakespeare's Last Plays* (London: Chatto & Windus, 1958), pp. 73–78.

CHAPTER VIII. *Congreve's Apprenticeship*

1. In their study of *The Way of the World* as a commentary on adulteries, Paul and Miriam Mueschke suggest that Ben Jonson is the most significant influence on Congreve; but while it is certainly true to say that both thought of "comedy at its best as an exalted form of poetry; and of poetry as sovereign of the arts," it does not necessarily follow that their comic visions must be identified. Whatever his "aesthetic creed," Congreve is, in fact, much closer in tone and spirit to Etherege than to either Wycherley or Jonson, although with an added dimension of seriousness. As has been so often true with critics of Congreve, the Mueschkes feel that he is in need of defense and therefore that they must define him as in some saving sense a moralist. Hence they see *The Way of the World* as centrally concerned with "the gradual regeneration of the former rake and his cast mistress . . . from an acceptance of a social and ethical norm through which they achieve self-knowledge and self-mastery," and more often than not they seem to be talking about some other play altogether. See *A New View of Congreve's Way of the*

*World* (Ann Arbor: Univ. of Michigan Press, 1958), pp. 78, 81. For a comprehensive survey of the varied critical positions taken over the years on this point and related ones in Congreve's plays, see Norman Holland's and Thomas Fujimura's very helpful and adequate summaries.

2. Bonamy Dobrée, *William Congreve: A Conversation between Swift and Gay* (Seattle: University of Washington Chapbooks, No. 26, 1929), p. 15.

3. Dragosh Protopopesco, *Un Classique moderne: William Congreve, sa vie, son oeuvre avec une lettre* (Paris: Les Éditions de "La Vie Universitaire," 1924), p. 54.

4. Bonamy Dobrée, *Restoration Comedy 1660–1720* (Oxford, Clarendon Press, 1924), p. 125.

5. The quotations from Congreve's plays are all taken from *Comedies by Congreve,* ed. Bonamy Dobrée (London: Oxford Univ. Press, n.d.).

6. Clarence deWitt Thorpe, *The Aesthetic Theory of Thomas Hobbes: With Special Reference to his Contribution to the Psychological Approach in English Literary Criticism* (Ann Arbor: Univ. of Michigan Press, 1940), p. 97.

7. Bonamy Dobrée, *William Congreve* (London: Longmans, Green, 1963), p. 15.

8. Norman Holland, *The First Modern Comedies: the Significance of Etherege, Wycherley, and Congreve* (Cambridge, Mass.: Harvard Univ. Press, 1959), p. 139.

9. Ibid., pp. 140, 141.

10. Quoted from Congreve's Prologue to *Love for Love, Comedies by Congreve,* ed. Bonamy Dobrée, p. 217.

11. William Van Voris, *The Cultivated Stance: The Design of Congreve's Plays* (Oxford: Dolman Press, 1965), p. 77.

12. *Aesop without Morals,* trans. and ed. Lloyd W. Daly (New York and London: Thomas Yoseloff, 1961), p. 95.

13. *The History of Reynard the Fox,* ed. William J. Thoms (London: Reprinted from the Percy Society, T. Richards, 1844), p. ix.

14. Congreve's characterization of Heartwell is clearly inspired by Wycherley's of Manly, but the differences are perhaps greater than the similarities, since although both are easily "duped" by a hypocritical society, there may be ambivalence but there is no pretense in Manly's hatred and he is, in the last analysis, a far more complicated character.

15. Johan Huizinga, *Homo Ludens, A Study of the Play Element in Culture* (Boston: Beacon Press, 1956), p. 3.

16. Quoted in John Palmer, *The Comedy of Manners* (London: G. Bell & Sons, 1913), p. 144.

17. Bernard Spivack, *Shakespeare and the Allegory of Evil* (New York: Columbia Univ. Press, 1958), pp. 424, 425.

18. Van Voris confirms this point by asserting that Maskwell "even usurps the role of the dramatist, disposes the characters about Lady Touchwood's bedroom, times their entrances and exits and provides that 'ocular proof' necessary to fool Lord Touchwood." *The Cultivated Stance,* p. 69.

19. John Wilcox, *The Relation of Molière to Restoration Comedy* (New York: Columbia Univ. Press, 1938), p. 159.

CHAPTER IX. *Love for Love*

1. William Van Voris, *The Cultivated Stance: The Design of Congreve's Plays* (Oxford: Dolmen Press, 1965), p. 77.

2. Dragosh Protopopesco, *Un Classique Moderne, William Congreve: sa· vie, son oeuvre* (Paris: Les Éditions de "La Vie Universitaire," 1924), pp. 119, 120.

3. Van Voris, *The Cultivated Stance,* p. 89.

4. Van Voris argues that certain of Valentine's lines in this scene ("a thoughtless two handed Whore, she knows my Condition well enough, and might have overlaid the Child a Fortnight ago, if she had had any forecast in her") suggest his fundamental hardness and cruelty; but there is nothing else in the play which attributes such characteristics to him, and presumably, therefore, the passage is not meant to be taken literally but rather is meant to suggest Valentine's cynicism of the moment and the extreme anger to which his frustrating confinement has pushed him—hence pointing up all the more sharply his later generosity of response (as opposed to his own father's totally ungenerous response when aroused to a similar anger). The lines, however, are admittedly puzzling and were omitted in the 1966 London production of *Love for Love.*

5. Norman Holland, *The First Modern Comedies: the Significance of Etherege, Wycherley, and Congreve* (Cambridge, Mass.: Harvard Univ. Press, 1959), p. 162. In fact, Holland goes on to spin out a fairly elaborate theory on the basis of this mistaken attribution: "His failure to realize that outside society there is a difference and his related failure to seek Angelica through something other than a show of 'affectation' are what keep him from winning her. *Love for Love,* like most of the comedies we have considered, is based on the idea of an education or therapy, and this is the point at which Valentine needs education: that there is a reality which is higher and larger than 'continued Affectation.'"

6. Van Voris, *The Cultivated Stance,* p. 89.

7. Ibid., p. 101.

CHAPTER X. *The Way of the World*

1. John Palmer, *Comedy* (New York: George H. Doran, 1919), pp. 37, 38.

2. Ibid., p. 35. Palmer actually refers to an "absence of feeling."

3. Kathleen M. Lynch, *The Social Mode of Restoration Comedy* (New York: Macmillan, 1926), p. 8.

4. Quoted in K. M. P. Burton, *Restoration Literature* (London: Hutchinson Univ. Library, 1957), p. 40.

5. Johan Huizinga, *Homo Ludens, A Study of the Play Element in Culture* (Boston: Beacon Press, 1956), p. 187.

6. Ashley H. Thorndike, *English Comedy* (New York: Macmillan, 1929), p. 327.

7. George Santayana, "Carnival," *Theories of Comedy,* ed. Paul Lauter (Garden City, N.Y.: Doubleday Anchor Books, 1964), p. 419.

8. Elinor C. Fuchs, "The Moral and Aesthetic Achievement of William Congreve" (Cambridge, Mass.: 1955, unpub.), pp. 49, 50. Quoted in Norman Holland, *The First Modern Comedies: the Significance of Etherege, Wycherley, and Congreve* (Cambridge, Mass.: Harvard Univ. Press, 1959), p. 192.

9. William Van Voris would presumably identify the contrasting scenes as an aspect of what he calls Congreve's " 'montage' technique," although he generally recognizes Congreve's use of it only in more clear-cut instances, as in his "alternating increasingly raucous scenes with those of increasingly stylized urbane dialogue" and placing "scenes of brightly witty scheming beside scenes of increasingly violent extravagance." "Congreve's Gilded Carousel," *Educational Theater Journal,* X (October, 1958), 214, 215.

10. Or at least so Congreve seems to want us to believe in thematic terms. The fact is, however, that as in the case of Etherege's Sir Fopling and his own Tattle, Witwoud, if ridiculous, is still an extremely engaging fellow, and as we are laughing at him along with Mirabell, we cannot fail to feel that he is himself no mean wit. Indeed his lines are among the best in the play, conveying as they do always a sense of being pearls of wit, each one strung with delighted self-congratulation and presented with a flourish. And we would have far to seek for any comic poetry equal to his description of Petulant's deceits: "why he wou'd slip you out of this Chocolate-house, just when you had been talking to him—As soon as your Back was turn'd—Whip he was gone;—Then trip to his Lodging, clap on a Hood and Scarf, and a Mask, slap into a Hackney-Coach, and drive hither to the Door again in a trice; where he wou'd send in for himself, that I mean, call for himself, wait for himself, nay and what's more, not finding himself, sometimes leave a

Letter for himself" (354). The breakneck pace of the passage (achieved by insistent parallel constructions and by the heavy concentration of one-syllable verbs—among which the "slip . . . Whip . . . trip" and "clap . . . slap" have a comically reductive effect) gives us the impression of actually witnessing a piece of wildly hilarious stage farce in which one harried character is frantically playing all the parts at once and for his pains is, at the same time, receiving a verbal wallop from his best friend.

11. Holland, *The First Modern Comedies,* p. 191.

12. Havelock Ellis, *The Dance of Life* (Boston and New York: Houghton Mifflin, 1923), pp. 64, 65.

## Chapter XI. *Epilogue*

1. "A Comparison between Laughing and Sentimental Comedy" (1773), *Theories of Comedy,* ed. Paul Lauter (Garden City, N.Y., Doubleday Anchor Books, 1964), p. 262.

2. Louis Cazamian, *The Development of English Humor, Parts I and II* (Durham, N.C.: Duke Univ. Press, 1952), p. 42.

3. Joseph Wood Krutch, *Comedy and Conscience after the Restoration* (New York: Columbia Univ. Press, 1924), p. 157.

4. Ibid., p. 155.

5. George Santayana, "The Comic Mask," *Theories of Comedy,* p. 416.

# INDEX

Alithea (*The Country Wife*): characterized, 137–38; idealism of, 139–40; and Margery, 141; and Sparkish, 141–42; and disease imagery, 142; honor in, 144

Ambidexter (*Cambises*), 29

Angelica (*Love for Love*): and comic spirit, 209; and Foresight, 210; and Valentine, 210, 222, 223–24, 225; design in, 217–18; as romance character, 226

Araminta (*The Old Batchelor*), 183

Ariana (*She wou'd if she cou'd*): and Gatty, 63; imagery of, 64; and battle of sexes, 65–67; and religious vocabulary, 67–68; and lovers' game, 68

Baudelaire, 5

Belinda (*The Old Batchelor*): role of, 183; as antiromantic, 184–85; characterized, 192–94

Bellair, Old (*The Man of Mode*), 89

Bellair, Young (*The Man of Mode*), 82–83

Bellinda (*The Man of Mode*), 86–87

Bellmour (*The Old Batchelor*): characterized, 180–82, 193–95; and Vainlove, 182, 183; lack of illusion in, 184; realism in, 185; philosophy of, 187; pretending in, 192; and Maskwell, 199, 201–202

Ben (*Love for Love*): and Sir Sampson, 214; and Prue, 215; characterized, 215–16; as innocent, 217, 220–21

Bentley, Eric, 5, 29

Bergson, Henri, 27, 79

Blackacre, Jerry (*The Plain Dealer*), 170–71

Brisk, Mr. (*The Double-Dealer*), 203, 204, 207

Cain (*The Killing of Abel*), 6

Careless (*The Double-Dealer*), 203, 206–207

Caution, Mrs. (*The Gentleman Dancing-Master*), 126, 129–30

Cazamian, Louis, 6, 7, 250

Charles II, 3, 32

Christina (*Love in a Wood*), 111–12, 119–20

Cockwood, Lady (*She wou'd if she cou'd*): position in play, 58; home of, 58; and *précieux* convention, 58; and Sentry, 59; and Courtall, 59–60, 72; and honor, 59–60; aggressiveness of, 60; and young lovers, 60–61; and Sir Oliver, 73–75; and other characters, 75

Cockwood, Sir Oliver (*She wou'd if she cou'd*): and *précieux* convention, 58; characterized, 72–75; imagery of, 72–73; and Lady Cockwood, 73–75; and love, 74

comedy: and fertility theme, 20; drawing-room, 23; Falstaffian, 23. *See also* English comedy, Restoration comedy

*Comical Revenge, The* (Etherege): critical attention to, 41–42; theme of, 42; modes of life in, 42, 44–45; *précieux* convention in, 44; imagery in, 45; warfare imagery in, 45–48; death imagery in, 48–49; pastoral